W9-BXQ-464

INTRODUCTION TO
DWDM TECHNOLOGY

Books of Related Interest from IEEE Press

UNDERSTANDING SONET/SDH AND ATM: *Communications Networks for the Next Millennium*
Stamatios V. Kartalopoulos
A volume in the IEEE Press Understanding Science & Technology Series
1999   Softcover   288 pp   IEEE Order no. PP5399   ISBN 0-7803-4745-5

PHOTONIC SWITCHING TECHNOLOGY: *Systems and Networks*
Hussein T. Mouftah and Jaafar M. H. Elmirghani
1998   Hardcover   612 pp   IEEE Order No. PC5761   ISBN 0-7803-4707-2

UNDERSTANDING LASERS: *An Entry-Level Guide*, Second Edition
Jeff Hecht
A volume in the IEEE Press Understanding Science & Technology Series
1994   Softcover   448 pp   IEEE Order No. PP3541   ISBN 0-7803-1005-5

INTRODUCTION TO DWDM TECHNOLOGY

Data in a Rainbow

Stamatios V. Kartalopoulos
Lucent Technologies, Inc.

IEEE Communications Society, *Sponsor*

SPIE OPTICAL ENGINEERING PRESS

A publication of SPIE—The International Society for Optical Engineering
Bellingham, Washington USA

The Institute of Electrical and Electronics Engineers, Inc., New York

This book and other books may be purchased at a discount
from the publisher when ordered in bulk quantities. Contact:

IEEE Press Marketing
Attn: Special Sales
445 Hoes Lane, P.O. Box 1331
Piscataway, NJ 08855-1331
Fax: +1 732 981 9334

For more information about IEEE Press products,
visit the IEEE Press Home Page: http://www.ieee.org/press

SPIE—The International Society for Optical Engineering
P.O. Box 10
Bellingham, Washington 98227-0010
Phone: 360/676-3290
Fax: 360/647-1445
Email: spie@spie.org
WWW: http://www.spie.org

Printed in the United States of America

10   9   8   7   6   5   4   3   2   1

An IEEE Press book published in cooperation with SPIE Optical Engineering Press.

IEEE ISBN 0-7803-5399-4
IEEE Order Number: PC5831

SPIE ISBN 0-8194-3620-8
SPIE Order Number: PM78

Library of Congress Cataloging-in-Publication Data

Kartalopoulos, Stamatios V.
  Introduction to DWDM technology: data in a rainbow / Stamatios V. Kartalopoulos
      p. cm.
  "IEEE Communications Society, sponsor."
  Includes bibliographical references and index.
  ISBN 0-7803-5399-4
    1. Optical communications. 2. Multiplexing. 3. Fiber optics. I. IEEE Communications
Society. II. Title.
TK5103.59 K36 2000
621.382'7--dc21

                                                                99-049676
                                                                    CIP

Dedicated to my wonderful family:
to my wife Anita with deep love and appreciation
for her continuous encouragement in endeavors far beyond academic,
and with the greatest love to our children William and Stephanie
who have brought both happiness and pride to our lives.

CONTENTS

PREFACE

Thousands of years ago someone tried to answer the question: Does light travel always in a straight line, even if in a transparent medium, or can it follow its curvature? Using a bucket of water with a hole at the bottom, he discovered the latter—how simple!

Sunlight rays crossing the morning dew droplets formed a rainbow of colors. Thus the sun rays, composed of many colors, were demystified—what a simple observation! Sun rays, when reflected with shining bronze shields, were redirected to selected points called *estiai* or *foci*. Furthermore, concentrated rays had so much energy that they could warm up things or burn them. Soon thereafter, the glassy optical lens was produced.

It was found that rays passing through a spherical lens did not create the best focal point; today, this imperfection is known as *lens sphericity*. It was also discovered that shapes based on hyperbolas or parabolas were better suited to optical applications than those based on circles or spheres.

Simple experiments and observations of the past have helped our understanding about the nature of things. Yesterday's science fiction is today's reality. The electronic properties of conductors and semiconductors help to create or detect light. Three crystals, each with different impurities and fused together, created a transistor, which within a few years revolutionized the way we live. The wrist-size communicator is no longer just fantasy in comic books. Pocket-size powerful computers and credit-card-size communication devices are a reality. Low earth orbit satellite (LEOS) communication networks are not "pie in the sky," but they are roaming the silent skies. At the click of a button, one can access virtually any part of the globe and hear and see events as they happen. Optical fiber has wrapped around the globe like a ball of yarn connecting all continents and transporting data at the speed of light. Direct-to-satellite communication enables anytime-wireless connectivity between any two places in the world, as well as providing global positioning services with accuracy of a few feet or inches! A single optical fiber can transport the information of hundreds of thousands of volumes within a second.

ABOUT THIS BOOK

My interest in this field began early in my life when I pursued an undergraduate degree in physics. My interest in optics continued during my graduate work when I combined electronics, materials, and interferometric techniques. During the last few years, I have been working on the subject of optical communications, both SONET/SDH and ATM over SONET/SDH. My work on this subject culminated into a book titled *Understanding SONET/SDH and ATM* (IEEE Press, 1999). Subsequently, I had the opportunity to expand my understanding of multiwavelength transmission in optical media, now known as *wavelength division multiplexing* (WDM), mainly through my active interest in this subject during my undergraduate and graduate studies. Recently, I discovered that the notes I had been compiling over the years had current educational value, particularly in the area of DWDM.

The intention of this book is to explain in simple language the properties of light, its interaction with matter, and how it is used to develop optical components such as filters, multiplexers, and others that are used in optical communications. In addition, the book provides an introduction to DWDM technology and to DWDM communications systems. This book is not meant to replace related standards or to provide a complete mathematical analysis of each optical device, although mathematical relationships support some device functionality. DWDM is still evolving, and it is strongly recommended that the reader interested in the details of DWDM consult the most current updated standards. I wish you happy and easy reading.

Stamatios V. Kartalopoulos
Lucent Technologies, Inc.

ACKNOWLEDGMENTS

Throughout time, few noted achievements have been the product of an individual's effort. Instead, they have been accomplished through the efforts of many. Similarly, the fruition of this book would have been impossible without the cooperation, diligence, understanding, and encouragement of a number of people.

First, I would like to extend my thanks and appreciation to my wife Anita for her patience and encouragement. Second, I express my appreciation to my colleagues for creating an environment that fosters learning, collaboration, and encouragement—in particular, Wayne H. Knox, Martin C. Nuss, Joseph E. Ford, Martin Zirngibl, Rod Alferness, Tom J. Ciaccia, and David J. Smith. Finally, to the anonymous reviewers for their comments and constructive criticism; to the IEEE Press staff for their enthusiasm, suggestions, creativity, and project management; and to all those who diligently worked during all phases of this production, I offer my humblest gratitude.

Stamatios V. Kartalopoulos
Lucent Technologies, Inc.

INTRODUCTION

Light has fascinated mankind since the very beginning of time. Light enables us to see things—uplifting rainbows, dramatic colors at dawn or sunset, vibrant colors of flowers and birds. Thus, it is no accident that light was held in a prominent position in most philosophies and religions.

The fascination with light has also sparked the curiosity of many scientists. Since ancient times, they have tried to decipher the nature of light and over the centuries, like masons laying one brick at a time to complete a wall, they have added to this body of knowledge. Today, we know that light is an electromagnetic wave which, like radio waves, is subject to all laws of physics on propagation and interaction.

Electromagnetic waves extend over a wide spectrum of frequencies (or wavelengths). However, this spectrum is not entirely visible to the human eye. The part of the spectrum that we call *visible light* is in a narrow range (of wavelengths), from 0.7 μm (7000 nm) to 0.4 μm (4000 nm) and from the deep red to the dark violet-blue. As an example, the yellow light of a sodium lamp is 5890 nm. It just happens that this part of the spectrum is in the response range of our eye receptors (the retinal cones and rods). The cones enable us to perceive color, and the rods enable us to detect such miniscule quantities of light that we can see a lit candle in the dark many miles away. Our eye receptors do not respond to frequencies below red (known as *infrared* or *IR*) or to frequencies above violet-blue (known as *ultraviolet* or *UV*), although the eye receptors of certain animals do. If we were to ask a cat or an owl what its visible range is or what it sees through its eyes, we would certainly hear a different answer.

Since ancient times, a great deal of research has revealed that light propagates in a straight line. However, when light is in an optically transparent *pipe,* then it is guided by the pipe and follows its curvature. This observation was demonstrated with a very simple and convincing experiment. Heron of Alexandria took a bucket with a hole in the bottom and filled it with water. As the water was gushing out of the hole, a curved stream of water was formed. As sunlight entered at an angle from the top of the bucket, it propagated through the hole following the curvature of the stream. This experiment and others have been repeated throughout the centuries, and new observations on the reflection and refraction of light led scientists to concentrate on light rays, which could be focused on a desired spot. (It is said that Archimedes was able to burn the enemy's wooden fleet doing so.)

The quest for unveiling the secrets of light did not stop. Huygens studied the wave nature of light, and Fabry and Perot studied interactions of light and explained its interferometric properties. In addition to the wave nature of light, it has been found that light exhibits particle properties. Initially, this raised many eyebrows as it was met with skepticism. However, Compton's demonstration of a small lightweight propeller in a vacuum, one side of which was black (for high absorption) and the other shiny (for high reflectance), was very convincing when light caused the propeller to rotate—a mechanical reaction that could not be explained with only wave theory.

Furthermore, many scientists studied the composition of light, and it was separated into its component wavelengths. Similarly, Zeeman studied the interaction of light with other fields, and he split the chlorine yellow line with a strong magnetic field. The propagation properties of light in transparent materials and in optical wavelengths were also studied. Today, many interesting materials have been developed, and glass fiber is the chosen transmission medium for high-speed, high-reliability, and long-distance terrestrial and submarine communications. Currently, bit rates of up to 40 Gb per second are used in a single fiber. With wavelength multiplexing, dubbed *dense wavelength division multiplexing* (DWDM), the aggregate bandwidth has exceeded the Terabit per second. DWDM systems with up to 128 wavelengths have been announced, and DWDM with 206 wavelengths has already been experimentally demonstrated. A 40-wavelength DWDM system, at 10 Gbps per wavelength, has an aggregate bandwidth of 400 Gb per second—a bandwidth that can transport in a single fiber the contents of more than 11,000 volumes of an encyclopedia in a second. DWDM systems with 40 Gb per second per wavelength have already been announced, and the trend continues to increase both the wavelength density and the bit rate, as illustrated in Figure I.1.

IN THIS BOOK

This book is organized into five parts and each part into chapters. Part I reviews the physics of light; interferometry, diffraction, refraction, and so on, are important to understand before the Mach-Zehnder or Fabry-Perot interferometers are described. The optical properties of matter including nonlinear effects is also important to understand before we describe the transmission properties of light in fiber. Part II describes the fundamentals of the optical glass fiber as a transmission medium and the transmission properties of light through it. It also describes the fundamentals of many optical devices such as filters, multiplexers and demultiplexers, switches, polarizers, light sources, and optical receivers. Part III reviews various coding tech-

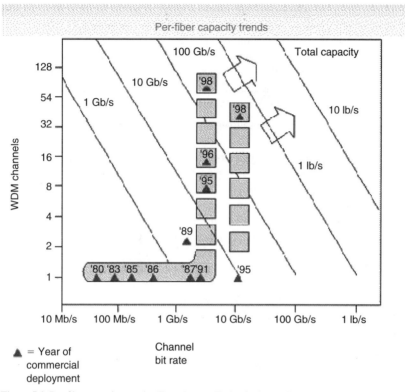

Figure I.1 Per-fiber capacity trends. (From Lucent Technologies, *Bell Labs Technology*, vol. 2 no. 2, Fall 1998, p. 3.)

niques that are used in both digital and optical transmission. Part IV provides a comprehensive, yet simplified, description of wavelength digital multiplexing (WDM) and DWDM. It also discusses DWDM system design issues, network topologies, and fault avoidance. Finally, Part V provides a discussion on the current research in this area. At the end of each chapter are problems and review questions, as well as answers. Related references are provided at the end of each part.

STANDARDS

Optical transmission is specified in detail in several documents published by various International Standards bodies. These documents are official and voluminous, and this relatively brief book can be only considered a high-level *tutorial* that is designed to help readers understand the workings of DWDM technology. Consequently, we strongly recommend that system designers consult these standards for details. The key International Standards bodies in DWDM optical communications are as follows:

- **ITU-T** and **ITU-R** stand for International Telecommunications Union-Telecommunications Standardization Sector and International Telecommunications Union-Radio-Communications Sector, respectively. ITU has published several documents identified by "ITU-T Recommendation G.nnn" where nnn is a number that refers to a specific aspect of the system. For example, ITU-T Recommendation G.774.01 describes the synchronous digital hierarchy (SDH) performance monitoring for the network element.

- **Bellcore** was a US-based organization that contributed to standards and also published recommendations.

- **Some other known standards bodies are as follows:** American National Standards Institute (ANSI), Association Française de Normalisation (AFNOR), ATM-Forum, British Standards Institution (BSI), Consultative Committee International Telegraph and Telephone (CCITT, a former name of ITU), Deutsches Institut fuer Normung EV (DIN), European Association for Standardizing Information and Communication Systems (ECMA), Electronics Industry Association/Telecommunications Industry Association (EIA/TIA), European Telecommunications Standardization Institute (ETSI), Frame-Relay Forum (FRF), Institute of Electrical and Electronics Engineers (IEEE), Internet Engineering Task Force (IETF), Motion Picture Experts Group (MPEG), International Standards Organization (ISO), Telecommunications Information Networking Architecture (TINA) consortium, Comit Europ en de Nolmalisation Electrotechnique (CENELEC), Personal Computer Memory Card International Association (PCMCIA), and World Wide Web Consortium (W3C).

PART I
FUNDAMENTALS OF LIGHT

INTRODUCTION

Part I provides a brief introduction to optical physics. It is the minimum prerequisite to the understanding of optical devices. It examines the nature of light, its propagation characteristics in vacuum and through matter, as well as its interaction with matter.

For example, interferometry must be first understood before the Mach-Zehnder or Fabry-Perot interferometers can be explained. Refraction and diffraction must be understood, before Bragg gratings and filters are explained. Similarly, the nonlinear properties of matter must be understood before nonlinear fiber-transmission phenomena are explained.

For simplicity, we have avoided complex mathematical derivations and have listed the minimum possible number of formulas needed to explain the operation of certain optical devices. The interested reader may consult advanced and specialized textbooks as well as other publications that provide full mathematical derivations. Our purpose is to provide a broad, yet thorough understanding of the workings of optical devices that are used in optical communications and in dense wavelength division multiplexing (DWDM) in Part II.

This part consists of two chapters. Chapter 1 describes the nature of light and its propagation characteristics. Chapter 2 provides a description of the interaction of light with matter.

CHAPTER 1

THE NATURE OF LIGHT

1.1 INTRODUCTION

Fiber has been the long-haul transmission medium of choice for several years as well as for metropolitan area networks (MAN) in inner-city and inner-campus applications. Based on a demand by end-customers for higher bandwidth, fiber penetration in the loop plant starts becoming noticeable as well.

Synchronous optical network/synchronous digital hierarchy (SONET/SDH) technologies have paved the fiber-way for ultra-high bit rates and ultra-bandwidths. Many thousands of kilometers of fiber are installed each year around the world. Advances in solid-state and photonic technology have transformed what once "could not be done" (i.e., bit rates at 40 Gbps over many kilometers of single-mode fiber) into a reality.

In addition to traditional time division multiplexing (TDM) services (e.g., voice, low-speed data), new services (e.g., Internet, high-speed data, video, wireless, etc.) have triggered a voracious appetite for bandwidth that legacy communications networks have a hard time delivering. Currently, voice traffic is increasing at a rate of 10% per year. Data traffic increases at a rate of 80% per year.

New communications systems have been designed and new standards have been recommended that promise prompt and reliable delivery of large volume of customer bits. However, although new systems are able to process a large quantity of data, the network must be able to transport and manage the increasing traffic, as well as the communication conduits that pass bits from one system to another. Therefore, a question arises: As the bandwidth keeps increasing, how do we assure that the transmission medium has a scalable bandwidth capacity? There are *two choices* to meet this demand:

1. Install more fiber, and/or
2. Increase the transportable bandwidth of an existing fiber.

Currently, depending on technology and economics, both choices are pursued. We examine the second.

1.2   INCREASING THE TRANSPORTABLE BANDWIDTH OF A FIBER

There are two methods to increase bandwidth in a single fiber:

1. *Increase the bit rate.* An increase to 10 Gbps and up to 40 Gbps is currently feasible for transporting SONET/SDH optical carrier-192 (OC-192) and optical carrier-768 (OC-768) signals, or their aggregate equivalent. However, the electronic circuitry (transmitters, receivers, etc.) that makes this possible is neither trivial nor cost-effective. In addition, transmitting a reliable error-free signal beyond 40 Gbps is a technology currently in experimental phase, and it does not seem likely that it will be incorporated into commercial systems soon.

2. *Increase the number of wavelengths in the same fiber.* This is a viable solution that capitalizes on advances in solid-state and photonic technology. Several wavelengths, each transporting data at 10 or 40 Gbps would increase the transportable bandwidth by a factor as large as the number of wavelengths. Systems with 40, 80, and 128 wavelengths per fiber have been designed, and systems with more wavelengths are in planning or experimental phase.

1.3   WHAT IS DWDM?

Wavelength division multiplexing (WDM) is an optical technology that couples many wavelengths in the same fiber, thus effectively increasing the aggregate bandwidth per fiber to the sum of the bit rates of each wavelength. As an example, 40 wavelengths at 10 Gbps per wavelength in the same fiber raise the aggregate bandwidth to 400 Gbps, and astonishing aggregate bandwidths at several terabits per second (Tbps) are also a reality.

Dense WDM (DWDM) is a technology with a larger (denser) number of wavelengths coupled into a fiber (>40) than WDM. However, as the number of wavelengths increases, several issues need attention, such as channel width and channel spacing, total optical power launched in fiber, nonlinear effects, cross-talk, span of fiber, amplification, and so on (we define these terms in subsequent sections). An earlier WDM technology with a small number of wavelengths (<10), larger channel width, and channel spacing is termed *coarse WDM* (CWDM). Here, we use the terms WDM and DWDM indistinguishably.

DWDM technology was made possible with the realization of several optical components. Components that were previously an experimenter's curiosity are now compact, of a high quality, commercially available, and increasingly inexpensive. It is also expected that several optical functions will soon be integrated to offer complex functionality at a cost per function comparable to electronic implementation. The following provides a snapshot of what has enabled the DWDM technology to become reality.

- Optical fiber has been produced that exhibits low loss and better optical transmission performance over the wavelength spectrum of 1.3 μm and 1.55 μm.
- Optical amplifiers with flat gain over a range of wavelengths and coupled in line with the transmitting fiber boost the optical signal, thus eliminating the need for regenerators.
- Integrated solid-state optical filters are compact and can be integrated with other optical components on the same substrate.
- Integrated solid-state laser sources and photodetectors offer compact designs.
- Optical multiplexers and demultiplexers are based on passive optical diffraction.
- Wavelength selectable (tunable) filters can be used as optical add-drop multiplexers.
- Optical add-drop multiplexer (OADM) components have made DWDM possible in MAN ring-type and long haul networks.
- Optical cross-connect (OXC) components, implemented with a variety of technologies (e.g., lithium-niobate), have made optical switching possible.

In addition, standards have been developed so that interoperable systems can be offered by many vendors. As DWDM technology evolves, existing standards are updated or new ones are introduced to address emerging issues.

DWDM finds applications in ultra-high bandwidth long haul as well as in ultra-high-speed metropolitan or inner-city networks and, at the edge of other networks (SONET, Internet protocol [IP], and asynchronous transfer mode [ATM]).

As DWDM deployment becomes more ubiquitous, DWDM technology cost decreases, primarily due to increased optical component volume. Consequently, DWDM is also expected to become a low-cost technology in many access-type networks, such as fiber-to-the-home (FTTH), fiber-to-the-desktop PC (FTTPC), and others.

1.4   WHAT IS OFDM?

Optical frequency-division multiplexing (FDM or OFDM) is an earlier acronym for WDM. However, the term FDM was already in use by non-optical systems (e.g., radio systems), whereas the terms WDM and DWDM have been exclusively used in optical communications systems. There is also an unofficial, subtle difference between the two: In WDM systems the spacing between wavelengths is in the order of 1 nm whereas in (optical) FDM is in the order of the bit rate of the signal.

In DWDM, each channel represents a bit stream that is carried over a different wavelength (λ_i). Different channels may carry data at different bit rates and of different services (e.g., voice, data, video, IP, ATM, SONET, etc.). An end-to-end simplistic view of a DWDM system with an optical amplifier is shown, Figure 1.1.

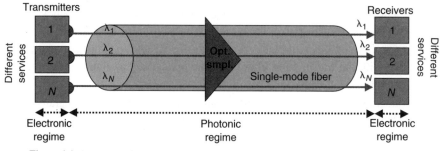

Figure 1.1 A conceptual DWDM system with many wavelength-channels in the same fiber.

1.5   OPAQUE VERSUS TRANSPARENT WDM SYSTEMS

There are two types of WDM systems. *Opaque* systems receive photonic information from the fiber, they photonically demultiplex each wavelength channel, and then each photonic channel is converted into electronic. Within the system, signal processing for each channel (payload multiplexing/demultiplexing, error control, routing, switching, etc.) takes place electronically. At the output port of the system, electronic information is converted back to photonic, wavelengths are multiplexed, and the WDM signal is launched into the fiber. Thus, from an observer's viewpoint, photons do not go through the system; hence the term *opaque*.

Optical devices are used throughout *transparent* systems. That is, received photons are never converted into electrons, including functions such as switching, multiplexing and demultiplexing. Thus, from an observer's viewpoint, photons go through the system; hence the term *transparent*.

1.6   DWDM DEVICES

DWDM technology requires specialized optical devices that are based on properties of light and on the optical, electrical, and mechanical properties of semiconductor materials. Such devices must provide the equivalent functionality of electrical/electronic (opaque) communications systems. These devices include optical transmitters, optical receivers, optical filters, optical modulators, optical amplifiers, OADM, and OXC. A quick review of the nature and properties of light in both free-space and in transparent material is therefore critical to a better understanding of WDM components, technology, and networks.

1.7   FUNDAMENTALS OF LIGHT

Light possesses two natures, a wave nature and a particle nature.

1.7.1   The Wave Nature of Light

Like radio waves or x-rays, light is electromagnetic radiation that is subject to reflection, refraction, diffraction, interference, polarization, fading, loss, and so on. Light of a single frequency is termed *monochromatic,* or single color. Light is described by the Maxwell's wave equations:

$$\nabla^2 E = \left(\frac{1}{v^2}\right)\left(\frac{\partial^2 E}{\partial t^2}\right) \quad \text{and} \quad \nabla^2 H = \left(\frac{1}{v^2}\right)\left(\frac{\partial^2 H}{\partial t^2}\right),$$

where ∇^2 is the second order Laplacian operator, v is the speed of the wave (in an isotropic medium) and E and H are the electric and magnetic fields, respectively. Note that Maxwell's equation refers to monochromatic light.

Light as a wave is characterized by frequency (and wavelength), phase, and propagation speed. *Frequency* is the number of waves in a second, and *wavelength* is the distance of a complete wave (e.g., peak-to-peak) in a medium or in vacuum. Frequency is described in cycles per second or Hertz, and wavelength in nanometers (nm) or micrometers (mm). Another unit that occasionally is encountered is the Angstrom; an *Angstrom* (Å) is 10^{-10} meters.

1.7.2   The Particle Nature of Light

Like all moving particles, light too can exert pressure and cause a wheel to spin (Compton's experiment). Thus, light is also described in number of particles. The smallest quantity of monochromatic light, known as a *photon*, is described by the energy (E) equation:

$$E = h\nu$$

where h is Planck's constant, $6.6260755 \times 10^{-34}$ (Joule-second), and ν is the frequency of light.

Light (from an incandescent light bulb) consists of a continuum of wavelengths that spans the complete optical spectrum from deep red (700 nm) to deep violet-blue (400 nm), as shown in Figure 1.2.

Light does not travel at the same speed in all media. In vacuum, it travels in a straight path at a constant maximum speed defined by Einstein's equation

$$E = mc^2$$

Figure 1.2 The visible spectrum is in the range from 0.7 μm (700 nm) to 0.4 μm (400 nm). The yellow light of sodium lamp is 589 nm.

Where $c = 2.99792458 \times 10^5$ km/s, or ~30 cm/ns.

The relationship between frequency, speed of light and wavelength is given by

$$v = c/\lambda$$

From the two energy relations $E = mc^2 = hv$, and the last one, certain interesting relationships are obtained, such as the frequency in terms of photon mass and speed ($v = mc^2/h$), and the mass of a photon ($m = hv/c^2$).

When light passes by a strong electromagnetic field, it interacts with it and its trajectory changes direction. The stronger the field the larger the change (Figure 1.3). When light travels in an optically denser (than vacuum) medium (e.g., water, glass, transparent plastic), then its speed becomes slower.

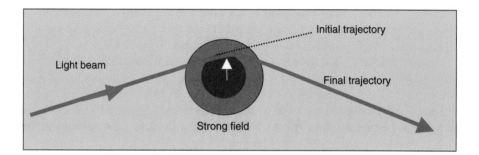

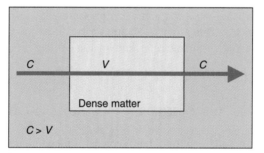

Figure 1.3 Light passing by a strong electromagnetic field, and light traveling through optically denser (than vacuum) medium (e.g., water, glass, transparent plastic).

1.8   PHOTOMETRIC TERMS: FLUX, ILLUMINANCE, AND LUMINANCE

When looking at two light sources or two illuminated objects, by comparison, it is possible to determine which is brighter. Although such comparisons are useful, absolute units of the brightness of light sources are very important. In the following, we list some key definitions.

The rate of optical energy flow (or number of photons per second) that is emitted by a point light source in all directions is known as the (total) *luminous flux, Φ*, measured in lumens (lm). In radiometric terms this is known as power, measured in *Watts*.

Most known sources of light do not emit at the same rate in all directions. The rate emitted in a solid angle of a spherical surface area equal to its radius (e.g., radius = 1 m, surface area = 1 m^2) is known as *luminous intensity*, I. Luminous intensity is measured in *candelas* or *candles* (cd). The luminous intensity of a sphere is $\Phi/4\pi$.

The flux density at an area A (m^2), or the luminous flux per unit area, is defined as *illuminance, E,* and it is measured in *lux* (lx). The illuminance at a point of a spherical surface is $E = \Phi/4\pi R^2$. Because the luminous intensity I of the sphere is $\Phi/4\pi$, then $E = I/R^2$. This is known as *the law of inverse squares* (Figure 1.4).

Illuminance refers to light received by a surface. The amount of optical energy emitted by a lighted surface per unit of time, per unit of solid angle, and per unit of projected area is known as *luminance, B*. Luminance is measured in cd/m^2, and is also known as *nit* (nt). Some examples of luminance are (in cd/m^2):

Clear blue sky:	10^4
Sun:	1.6×10^9
Candle:	2×10^6
Fluorescent lamp:	10^4

Table 1.1 summarizes photometric units that are used in optics and optical communications, their measuring units, and their dimensions.

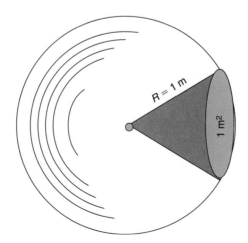

Figure 1.4 Definition of luminous (or candle) intensity.

Table 1.1 Summary of Photometric Units

Definition	Photometric Unit	Dimensions*
Energy	Luminous energy (talbot)	ML^2T^{-2}
Energy per unit area	Luminous density (talbot/m^2)	MT^{-2}
Energy per unit time	Luminous flux (lumen)	ML^2T^{-3}
Flux per unit area	Luminous emittance (lumen/m^2 or lambert)	MT^{-3}
Flux per unit solid angle	Luminous intensity (lumens/steradian)	ML^2T^{-3}
Flux per unit solid angle per unit projected area	Luminance (candela/m^2)	MT^{-3}
Flux input per unit area	Illuminance (meter-candela)	MT^{-3}
Ratio of reflected to incident flux	Luminous reflectance	
Ratio of incident flux to output flux	Luminous transmittance	
Ratio of absorbed to incident flux	Luminous absorptance	

*M = mass, T = time, L = length.

EXERCISES

1. Two nodes are linked with a 50-km single-mode fiber cable and communicate at a bit rate of 1 Gbps. The wavelength over which data is carried is 1310 nm. The two nodes are upgraded to 10 Gbps. The fiber capacity must be increased to 10 Gbps. What would you recommend if:
   (a) The fiber is part of a seven-fiber cable (not all used) routed via an underground 10-cm diameter pipe?
   (b) The fiber is part of a seven-fiber cable (all used) routed via an underground 10-cm diameter pipe?
   (c) The fiber is part of a seven-fiber aerial cable (all used)?
2. A glass plate has blue color. Is it transparent or opaque?
3. A glass plate has blue color. Another glass plate of red color is placed on top of it. A flashlight is placed behind the two plates. What color do you expect to see?
4. A surface is made such that half is covered with aluminum foil and the other half is painted black. If the surface is exposed to the sun, what do you expect to find after 1 hour?

CHAPTER 2

INTERACTION OF LIGHT WITH MATTER

2.1 INTRODUCTION

When light enters matter, its elecromagnetic field interacts with the localized electromagnetic field of atoms. The result is that if and when light emerges from matter, its characteristics and properties may not be the same. How light is affected by matter depends on the strength of the field of the light, its wavelength, and the matter itself. In addition, external influences on matter, such as temperature, pressure, and other external fields (electrical, magnetic), influence the interaction of light with matter. The interaction of light with matter may be undesirable, but it may also be taken advantage of to construct optical devices.

In this chapter, we examine the interaction of light with matter.

2.2 TRANSPARENT VERSUS OPAQUE MATTER

Some matter allows all light energy (all photons) to propagate through it and it is called *optically transparent.* In contrast, *opaque* matter does not.

Example

Clear glass is transparent; a sheet of iron is not.

Semi-transparent matter passes a portion of light energy through it, and absorbs the remainder. Such matter attenuates the optical power of light and it may be used to make an optical device known as *optical attenuator.* ∎

Example

Most transparent matter, semi-transparent mirrors.

An *optical filter* allows selected frequencies to be propagated through it. ∎

Example

Red, green, yellow, or blue glass (each allows a selected range of frequencies to be propagated through it).

Some matter in ionized state absorbs selected frequencies and passes all others.   ■

Example

The sun's ionized surface.   ■

2.3 PROPERTIES OF OPTICALLY TRANSPARENT MATTER

When light enters matter, its electromagnetic field reacts with the near fields of its atoms. In dense matter, light is quickly absorbed within the first few atomic layers and, because it does not emerge from it, that matter is termed *non-optically transparent*. In contrast to this, some types of matter do not completely absorb light, letting it propagate through it and emerge from it. This is termed *optically transparent* matter. Examples of optically transparent matter include water, clear glass, and so on. We are more interested in optically transparent matter; thus, we examine the interaction of light with it. In particular, we examine the following:

- Reflection and refraction
- Diffraction
- Interference
- Holography
- Polarization
- Birefringence
- Dispersion
- Non-linear phenomena
- Optical isotropy and anisotropy
- Optical homogeneity and nonhomogeneity
- Effects of impurities and microcracks
  - Absorption
  - Scattering

2.3.1 Reflection and Refraction—Index of Refraction

The *index of refraction* of a transparent medium (n_{med}) is defined as the ratio of the speed of light in vacuum (c) over the speed of light in a medium (v_{med}).

$$n_{med} = c/v_{med}$$

Then, between two mediums (1 and 2) the relationship:

$$n_2/n_1 = v_1/v_2$$

is true (Figure 2.1), where n_1, v_1, and n_2, v_2 are the index of refraction and speed of light in the two media, respectively. The index of refraction, or refractive index, for vacuum is 1; for other materials it is greater than 1, typically between 1 and 2. For example, polyurethane has $n = 1.46$.

The following basic relationships are useful:

speed of light in vacuum: $c = \lambda f$

speed of light in medium: $v_{\text{med}} = \lambda_{\text{med}} f$

index of refraction: $n_1/n_2 = \lambda_2/\lambda_1$

where f is the frequency of light and λ the wavelength. Usually, letters, f or the Greek letter v are used for frequency. Here, we use f to eliminate confusion between v (for speed) and v (for frequency).

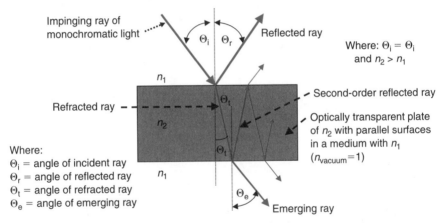

Figure 2.1 Reflection and refraction.

2.3.2 Snell's Law

Snell's law links the ratio of index of refraction with the angle of the incident (Θ_i) and of the refracted (Θ_t) rays:

$$n_2/n_1 = \sin \Theta_i/\sin \Theta_t$$

where Θ_i and Θ_t are defined in Figure 2.1.

2.3.3 Critical Angle

The *critical angle*, Θ_{critical}, is the (maximum) angle of incidence of light (from an optically denser to optically thinner material) at which light stops being refracted and is totally reflected (Figure 2.2). The critical angle depends on the refractive index and the wavelength of light.

$$\sin \Theta_{\text{critical}} = n_1/n_2$$

for $n_1 = 1$ (air), then

$$\sin \Theta_{\text{critical}} = 1/n_2.$$

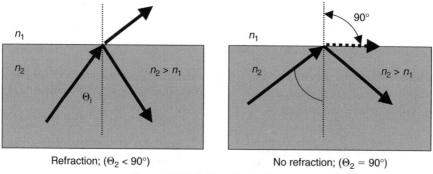

| Refraction; ($\Theta_2 < 90°$) | No refraction; ($\Theta_2 = 90°$) |

Figure 2.2 Definition of critical angle.

In certain cases, a continuous change of the refractive index may take place. When light rays enter from one side, the rays are refracted and they may emerge from the same side (Figure 2.3).

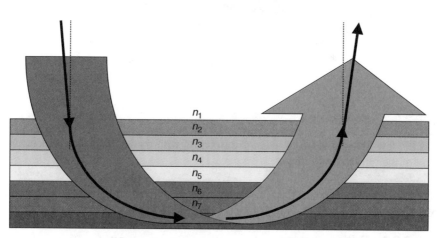

Where: $n_1 < n_2 < n_3 < n_4 < n_5 < n_6 < n_7 < n_8$

Figure 2.3 Refraction through variable refractive index.

2.3.4   Optical Prisms

Consider that two planes of a plate intersect each other to form a *prism* at an angle Θ_2. When a polychromatic narrow beam of light impinges one of the prism surfaces, then each frequency component is refracted differently. When each frequency reaches the other surface it is refracted again.

The output light from the second surface of the prism consists of the frequency components separated by a small angle. The angle of each frequency component with the original composite beam is known as the *angle of deflection, ϵ.* That is, the angle of deflection varies with frequency (Figure 2.4).

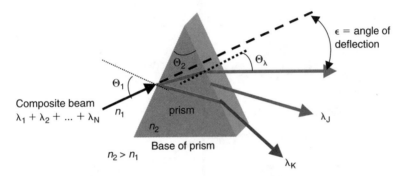

Figure 2.4 The angle of deflection is different for each frequency component.

In Figure 2.4, when $n_1 = 1$, the Snell's law derives:

$$n_2 = \{\sin[(\Theta_2 + \epsilon)/2]\}/\sin(\Theta_2/2)$$

The following prism laws hold:

- The angle Θ_λ increases as the index of refraction increases.
- The angle Θ_λ increases as the prism angle Θ_2 increases.
- The angle Θ_λ increases as the angle of incidence Θ_1 increases.
- The angle Θ_λ increases as the frequency of light increases (or the wavelength decreases).

The angular variability of each frequency component of the prism is known as *angular dispersion* and it is given by

$$d\theta/d\lambda = [(d\theta/dn)(dn/d\lambda)]$$

where n is the index of refraction and λ the wavelength. The first term depends on the geometry of the prism, whereas the second term depends on the material.

2.3.5   Diffraction

Consider a parallel beam of light that impinges on a screen with a small round hole in it, and a second screen behind the first at a distance d (Figure 2.5). Although light travels in a straight line and a small round projection is expected, D_{EXP}, a wider projection is seen instead, D_{ACT}. This phenomenon is due to the edge of the hole that diffracts light. This is known as *diffraction of light* or the *phenomenon of Fresnel*. The smaller the diameter, the wider the projection. If the hole were a narrow rectangle, what would the projection look like?

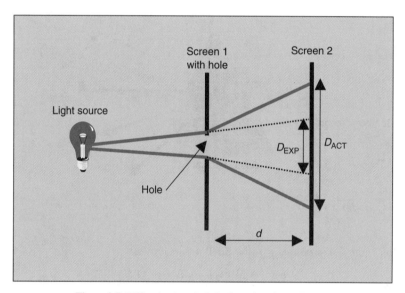

Figure 2.5 Diffraction by a hole in the order of wavelength.

2.3.6   Diffraction at Infinity

Let parallel (collimated) light, also known as *light from a source at infinity,* pass through a rectangular slit of height h and width w. Then, due to diffraction, the projection on a screen is a rectangle rotated by 90°. That is, the diffracted pattern is narrow in the direction in which the aperture of the slit is wide (see Section 2.3.5) (Figure 2.6). In addition, because of two-dimensional (2-D) Fourier expansion, the diffracted light forms many rectangles on the screen in the x–y plane with an intensity that fades as one moves away from the axis of symmetry. The condition of rectangles on the screen are

$R(x, y) = \text{Rect}(x/w_o)\text{Rect}(y/h_o) = 1$, for $|x| < w_o/2$ and $|y| < h_o/2$, and $R(x, y)$
$\quad = 0$ elsewhere.

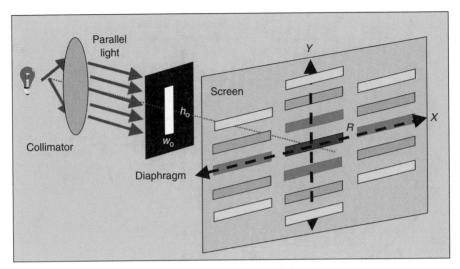

Figure 2.6 Diffraction at infinity.

2.3.7   Diffraction Gratings

A *diffraction grating* is a passive optical device that diffracts incident parallel light in specific directions according to the angle of incidence on the grating, the optical wavelength of the incident light, and the design characteristics of the grating, *line spacing d,* and *blaze angle* Θ_B (Figure 2.7).

A common form of a diffraction grating consists of a glass substrate with adjacent epoxy strips that have been blazed. The number of strips per unit length is a parameter known as the *grating constant.* The blaze angle Θ_B, the wavelength λ, and the d are related by

$$\Theta_B = \sin^{-1}(\lambda/2d).$$

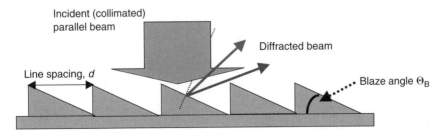

Figure 2.7 When collimated light falls on a grating, each frequency is diffracted differently.

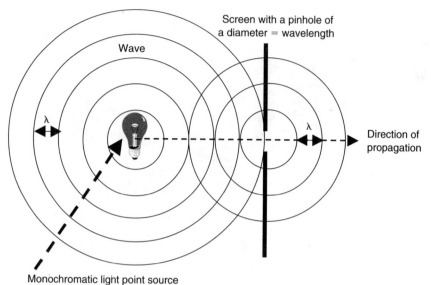

Figure 2.8 Principles of Huygens-Fresnel.

2.3.8   Principle of Huygens-Fresnel

Let the light from a monochromatic point source impinge on a screen having a small round hole in the order of the wavelength. The hole then behaves like a source of light of the same wavelength (Figure 2.8). This is known as the *Huygens-Fresnel principle,* a key principle in the study of *interference of light.*

2.3.9   Interference of Light

Consider a monochromatic light source, a screen with two pinholes equidistant from the axis of symmetry, and a second screen behind the first and parallel to it (Figure 2.9). Based on the Huygens-Fresnel principle, the two pinholes become two sources of coherent light, and alternating bright and dark zones are seen on the second screen. Bright zones (*constructive interference*) are formed when the travel difference between two rays $\Delta = |r_2 - r_1|$ or $\Delta = |r_4 - r_3|$ is an integer multiple of λ, and dark zones (*destructive interference*) are when the travel difference between two rays is half-integer multiple of λ. The Mach-Zehnder filter is based on this principle.

2.3.10   Antireflection Coatings

Many optical devices or components require the maximum possible optical power of a specific wavelength range to be coupled in, and thus zero or a minimal reflected power. This is accomplished by using *antireflection coatings* at the interface air-component. Antireflection coatings consist of one or more thin layers (films) of material, each layer having a specific thickness and a specific refractive index. As an example, to minimize the reflected optical power on incident light on glass, the layer

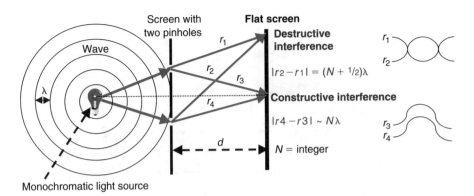

Figure 2.9 Interference (constructive or destructive) of two coherent sources of the same wavelength.

that interfaces glass with air has a low refractive index. Such material is MgF_2 ($n = 1.38$). The next layer (in a two-layer coating system) may be PbF_2 ($n = 1.7$), and the last is glass ($n = 1.5$). Each layer has a quarter-wavelength thickness so that rays reflected by each layer interfere destructively and thus the *extinction of reflection* at the designed wavelength is complete. This means that the antireflection coating is also wavelength selective (Figure 2.10). Because of the wavelength selectivity of coatings, they are also used as optical filters (see filters, Section 4.6).

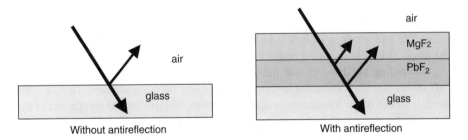

Figure 2.10 Refraction by a glass plate without and with antireflection coating.

2.3.11   Holography

Holography is a method by which, using coherent light (laser light), the phase and amplitude characteristics of a three-dimensional (3-D) object is captured on a 2-D photographic plate. Both diffraction and interference of light are employed in holography.

Consider a monochromatic coherent light source split into two beams A and B. Beam A impinges the 3-D object and it is diffracted on a photographic film (Figure 2.11). Beam B is reflected by a prism and it, too, impinges the photographic plate. At the plate, beams A and B interfere and, depending on the travel difference of rays in the two beams, because of the three-dimensionality of the object, the amplitude and phase difference from each point of the object are recorded on the photographic

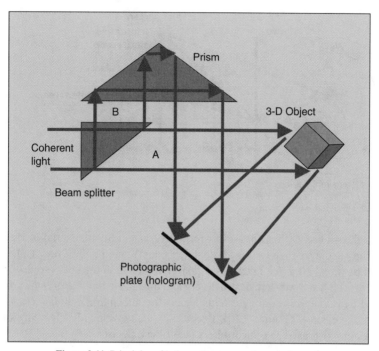

Figure 2.11 Principles of holography—generating a hologram.

plate. The end result is an incomprehensible image of dense stripes and whorls on the plate. This is known as a *hologram*.

According to "diffraction at infinity," the phase and amplitude information of a 3-D object has been recorded in a myriad of places on the hologram. Thus, even a small segment of the hologram contains all information (phase and amplitude) of the 3-D object.

To recreate an image of the 3-D object, the process of holography is reversed. That is, the hologram is illuminated with coherent light (Figure 2.12). The dense stripes and whorls in the plate act as a diffraction grating that interacts with the incident coherent beam and it decodes the phase and amplitude information to recreate an image replica of the original 3-D object.

One of the salient features of holography is its image recognition. When coherent light passes through a transparent plate with a set of images, then through a hologram, an image is seen on a screen, one that matches an image previously recorded, in the hologram. It turns out that two conjugate inverted images appear about the axis of symmetry. If there is no match, then a blurred dot is seen (Figure 2.13).

Holograms are so small that many thousands may be contained in a square millimeter of a holographic plate. Thus, if each hologram contains an individual image, then thousands of different images may be stored in few square millimeters of a holographic plate. If these images correspond to the frames of a movie, or the pages

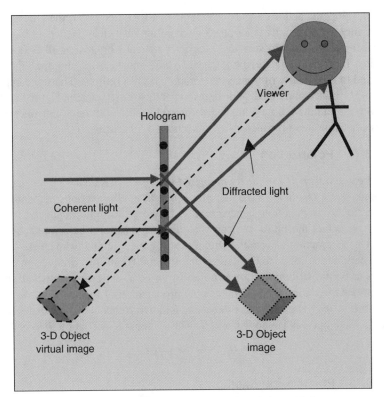

Figure 2.12 Principles of holography—creating a holographic image.

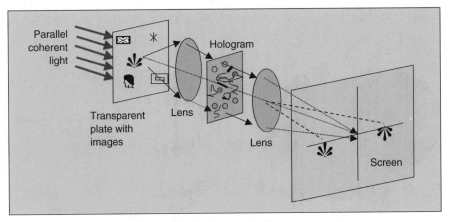

Figure 2.13 Application of holography in image recognition.

of an encyclopedia and if they are selectable in a specified order, then the enormous applicability of holograms in storage is becoming very clear. Hence, holography is a promising technology in very large capacity optical storage as well as in communications. In optical storage, Fe-doped $LiNbO_3$ and organic photopolymers have been used to construct write-once, read many (WORM) times. The write capability in WORMs is accomplished with high-power low-cost semiconductor lasers (see Section 6.2), and the holographic frames are selectable with micromirrors that have been made using nano-technology (see Sections 11.4 and 11.5).

2.3.12   Polarization

Typical created light is *circularly polarized* or *unpolarized*. That is, its electric (E) and its magnetic (H) fields have the same strength in all directions perpendicular to the direction of propagation, hence *circular*. However, as light propagates through a medium, it enters the fields of nearby atoms and ions, and field interaction takes place. This interaction affects the strength of the electric and/or magnetic fields of light in certain directions to the degree that the end-result may produce an elliptical or a linear field distribution. Linear polarization is an extreme case where the field exists in one direction perpendicular to the propagation of light.

Consider that polarized light is separated into two components, one that is fully polarized, I_P, and one that is unpolarized, I_U. The degree of polarization, P, is defined by

$$P = I_P/(I_P + I_U)$$

2.3.13   Polarization Examples

Figure 2.14 illustrates some polarization distributions (polarization modes) around the axis of propagation of a ray.

2.3.14   Polarization by Reflection and Refraction

Polarization may take place by reflection, by refraction, and by scattering. When unpolarized light impinges a surface, its reflection is polarized. The degree of

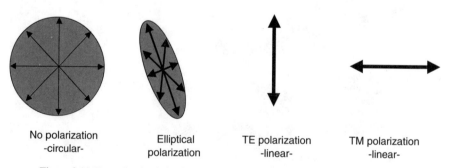

| No polarization -circular- | Elliptical polarization | TE polarization -linear- | TM polarization -linear- |

Figure 2.14 Example of polarization modes (direction of light is perpendicular to page).

polarization depends on the angle of incidence and the refractive index of the material, given by the *Brewster's Law* $\tan(I_P) = n$, where n is the refractive index and I_P the polarizing angle. Figure 2.15 illustrates some reflected and refracted polarization examples.

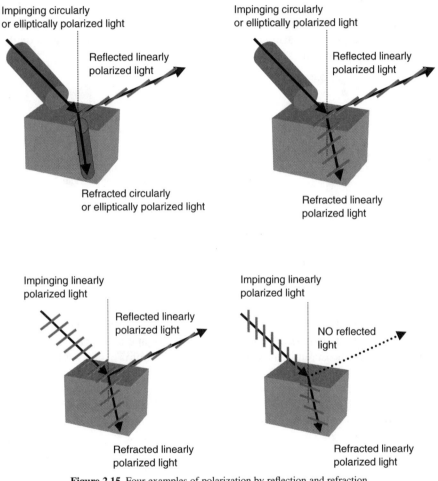

Figure 2.15 Four examples of polarization by reflection and refraction.

2.3.15 Extinction Ratio

Consider polarized light traveling *through a polarizer*. When transmittance is maximum, T_1, it is termed major *principal transmittance*, and when minimum, T_2, it is termed *minor principal transmittance*. The ratio major to minor *principal transmittance* is known as *principal transmittance*. The inverse, minimum to maximum is known as *extinction ratio*.

Consider two polarizers in tandem, one behind the other with parallel surfaces. If their polarization axes are parallel, the transmittance is $T_1^2/2$. If their axes are crossed (perpendicular), the transmittance is $2T_2/T_1$. This is also (but incorrectly) termed as *extinction ratio*.

2.3.16   Polarization Mode Shift: The Faraday Effect

Some materials shift the direction of polarization of transmitted light through it (Figure 2.16). This shift is also known as the *Faraday effect*. Devices based on the Faraday effect are known as *rotators*.

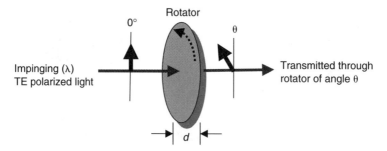

Figure 2.16 Principle of polarization rotator–Faraday effect.

The amount of the rotation angle or *mode shift*, θ, depends on the thickness of material d (cm), the magnetic field H (Oersted [Oe]), and a constant V, known as Verdet constant (measured in min/cm-Oe). The mode shift is expressed by

$$\theta = VHd$$

Devices with a strong Verdet constant, magnetic field, and length may also shift the TE polarization mode to TM polarization mode (Figure 2.17).

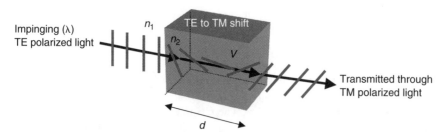

Figure 2.17 Polarization shift from TE to TM mode.

2.3.17   Phase Shift

Some dielectric materials shift the phase of transmitted light through it (Figure 2.18). The amount of phase shift $\Delta\phi$ depends on the wavelength λ, the dielectric constant ϵ, the refractive index ratio n_1/n_2, and the optical path (thickness) of material.

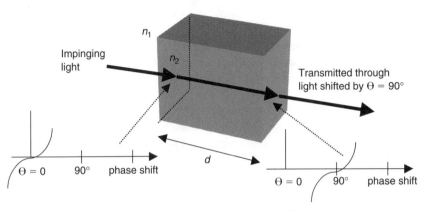

Figure 2.18 Principle of phase angle shift.

2.3.18   Isotropy and Anisotropy

Isotropic optically transparent materials are those that have the same index of refraction, same polarization, and same propagation constant in every direction throughout the material. Materials that do not exhibit these properties are known as *anisotropic* (Figure 2.19).

In crystals (such as calcite–$CaCO_3$), electrons move with different amounts of freedom in specific directions, as compared with other directions in the crystal. As a result, as rays of light enter the crystal, they interact differently in different directions of the crystal. Such crystal is also termed anisotropic.

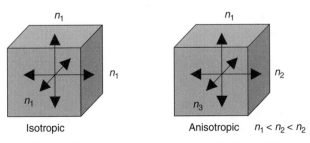

Figure 2.19 Principle of isotropic and anisotropic materials.

2.3.19 Birefringence

Anisotropic materials have a different index of refraction in specific directions. As such, when a beam of monochromatic light travels through it and in a specific direction, it is refracted differently along the directions of different indices (Figure 2.20). That is, when an unpolarized ray enters the material, it is separated into two rays, each with a different polarization, different direction, and different propagation constant, called the ordinary ray (O) and the extraordinary ray (E). This property of anisotropic crystals is known as *birefringence.*

Some optically transparent isotropic materials, when they are under stress, become anisotropic. Mechanical forces (pulling, bending, twisting), thermal forces (ambient temperature variations), and electrical fields may exert stress. Under such conditions, the index of refraction, polarization, and propagation characteristics become different in certain directions within the material.

Birefringence in fiber transmission is undesirable. Birefringence alters the polarization and the propagating characteristics of the transmitted signal and while the receiver expects one polarization, it receives another.

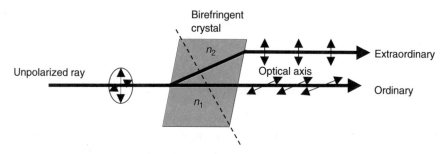

Figure 2.20 Birefringent materials split the incident beam in the ordinary and extraordinary rays, each with different polarization.

To minimize birefringence in fibers, several techniques have been devised. One technique monitors and controls the received polarization by changing the polarization of the receiver, or by using polarization-maintaining fibers. Another technique uses transmitting and receiving strategies to "immunize" the system from fiber polarization variations, such as polarization spreading (polarization scrambling, data-induced polarization), or polarization diversity.

However, birefringence has also been taken advantage of, to construct filters that may also be used as wavelength multiplexers and demultiplexers (see filters, Section 4.II). Figure 2.21 gives an example of a circularly polarized light ray traversing a birefringent plate.

2.3.20 Material Dispersion

The refractive index is related to the dielectric coefficient of the material and to the characteristic resonance frequencies of its dipoles. The dipoles of the material, there-

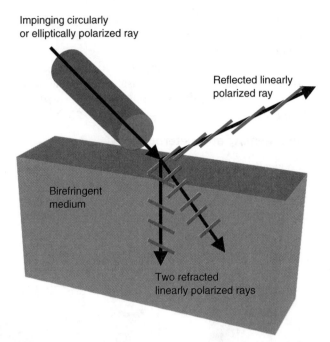

Figure 2.21 Example of birefringence on a non-polarized beam before and after.

fore, interact more strongly with (and absorb more) optical frequencies that are closer to their resonance frequencies. Consequently, the refractive index $n(\omega)$ is optical frequency–dependent. The dependency of the refractive index of the material on the optical frequency is termed *material dispersion.*

Silica, a key ingredient of optical fiber cable, has a refractive index that varies with optical frequency. Therefore, dispersion plays a significant role in fiberoptic communications.

2.3.21 Nonlinear Phenomena

The polarization of an *E-M* wave, *P*, which is induced in electric dipoles of a medium by an electric field, *E*, is proportional to susceptibility, $\varkappa$:

$$P = \epsilon_o\, [\varkappa^1 {\cdot} E + \varkappa^2 {\cdot} E.E + \varkappa^3 {\cdot} E {\cdot} E {\cdot} E + ...]$$

The factor ϵ_o is known as the permitivity in vacuum.

For an isotropic medium, the first-order term expresses the linear behavior of matter, and the second-order term is orthogonal. Therefore, the second-order term vanishes, and higher-ordered terms are negligible. Thus, for an isotropic medium the above series relation is simplified to $P = \epsilon_o\, \varkappa {\cdot} E$. However, nature is not so simple, and most materials are either not isotropic, or become anisotropic under certain conditions. In such cases, higher-order terms should also be considered. In particular, the third-order term becomes significant and it results in nonlinear effects that may affect and limit optical transmission.

The most influential nonlinear effects in optical transmission, particularly when many wavelengths at high optical power are transmitted over the same medium (e.g., DWDM), are *four-wave mixing* (FWM), *stimulated Raman scattering* (SRS), and *stimulated Brillouin scattering* (SBS).

2.3.22   Homogeneity and Heterogeneity

A *homogeneous* optically transparent medium has the same consistency (chemical, mechanical, electrical, magnetic, or crystallographic) throughout its volume (Figure 2.22). A *heterogeneous* optically transparent medium does not have the same consistency (chemical, mechanical, electrical, magnetic, or crystallographic) throughout its volume.

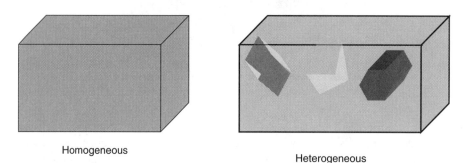

Homogeneous

Heterogeneous

Figure 2.22 Illustrative definition of homogeneous and non-homogeneous (heterogeneous) matter.

2.3.23   Effects of Impurities in Matter

An *impurity* is the presence of unwanted elements or compounds in matter. During the purification process of matter (e.g., Silica), certain elements cannot be removed in their entirety and some traces still remain. These undesired elements or compounds alter the optical characteristics of the transparent material (e.g., fiber), and have an absorptive effect or result in optical throughput loss by scattering photons in other directions. Figure 2.23 captures the absorptive and scattering effect of photons as they transverse matter.

Examples of impurities that affect optical transmission are the elements iron, copper, cobalt, and their oxides. The result is selective optical wavelength absorption. For instance, blue glass is the result of cobalt or copper in glass (it looks blue because it absorbs all wavelengths but the blue). One of the most difficult "impurities" to be removed from glass fiber is the OH radical. OH radicals in fiber cable are responsible for increased absorption in the range before 1400 nm (Figure 2.24).

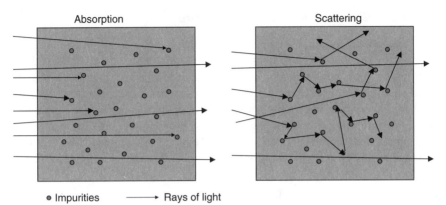

Absorption   Scattering

● Impurities   ⟶ Rays of light

Figure 2.23 Illustrative definition of matter with absorption center and with scattering centers.

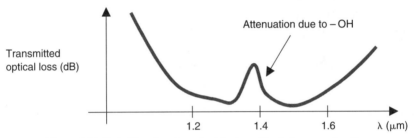

Transmitted
optical loss (dB)

Attenuation due to − OH

1.2   1.4   1.6   λ (μm)

Figure 2.24 Optical loss (or attenuation) by impurities in transparent matter.

2.3.24   Effects of Microcracks

Cracks may be viewed as discontinuities in the index of refraction of the material with planes that are not necessarily flat (Figure 2.25). Microcracks in the crystallized matrix of matter, or in amorphous solid matter, are generated by stresses (mechanical or thermal) or material aging. Microcracks are invisible to the naked eye and only become visible under a strong microscope or with specialized interferometric techniques. As light travels through matter with cracks, its propagation is disrupted or distorted.

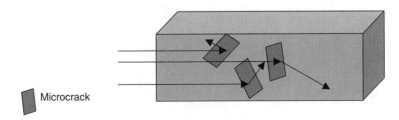

Microcrack

Figure 2.25 Illustrative definition of matter with microcracks.

2.3.25   Effects of Mechanical Pressure

When mechanical pressure is applied, the internal microstructure of the material is disturbed (Figure 2.26). As a result, there is a variation of the refractive index determined by the pressure distribution in the material. Mechanical pressure is also exhorted on fibers as they are pulled or bent. Thus, assuming a circular bend, the outer periphery experiences stretching points while the inner experiences compression points. Pressure and stretching points are clearly points of optical disturbances that are generally undesirable in optical communications. The safe bend radius has been recommended by ITU-T to be the widely accepted radius of 37.5 mm (ITU-T G.652, para. 5.5, note 2).

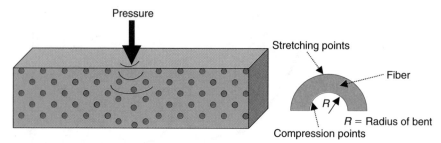

Figure 2.26 Dislocation of orderly molecules in matter by pressure distribution and pressure effects on fiber by bending.

2.3.26   Effects of Temperature Variation

The properties of materials vary as temperature varies. In addition to changing its physical properties, the electrical, magnetic, and chemical properties also change. As a result of this, the index of refraction is affected (Figure 2.27). Clearly, in optical communications, temperature variations are undesirable, although there are cases where temperature control has been used productively to vary the refractive index of optical devices.

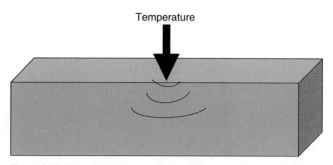

Figure 2.27 Dislocation of orderly molecules in matter by temperature distribution.

EXERCISES

1. Could a moving photon-particle stop moving in vacuum by itself?

2. When monochromatic light of frequency v travels in vacuum, then $E = mc^2 = hv$, and when it travels in dense matter then its speed changes but its energy is preserved. Then, what does it change?

3. Could the refractive index n be smaller than 1?

4. If in Figure 5, θ_i becomes zero (i.e., rays are perpendicular to surface), then would there be a reflected ray?

5. If, in Figure 2.6, $n_1 > n_2$, is $\Theta_t < \Theta_i$ or $\Theta_t > \Theta_i$?

6. If in the prism of Figure 2.4 $n_1 < n_2$, is $\lambda_K < \lambda_J$ or $\lambda_K > \lambda_J$?

7. Which physical phenomenon describes refraction through a continuously variable index of refraction?

8. A pond appears to be only 2 feet deep. A coin lies on its bottom. We try to reach the coin with a 2.5-foot long stick, but we discover that we cannot even reach the coin. Why?

9. Two coherent light sources impinge on a screen as shown (Figure 2.28). Identify points of minima and maxima contributions within the highlighted area.

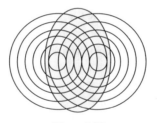

Figure 2.28

10. Consider the set up of Figure 2.29. Device G splits a monochromatic beam A into two, beams B and C. Beam B travels straight through and impinges at point F on a screen. Beam C is further reflected by mirror M. Mirror M, however, slowly moves vertically and simultaneously rotates so that the reflected ray C also impinges at point F on a screen. As the mirror moves, what is expected to be observed at point F?

11. Could a moving photon be captured and stored?

12. What happens when a photon interacts with an atom?

13. A monochromatic light source has a frequency $f = 192,843$ Ghz. Calculate the wavelength.

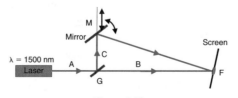

Figure 2.29

REFERENCES

[1] Members of the Technical Staff, *Transmission Systems for Communications*, Bell Telephone Laboratories, 1982.

[2] R. Handel and M.N. Huber, *Integrated Broadband Network*, Addison Wesley, 1991.

[3] R.D. Gitlin, J.F. Hayes, and S.B. Weinstein, *Data Communications Principles*, Plenum, New York, 1992.

[4] R. E. Matick, *Transmission Lines for Digital and Communication Networks*, IEEE Press, 1995.

[5] B. Furht, ed., *Handbook of Internet and Multimedia: Systems and Applications*, IEEE Press, New York, 1999.

[6] J. Nellist, *Understanding Telecommunications and Lightwave Systems*, IEEE Press, 1996.

[7] J. Hecht, *Understanding Fiber Optics*, Prentice Hall, Upper Saddle River, NJ, 1999.

[8] S.V. Kartalopoulos, *Understanding Neural Networks and Fuzzy Logic: Basic concepts and applications*, IEEE Press, New York, 1995.

[9] J.R. Freer, *Computer Communications and Networks*, IEEE Press, New York, 1996.

[10] E.B. Carne, *Telecommunications Primer*, Prentice Hall, New Jersey, PTR, 1995.

[11] A. Kastler, *Optique*, 6th ed., Masson & Cie, Paris, 1965.

[12] M.H. Freeman, *Optics*, 10th ed., Butterworths, London, 1990.

[13] E.B. Brown, *Modern Optics*, Reinhold Publishing Corp., New York, 1965.

[14] M. Francon, *Optique: Formation et Traitement des Images*, Masson & Cie, Paris, 1972.

[15] M. Francon, *Holographie*, Masson & Cie, Paris, 1969.

[16] P.M. Duffieux, *L'Integrales de Fourier et ses Application à l'Optique*, Masson & Cie, Paris, 1970.

[17] T.G. Robertazzi, ed., *Performance Evaluation of High Speed Switching Fabrics and Networks*, IEEE Press, New York, 1993.

[18] T. Wildi, *Units and Conversion Charts*, 2nd ed., IEEE Press, New York, 1995.

[19] R.H. Stolen, "Non-linear properties of optical fibers," in *Optical Fiber Telecommunications*, S.E. Miller and G. Chynoweth, Eds., Academic Press, New York, 1979.

[20] K. Maxwell, "Asymmetric digital subscriber line: interim technology for the next forty years," *IEEE Communications Magazine*, October 1996, pp. 100–6.

[21] D. Cotter, "Stimulated Brillouin scattering in monomode optical fiber," *Journal of Optical Communications*, vol. 4, 1983, pp. 10–19.

[22] G. Waarts, and R.P. Braun, "Crosstalk due to stimulated Brillouin scattering in monomode fibers," *Electronics Letters*, vol. 24, 1988, pp. 78–80.

[23] P.T. Thomas, et al., "Normal acoustic modes and Brillouin scattering in single-mode optical fibers," *Physics Review*, vol. B19, 1979, pp. 4986–98.

[24] K.O Hill, et al., "CW three-wave mixing in single-mode optical fibers," *Journal of Applied Physics*, vol. 49, 1978, pp. 5098–106.

[25] K. Inoue, "Four-wave mixing in an optical fiber in the zero-dispersion wavelength region," *Journal of Lightwave Technology*, vol. 10, no. 11, 1992, pp.1553–61.

[26] C.F. Buhrer, "Four waveplate dual tuner for birefringent filters and multiplexers," *Applied Optics*, vol. 26, no. 17, 1987, pp. 3628–32.

[27] S.R. Nagle, "Optical fiber—the expanding medium," *IEEE Circuits and Devices Magazine*, vol. 5, no. 2, 1989, pp. 36–45.

STANDARDS

[1] ANSI/IEEE 812-1984, *Definition of Terms Relating to Fiber Optics*, 1984.

[2] Bellcore, GR-1110-CORE, *Broadband Switching System (BSS) Generic Requirements*, 1995.

[3] Bellcore, TR-NWT-233, *Digital Cross Connect System*, November 1992.

[4] Bellcore, TR-NWT-499, *Transport Systems Generic Requirements (TSGR): Common Requirements*, issue 5, December 1993.

[5] IEC Publication 793-2, Part 2, *Optical Fibres—Part 2: Product Specifications*, 1992.

[6] ITU-T Recommendation G.650, *Definition and Test Methods for the Relevant Parameters of Single-Mode Fibres*, 1997.

[7] ITU-T Recommendation G.652, *Characteristics of a Single-Mode Optical Fibre Cable*, 1997.

[8] ITU-T Recommendation G.653, *Characteristics of a Dispersion-Shifted Single-Mode Optical Fibre Cable*, 1997.

[9] ITU-T Recommendation G.654, *Characteristics of a Cut-Off Shifted Single-Mode Optical Fibre Cable*, 1997.

[10] ITU-T Recommendation G.655, *Characteristics of a Non-Zero-Dispersion Shifted Single-Mode Optical Fibre Cable*, 1996.

[11] ITU-T Recommendation G.671, *Transmission Characteristics of Passive Optical Components*, 1996.

[12] ITU-T Recommendation G.702, *Digital Hierarchy Bit Rates*, 1988.

PART II
OPTICAL COMPONENTS

Legacy optical communications systems—systems that transmit data over a single wavelength—depend heavily on four components: the optical transmitter, the optical receiver, the optical fiber, and the optical amplifier. Although the bandwidth (bit rate) of the transmitted optical signal keeps increasing, it is predicted that bandwidth exhaust is inevitable. To respond to bandwidth exhaust and to also allow for service diversification (over the same fiber), more wavelengths are "squeezed" into the same fiber. In dense wavelength division multiplexing (DWDM) systems, in addition to the above four devices, more specialized optical devices are required to offer an all-optical connectivity between two points. Such devices are optical filters, add-drop multiplexers, tunable transmitters and receivers (that selectively can tune-in a wavelength), optical switches, and so on.

In Part II, we describe the optical components that are needed in optical DWDM systems. This technology is still evolving and thus, one would expect better performing and more compact devices to be seen. Nevertheless, the underlining principles remain the same.

CHAPTER 3

THE OPTICAL WAVEGUIDE— THE FIBER

3.1 INTRODUCTION

Fiber has become the transporting medium of choice for voice, video, and data, particularly for high-speed communications. Fiber is compact, as compared to copper cables (twisted pair and coax), and has many properties that copper solutions do not have. For example, fiber is immune to electromagnetic interference, does not corrode, and has (for all practical purposes) an almost unlimited bandwidth; for example, the useful bandwidth per single fiber strand is one thousand times the total radio bandwidth worldwide (i.e., 25 Tbps vs. 25 Gbps). However, fiber requires connectors, and specialized personnel to splice and connect fiber cables. Overall, the installation of fiber itself is dominated not by the cost of the fiber cable itself (which is a fraction of a US $ per meter) but by the cost of licenses needed to cross fields, underground conduits, in pipes or aerial cable, specialized installation equipment, and the cost of labor. Here, we examine the manufacturability of fiber and its ability to transmit light.

3.2 ANATOMY OF A FIBER CABLE

A typical single optical fiber consists of a strand of ultra-pure silica mixed with specific elements, the *dopants*. Dopants have been added to adjust the refractive index of silica and thus its light-propagation characteristics.

The optical cable is a single strand of fiber, many miles long. It consists of several layers. The innermost layer is the silica *core*. The core is covered by another layer of silica with a different mix of dopants, known as *cladding*. The cladding is covered with a buffer coating, which absorbs mechanical stresses during handling of the cable. The coating is covered by a strong material such as Kevlar™. Finally, a layer of plastic material covers these layers (Figure 3.1). The final fiber cable used in long-haul communications consists of a bundle of optical fibers. Some cables may have up to 432 fibers.

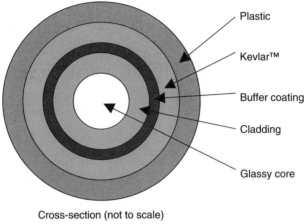

Plastic

Kevlar™

Buffer coating

Cladding

Glassy core

Cross-section (not to scale)

Figure 3.1 Anatomy of a fiber.

3.2.1 How Is Fiber Made?

Fiber is made by vertically drawing a cylindrical preform made of ultra-pure SiO_2 in which dopants (e.g., GeO_2) have been added in a controlled manner. The various dopants are homogeneously distributed in a tubular fashion and they determine the refractive index profile of the fiber. The base of the preform is heated at $2,000°C$ (where silica starts melting and becomes viscous) in a high-frequency doughnut-shaped furnace (Figure 3.2).

As the fiber is drawn, its diameter is continuously monitored and minute adjustments are made (via an automatic control mechanism) so that the fiber is produced with tight diameter tolerance.

3.2.2 How Is the Preform Made?

The cylindrical preform is made by one of several methods, such as vapor-phase axial deposition (VAD), outer vapor deposition (OVD), or modified chemical vapor deposition (MCVD), invented in 1970 by scientists at Bell Laboratories.

In the MCVD method, oxides and oxygen enter a rotating, highly pure silica tube in a specified sequence. The tube is maintained at a very high temperature so that chemical interaction with silica and dopant elements (Ge, B, etc.) takes place in a controlled manner. The products of reaction are deposited in the interior walls of the preform evenly. As deposition takes place, the opening of the tube closes in (Figure 3.3). The even and radial deposition of the elements in the preform determines the profile of index of refraction of the fiber, when it is drawn.

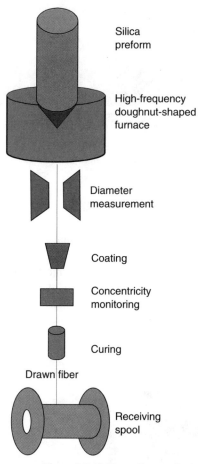

Silica
preform

High-frequency
doughnut-shaped
furnace

Diameter
measurement

Coating

Concentricity
monitoring

Curing

Drawn fiber

Receiving
spool

Figure 3.2 Making a fiber.

The highly pure silica tube is manufactured using a typically proprietary method. LUCENT Technologies uses a method called *sol gel* (described and illustrated in http://www.bell-labs.com/org/physicalsciences/projects/solgel). Sol gel is made in five phases. In phase 1, a colloidal suspension of silica particles is gelled and casted to form a tube. In phase 2, the gel is removed under water to produce a porous solid tube. In phase 3, the tube is slowly dried without cracking. In phase 4, the tube is placed in a furnace and heated in the presence of various gasses to remove water, organic compounds, and other impurities. In the last phase, the porous purified tube is sintered; that is, the purified tube is consolidated to clear glass in chlorine, oxygen, and helium gasses. Then, an MCDV rod is inserted in the core of the sol gel tube and both are collapsed to one solid preform. This preform is used to draw fiber from.

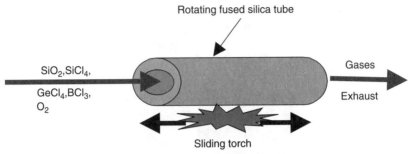

Figure 3.3 Making a preform with the MCDV method.

3.3   INDEX OF REFRACTION PROFILES

The refractive index of the core and the cladding of a fiber are radially controlled during the manufacturing phase to produce an index profile of a shape in one of several forms, such as *step, gaussian, triangular,* or more complex (Figure 3.4). The refractive index profile is formed by controlling the type and amount of dopants in the preform. Dopants increase or decrease the refractive index. For example, zinc sulfide increases the refractive index, whereas magnesium fluoride lowers it.

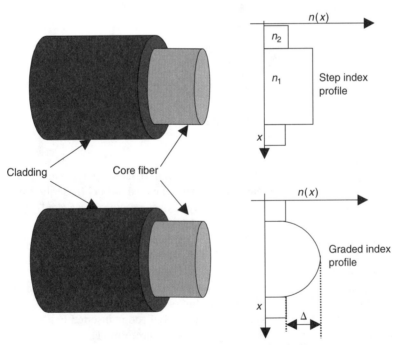

Figure 3.4 Step index and graded index profiles in fiber.

3.4   FIBER MODES

The propagation characteristics of light in silica fiber depend on the chemical consistency (silica + dopants) and the cross-sectional dimensions of core and cladding. Typically, core and cladding have a diameter of about 125 μm, but the core itself comes in two different dimensions, depending on the application the fiber is intended for. Fiber with a core diameter of about 50 μm is known as *multimode* fiber, whereas fiber with a core diameter of 8.6 to 9.5 μm is known as *single mode* (per ITU-T G.652) (Figure 3.5). In the following discussion, we will examine the reasons for having cores of different dimensions.

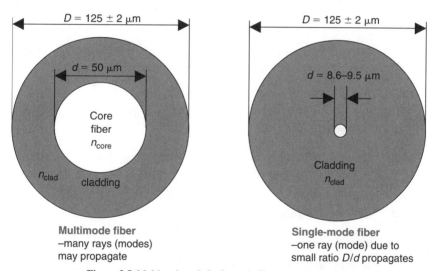

Figure 3.5 Multimode and single-mode fiber cross-section.

Optical fiber transmission takes place through guided modes. The modes are determined from the *eigenvalues* of second-order differential equations and their boundary conditions, a similar analysis to propagation in cylindrical waveguides. Solution of these equations also determines the *cut-off frequency*, beyond which the waveguide does not support transmission.

Modes are labeled as TE_{MN} or TM_{MN} (where M and N are integers), depending on the value of the *transverse electric field* ($E_Z = 0$) or the *transverse magnetic field* ($H_Z = 0$) at the surface of the fiber core (the boundary) in the transverse direction. Fibers, based on their dielectric constant and dimensions, support the fundamental mode TE_{11} (also known as HE_{11}) or higher modes. Fibers that support many modes are known as *multimode*, and those that support one (the HE_{11}) are known as *single mode*. A single-mode fiber supports transmission along its longitudinal axis (HE_{11}).

Modes may be thought of as specific path eigen-directions. The number of modes, M, of a multimode fiber with a step index profile (n_{core}, n_{clad}) is approximated by

$$M = \frac{1}{2} \{ (4\pi/\lambda)\, d \sqrt{(n_{core}^2 - n_{clad}^2)} \}^2$$

Where λ is the wavelength, and d is the core diameter.

Multimode and single-mode fibers have different manufacturing processes, different refractive index profiles, different dimensions, and therefore different transmission characteristics. Consequently, in optical transmission they find different applications. Some of the salient characteristics of multimode graded-index and single-mode fibers are summarized in the following sections.

3.4.1   Multimode Graded Index

- It minimizes delay spread, although the delay is still significant.

- A 1% index difference between core and cladding amounts to a 1 to 5 nsec/km delay spread (compare with step index that has about 50 nsec/km).

- It is easy to splice and to couple light into.

- The bit rate is limited; up to 100 Mbps for lengths up to 40 km; shorter lengths support higher bit rates.

- Fiber span without amplification is limited; up to 40 km at 100 Mbps (extended to Gbps for shorter distances for graded-index).

3.4.2   Single Mode

- It (almost) eliminates delay spread.

- It is more difficult to splice and to exactly align two fibers together.

- It is more difficult to couple all photonic energy from a source into it.

- It is difficult to study propagation with ray theory; it requires Maxwell's equations.

- It is suitable for transmitting modulated signals at 40 Gbps (or higher) and up to 200 km without amplification.

3.5   PROPAGATION OF LIGHT

The propagation of light in matter is typically shown using the ray technique. This is a graphical and visual technique that shows the paths of optical rays as they travel through the matter, and in our case through the fiber, depicting diffraction, refraction, polarization, and birefringence. Figure 3.6 shows two cases of light propaga-

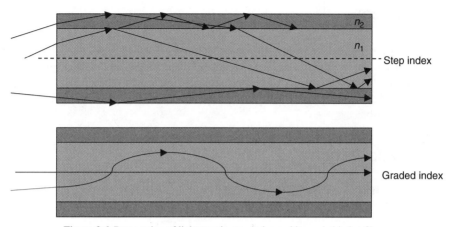

Figure 3.6 Propagation of light rays in step-index and in graded-index fibers.

tion in a step-index and in a graded-index fiber, using the ray technique. This technique is used extensively throughout this book.

3.6   CRITICAL CONE OR ACCEPTANCE CONE

Critical cone, also known as *acceptance cone*, is a cone of an angle within which all rays that are launched into the core are reflected at the core-cladding interface at or beyond the critical angle (Figure 3.7). The half angle of the critical cone, also known as *numerical aperture*, depends on the refractive index distribution function in the core and cladding, and is independent of the core diameter. For a step-index fiber, the numerical aperture is

$$NA = \sin \Theta_{NA} = \sqrt{(n_1^2 - n_2^2)}$$

where n_1 is for the core and n_2 for the cladding.

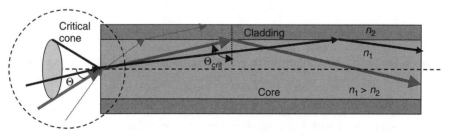

Figure 3.7 Illustrative definition of critical cone.

3.7   EXIT CONE

Similar to the critical or acceptance cone defined at the entry of the fiber, light emerges from the far-end of the fiber in a cone. This is known as the *emerging cone.* In single-mode fiber, the exit cone is approximately the same as the acceptance cone. Clearly, for best coupling results, the acceptance cone and the exit cone should be as acute as possible.

3.8   PHASE VELOCITY

A monochromatic wave (single ω or λ) that travels along the fiber axis is described by

$$E(t,x) = A^{[j(\omega t - \beta x)]}$$

where A is the amplitude of the field, $\omega = 2\pi f$, and β is the propagation constant.

Phase velocity, V_ϕ, is defined as the velocity of an observer that maintains constant phase with the traveling field, that is, $\omega t - \beta x =$ constant. Replacing the traveled distance x within time t, $x = V_\phi t$, then the phase velocity of the monochromatic light in the medium is

$$V_\phi = \omega/\beta$$

3.9   GROUP VELOCITY

A modulated optical signal contains frequency components that travel (in the fiber) with slightly different phase velocities. This is explained mathematically as follows. Consider an amplitude-modulated optical signal traveling along the fiber:

$$e_{AM}(t) = E[1 + m\cos(\omega_1 t)]\cos(\omega_c t)$$

where E is the electric field, m is the modulation depth, ω_1 is the modulation frequency, ω_c is the frequency of light (or carrier frequency), and $\omega_1 \ll \omega_c$. Trigonometric expansion of the above expression results in three frequency components with arguments:

$$\omega_c, \omega_c - \omega_1, \text{ and } \omega_c + \omega_1$$

Each component travels along the fiber at a slightly different phase velocity (β_c, $\beta_c - \Delta\beta$, $\beta_c + \Delta\beta$, respectively) accruing a different phase shift. Eventually, all three components form a spreading envelope that travels along the fiber with a phase velocity:

$$\beta(\omega) = \beta_c + (\partial\beta/\partial\omega|\omega, = \omega_c)\Delta\omega = \beta_c + \beta'\Delta\omega$$

Group velocity, $(v_g = c/n_g)$, is defined as the velocity of an observer that maintains constant phase with the group traveling envelope; that is, $\omega t - (\Delta\beta)x =$ constant. Replacing x by $v_g t$, then, the group velocity is expressed by

$$v_g = \omega/\Delta\beta = \partial\omega/\partial\beta = 1/\beta'$$

where β is the propagation constant, and β' is the first partial derivative w.r.t. ω.

Group velocity is particularly significant in optical data transmission where light is modulated.

3.10   MODAL DISPERSION

An optical signal that is launched into a fiber may be considered as a bundle of rays. Although a serious effort is made to launch all rays parallel into the fiber, due to imperfections of optical devices, rays are transmitted within a small cone. Because the rays in the fiber are not parallel, the transmission is affected. In the following sections, we examine the effect that this has on the quality of the signal and on the bandwidth (bit rate).

3.10.1   Intermodal Delay Difference

Consider an optical signal that is modulated so that optical pulses are coupled into the fiber. With reference to Figure 3.8, rays A and B are of the same wavelength, they belong to the same optical signal (pulse), but because they are not parallel, rays travel different paths along the fiber. These paths are also known as *modes*. Thus, ray A travels in a straight path along the core of the fiber (one mode), whereas ray B travels in an angle bouncing off the cladding (another mode). As a result, each ray travels a different total distance and arrives at a distant point of the fiber at a different time. Thus, the initial narrow pulse spreads out due to modal delays. This is known as *modal dispersion.*

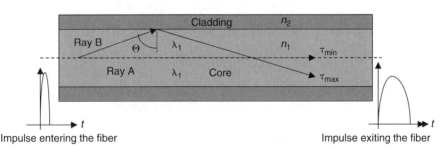

Figure 3.8 Initial narrow pulse spreads out due to modal dispersion.

Clearly, as a pulse spreads out (Figure 3.9), it reaches a point where it overlaps with the one that follows it. Obviously, this is highly undesirable in ultra-fast digital transmission where pulses are as narrow as few tens of picoseconds. In digital transmission, the rule of thumb for acceptable dispersion is:

$$\Delta\tau < T/k$$

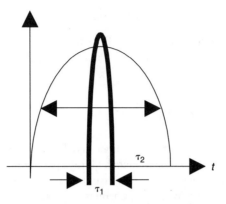

Figure 3.9 Modal dispersion, before and after.

and the information (bit rate) limit is expressed by

$$R_b < 1/(k\Delta\tau)$$

where $\Delta\tau = \tau_2 - \tau_1$, R_b is the information (bit) rate, T is the bit period, and k is the dispersion factor (a transmission design parameter, typically selected to $k = 4$). If $k = 5$, then less dispersion is acceptable; if $k = 3$, more is acceptable.

3.10.2   Maximum Bit Rate

The travel time of the two rays (see Figures 3.8 and 3.9) are

$$\tau_{min} = (Ln_1)/v, \text{ and } \tau_{max} = (Ln_1)/v \cos \Theta$$

for $\Theta = \Theta_{crit}$ (total reflection) and from Snell's law:

$$\cos \Theta_{crit} = n_1/n_2$$

The difference in travel time (assuming total reflection) is

$$\Delta\tau = \tau_{max} - \tau_{min} = \{(Ln_1)/v\}\Delta n/n_1$$

Hence, the maximum bit rate, R_b, is calculated from

$$R_b < 1/(4\Delta\tau) = (1/4)(v/Ln_1)(n_1/\Delta n)$$

3.10.3   Mode Mixing

Consider the case of two connected multimode fibers. Clearly, the connection of the two fibers presents a perturbation in the optical path. When light rays reach the end of the first fiber they are launched into the second. However, because there are many modes (i.e., different rays traveling in different angles), each ray enters the second fiber at a different angle and thus is refracted differently. Consequently, one mode may change into another mode. This is known as *mode mixing*, and it only occurs in multimode fibers.

Mode mixing affects the actual transmitted bandwidth (BW_{act}) over the length (L) of a multimode fiber. An empirical *scaling factor*, γ, has been devised to calculate the effective bandwidth:

$$BW_{eff} = BW_{act}/L^{\gamma}$$

where γ is between 0.7 and 1.0.

3.11   REDUCTION OF MODAL DISPERSION

The difference in travel time is improved if a graded-index fiber is used. For a graded index of refraction profile $n(r)$, dispersion is improved if the condition holds:

$$R_b \leq 2v_g/(n_gL\Delta^2)$$

where n_g is the group refractive index, Δ is the maximum relative index between core and cladding, and v_g is the group velocity in the medium.

Fibers with various graded-index profiles have been made. An example of a profile (Figure 3.10) is

$$n(r) = n_1\sqrt{\{1 - 2\Delta(r/a)^{\alpha}\}}, \text{ for } r < a$$

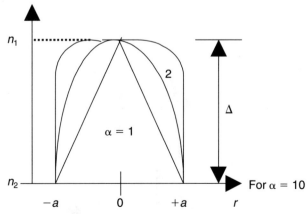

Figure 3.10 Index of refraction profiles to minimize modal dispersion.

3.12 CHROMATIC DISPERSION

The propagation characteristics of each wavelength depend on the refractive index of the medium and on the nonlinearity of the propagation constant. These dependencies affect the travel time of each wavelength through a fiber medium. As a result, an initially narrow pulse is widened. This is termed as *chromatic dispersion*, also known as intramodal dispersion (not to be confused with the intermodal dispersion). Chromatic dispersion consists of two contributions: (1) the dependence of the dielectric constant, ϵ, on frequency, ω, known as *material dispersion*; and (2) the nonlinear dependence of the propagation constant on frequency, ω, known as *wavelength dispersion*.

Dispersion is measured in psec/nm-km (i.e., delay per wavelength variation and fiber length). Material dispersion is the most significant. In the following section, we examine both.

3.12.1 Material Dispersion

The propagation characteristics of each wavelength depend on the refractive index of the medium. The refractive index is also related to the dielectric constant of the medium. Thus, there is a dependence of the dielectric constant on frequency and on wavelength. The propagation characteristics of each wavelength in a fiber are therefore different. Different wavelengths travel at different speeds in the fiber that result in dispersion due to the material.

Thus, when a narrow pulse of light, consisting of a narrow range of wavelengths, is launched in a medium, each individual wavelength arrives at the end of the fiber at a different time, even if all frequencies travel on the same straight path. The result is a dispersed pulse due to *material dispersion* (Figure 3.11).

3.12.2 Wavelength Dispersion

Consider that a narrow optical impulse consists of a narrow range of wavelengths. Thus, wavelengths λ_1 and λ_2 in the same impulse are slightly different. We assume

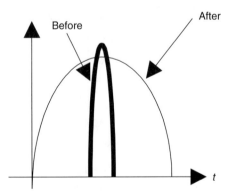

Figure 3.11 Material dispersion, before and after.

that both wavelengths travel (along the core of the fiber) in a straight path, but λ_1 travels faster than λ_2 ($\lambda_1 < \lambda_2$), due to the nonlinear dependence of the propagation constant on frequency ω (and on wavelength) (Figure 3.12). Thus, although the optical impulse is initially narrow, at a distant point of the fiber, the constituent wavelengths of the impulse arrive at different times due to propagation delays, termed *wavelength dispersion.*

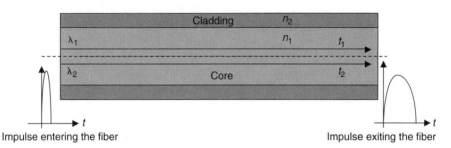

Figure 3.12 Principles of wavelength dispersion.

3.12.3   Chromatic Dispersion: Travel Time Variation

The travel time τ for a group of velocity v_g over a length of fiber L is

$$\tau = L/v_g \text{ , or } \tau = L\beta' = L\{\partial\beta/\partial\omega\}$$

where β is the propagation constant and β' is the first derivative with respect to ω. The variation of τ with respect to ω, ($\partial\tau/\partial\omega$), is

$$\partial\tau/\partial\omega = L\ \partial(1/v_g)/\partial\omega = L\ \partial^2(\beta)/\partial\omega^2 = L\beta''$$

where β'' is the second derivative with respect to ω.

For a signal with a spectral width $\Delta\omega$, then

$$\Delta\tau = (\beta'')\ L\ \Delta\omega$$

That is, the pulse spread (chromatic dispersion) depends on β'' and is proportional to the length of the fiber.

3.12.4   Chromatic Dispersion: Pulse Spread

The *group velocity dispersion* (GVD) coefficient, D, is defined as the variation of travel time due to the wavelength variation per unit length of fiber, L:

$$D = (1/L)(\partial\tau/\partial\lambda)$$

where ∂ is the partial derivative. The coefficient D is also known as the *chromatic dispersion coefficient.* It follows that

$$D = (1/L)\ (\partial\tau/\partial\omega)\ (\partial\omega/\partial\lambda).$$

However, $\partial\tau/\partial\omega = L\beta''$ and $\partial\omega/\partial\lambda = -2\pi v/\lambda^2$ and thus,

$$D = -(2\pi v/\lambda^2)\ \beta''$$

and

$$\Delta\tau = DL \{[-1/(2\pi v/\lambda^2)]\ \Delta\omega\}$$

Finally, the pulse spread, or chromatic dispersion, is expressed by

$$\Delta\tau = |D|L\Delta\lambda$$

where ∂ has been replaced by Δ and $\Delta\lambda$ is the optical spectral width of the signal (in nm units); chromatic dispersion is also denoted by the Greek letter σ (Figure 3.13).

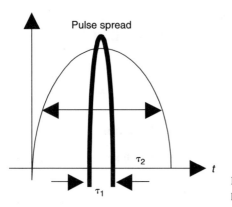

Figure 3.13 Pulse spread due to chromatic dispersion.

3.13   DISPERSION-SHIFTED AND DISPERSION-FLATTENED FIBERS

The dependency of the refractive index of Silica fiber is nonlinear. As such, at some wavelength, the derivative $d\{n(\omega)\}/d\lambda$ becomes zero; that is, material dispersion becomes zero. The wavelength where the derivative is zero is called *zero-dispersion wavelength.*

A conventional single-mode fiber with a core diameter of about 8.3 μm and an index of refraction variation of about 0.37% has a zero-dispersion at about 1.3 μm. Below this point, wavelength dispersion is negative and above it is positive.

For long-haul transmission, single-mode fibers with specialized index of refraction profiles (by controlling the dopant) have been engineered and manufactured.

A fiber with a zero-dispersion point shifted at 1550 nm (1.55 μm) (i.e, where the minimum absorption for Silica fiber is) is called *dispersion-shifted fiber* (DSF). These fibers are compatible with optical amplifiers that perform best at around 1550 nm. Dispersion-shifted fiber with low loss in the range of 1570 to 1610 nm, termed as *L-band*, provides a wide range of wavelengths making it suitable for DWDM applications. For example, DSF fiber has been installed extensively in Japan.

Another fiber type with near-zero dispersion in the range from 1.3 μm to 1.55 μm is called *dispersion-flattened fiber* (DFF). In this category, depending on the dispersion slope, there is *positive DFF* and *negative DFF*. There are also other types of fibers, such as *dispersion-compensated fiber* (DCF), *dispersion-flattened compensated fiber* (DFCF), *dispersion-slope compensated fiber* (DSCF), *dispersion-shift compensated fiber* (DSCF), and *nonzero dispersion fiber* (NZDF). There are even more specialized fiber types, in addition to erbium-doped fiber amplifiers (EDFA) that are used to amplify optical power.

The TrueWave™ fiber family of LUCENT Technologies is a two-member family of nonzero dispersion fibers optimized for wavelength division multiplexing (WDM) applications over long fiber span (long haul). The TrueWave™ RS (reduced slope) member is optimized for minimal dispersion to avoid cross-talk. In addition, the small dispersion amount it introduces is the same for all wavelengths of a broad spectrum making it suitable for WDM. TrueWave™ XL is optimized for high-power dense WDM (DWDM) signals suitable for undersea spans and at rates up to 10 Gbps per wavelength. Figure 3.14 illustrates the dependence of material and wavelength dispersion in both conventional and dispersion-shifted fibers, as well as a dispersion-flattened fiber.

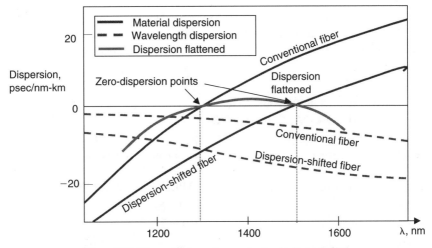

Figure 3.14 Chromatic dispersion graphs for single-mode fiber.

3.14   CHROMATIC DISPERSION LIMITS: ITU-T

The maximum *chromatic dispersion coefficient* (CDC), $D(\lambda)$, is specified by ITU-T G.652, G.653 and G.655. ITU-T G.652 recommends the limits of CDC for single-mode fiber and for wavelengths in the 1260 to 1360 nm range. In this case, the CDC limits are calculated by

$$D_1(\lambda) = (S_{0max}/4)[\lambda - (\lambda_{0min}^{4}/\lambda^{3})]$$

and

$$D_2(\lambda) = (S_{0max}/4)[\lambda - (\lambda_{0min}^4/\lambda^3)]$$

where S_{0max} is the maximum zero-dispersion slope set at $S_{0max} = -0.093$ ps/(nm^2·km), $\lambda_{0min} = 1300$ nm, and $\lambda_{0max} = 1324$ nm.

ITU-T G.653 recommends the chromatic dispersion coefficients for dispersion-shifted fiber cables. In this case, the CDC is calculated by

$$D(\lambda) = S_0 (\lambda - \lambda_0)$$

where S_0 is the zero-dispersion slope [typically equal or less than 0.085 ps/(nm^2·km)], λ_0 is the zero-dispersion wavelength in nm, and λ is the wavelength of interest. Assuming a zero-dispersion fiber at $\lambda_0 = 1550$, and λ is within the 1525 to 1575 nm range, then $D < 3.5$ psec/(nm^2·km).

ITU-T G.655 recommends the chromatic dispersion coefficients for nonzero dispersion-shifted fiber cables. In this case, the CDC should be within the range specified by

$$D_{min} \leq | D_{min}(\lambda) | \leq D_{max}, \quad \text{for} \quad \lambda_{min} \leq \lambda \leq \lambda_{max}$$

where 0.1 psec/(nm^2·km) $\leq D_{min} \leq D_{max} \leq 6$ psec/(nm^2·km), and 1530 nm $\leq \lambda_{min} \leq \lambda_{max} \leq 1565$ nm.

Fiber cable manufacturers provide chromatic dispersion coefficients by wavelength regions and for each cable type. The total dispersion over a fiber span is calculated assuming a linear dependence on length; that is, the coefficient is multiplied by the fiber length in km.

3.15   SINGLE-MODE CHROMATIC DISPERSION CALCULATIONS

The following is a rough example of dispersion calculations over a fiber link.

Equipment manufacturer model:	"APEX, Inc.," model F145X	
Bit rate:	1.2 Gbps	
Maximum allowable dispersion:	220 psec	
Transmitter wavelength (nominal):	λ_{nom}	1310 ($\pm$20) nm
Total fiber span length:	L	45 km
Zero dispersion wavelength:	λ_0	1310 nm
Dispersion slope at nominal wavelength:	S_0	0.1 psec/nm-km
Source spectral line width:	$\Delta\lambda$	0.5 nm
Chromatic dispersion coefficient @ λ_{max}:	$D(\lambda_{max})$	2.9 psec/nm-km
(provided by manufacturer or		

calculated by equation: $D(\lambda) =$
$[S_0\lambda/4][1 - (\lambda_0^4/\lambda^4)])$

Chromatic dispersion (calculated):   σ $\Delta\lambda \times D \times L = 0.5 \times 2.9 \times 45$
                                                                                $= 65.25$ psec

The calculated chromatic dispersion, 65.25 psec, is within the system manufacturer's allowable dispersion of 200 psec.

3.16   CHROMATIC DISPERSION-COMPENSATION

Clearly, chromatic dispersion has an adverse effect on the ability to transmit at very high bit rates. However, chromatic dispersion is by a good approximation a linear phenomenon, and therefore relatively simple dispersion compensating methods may be applied. A typical dispersion value in standard single-mode fibers is 1 psec/(km-nm).

One of the popular methods is DCF. A DCF is a fiber with a defractive index profile that has an opposite effect (on a specific range of wavelengths) than conventional fibers. Thus, when a DCF fiber is coupled to the transmitting (conventional single mode) fiber, chromatic dispersion is compensated for the group of wavelengths that the DCF is designed for.

Chromatic dispersion is also compensated by using chirped in-fiber Bragg gratings (see Section 4.3). According to this, adjacent wavelengths in a channel are reflected at different depths of the fiber Bragg grating, thus compensating for the wavelength travel-time variation.

Example (see Onaka)

55 λs, each at 20 Gbps (at an aggregate bandwidth of 1.1 Tbps) were transmitted for 150 km using a zero-dispersion fiber designed at 1.3 μm. To use EDFAs, which operate best in the range 1.55 μm, the transmitted wavelengths were selected in this range. The resulting chromatic dispersion would be +15.2 psec/(km-nm) with a dispersion slope of +0.064 psec/(nm²-km).

However, a DCF was used with a large negative dispersion of −103 psec/(km-nm) and a large negative dispersion slope of −0.18 psec/(nm²-km). Every 50 km of fiber span, a segment of DCF was inserted, a total of three segments each with dispersion of −800, −700, and −650 psec/nm at 1545 nm, respectively. Thus, the chromatic dispersion was compensated for, as well as both β′ and β″, and D and D′, leading to a small total chromatic dispersion of 191 psec/nm for a total of 150 km length fiber.   ■

3.17   POLARIZATION MODE DISPERSION

When a stream of very narrow (few picoseconds) polarized pulses with separation of few tens of picoseconds is transmitted in a fiber, then two sequential pulses interact and generate a stream of pulses at lower amplitude and different polarization. This phenomenon is encountered in ultra-high bit rates in fiber transmission and is known as *polarization mode dispersion* (PMD). This phenomenon is not well understood or theoretically explained, although it is known and demonstrated via experiments. It is plausible that due to manufacturing imperfection, the noncircular (but elliptical) core of the fiber, may contribute to PMD. In Figure 3.15, two consecutive pulses, one polarized at $+45°$ and the other at $-45°$ produce a third, linearly polarized signal at lower amplitude. It has been shown that as the separation between the two pulses increases, the PMD-generated signal decreases. Optical fibers have a polarization mode dispersion coefficient of less than 0.5 psec/km$^{1/2}$ (see ITU-T G.652, G.653, and G.655). For an STS-192/STM-64 signal (~10 Gbps), this PMD coefficient value limits the fiber length to 400 km.

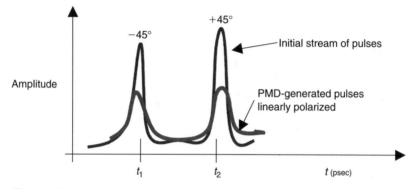

Figure 3.15 In polarization mode dispersion, sequential polarized pulses interact to generate another stream of linearly polarized pulses.

3.18   FIBER ATTENUATION OR LOSS

Fiber attenuation or *loss* is a very important transmission characteristic that imposes a limiting effect on the fiber. Fiber loss, for a given launched optical power into the fiber, $P(0)$, affects the total power arrived at the receiver, P_r, and thus, it limits the fiber span, L_{max}, without amplification.

Fiber attenuation depends on scattering on fluctuations of the refractive index, on imperfections in the fiber, and on impurities. Metal ions and OH radicals have a particular effect, particularly in the range of 1.4 μm, although fiber cable that is almost free of OH radicals has been successfully manufactured.

Assuming a fiber with an optical power attenuation constant, $\alpha(\lambda)$, the optical power attenuation at a length L is expressed by

$$P(L) = P(0)\ 10^{-\alpha(\lambda)L/10}$$

Where $P(0)$ is the launched power into the fiber. If we replace $P(L)$ with P_r, the minimum acceptable power at the receiver, then the (ideal) maximum fiber length is

$$L_{max} = [10/\ \alpha(\lambda)]\log_{10}[P(0)/P_r]$$

Note: We will see that there are more limiting factors (e.g., dispersion and bit rate) that further limit the (ideal) maximum fiber length.

In general, the optical power attenuation constant, $\alpha(\lambda)$, is nonlinear and depends on the wavelength:

$$\alpha(\lambda) = C_1/\lambda^4 + C_2 + A(\lambda)$$

where C_1 is a constant (due to Raleigh scattering), C_2 is a constant due to fiber imperfections, and $A(\lambda)$ is a function that describes the absorption of wavelengths by impurities in the fiber.

The optical power attenuation constant (in dB/km) of a fiber is typically plotted as a function of the wavelength (Figure 3.16). Conventional single-mode fibers have two low attenuation ranges, one about 1.3 μm and another about 1.55 μm. Between these two ranges, and about 1.4 μm, there is a high attenuation range (1350–1450 nm) due to the OH radical with a peak at 1385 nm. This high attenuation range is also known as the "fifth window." Dispersion-shifted fiber has a third low attenuation region in the range above 1550 and below 1625 nm.

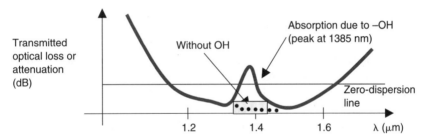

Figure 3.16 Typical single-mode fiber attenuation graph (for reference, a zero-dispersion level is also included). The LUCENT Technologies AllWave™ fiber has eliminated losses due to OH (dotted line).

If the OH radical could be eliminated from the fiber material, then the high attenuation unused region, about 1.4 nm, could be utilized. Clearly, this would make more wavelength channels available. Such a fiber, known as AllWave™ Fibre, has been manufactured by LUCENT Technologies and it has increased the number of wavelengths by over 50% by opening the previously unavailable 1350 to 1450 nm range (fifth window), thus making all wavelengths, from 1335 nm to 1625 nm, usable. This corresponds to about 500 channels with 100 Ghz channel spacing. This type of fiber is suitable for metropolitan area network (MAN) applications.

Fiber attenuation is measured in dB per kilometer. ITU-T G.652 recommends losses below 0.5 dB/km in the region 1310 nm, and below 0.4 dB/km in the region 1500 nm. Some typical values are 0.4 dB/km at about 1310 nm, and 0.2 dB/km at about 1550 nm. To appreciate the low fiber attenuation, compare it with 1 dB per cm thickness of ordinary clear glass or with the 3 dB of ordinary sunglasses.

3.18.1   The Decibel

Optical power attenuation over a fiber span is measured in decibel units (dB). A *decibel* is the logarithmic ratio of received power over transmitted power. Both received and transmitted power is expressed in the same units and therefore their ratio is dimensionless. Hence, attenuation over a fiber span in dB is expressed by:

$$\alpha(\lambda) = 10 \log P_1/P_2 \quad \text{(dB)}$$

Thus, a power ratio of 1,000 is 30 dB, a power ratio of 10 is 10 dB, a power ratio of 2 is 3 dB, a power ratio of 0.1 is -10 dB, and so on. Similarly, the signal-to-noise (power) ratio is expressed in dB units.

In communications, transmitted signals are at extremely low power, in the order of milliwatts. To denote that, the reference power point (P_2) is in milliwatts, the decibel unit is expressed in dBm.

Attenuation of several concatenated components, each expressed in decibel units, is additive. Thus, the net power loss of two concatenated components, one with 25.5 dBm and the other with -15.0 dBm is $(25.5 - 15.0) = 10.5$ dBm.

3.19   FIBER SPECTRUM UTILIZATION

Based on optical power loss of fiber, spectrum ranges have been characterized for compatibility purposes with light sources, receivers, and optical components, including the fiber. Thus, the low-loss spectrum for single-mode fiber has been subdivided into smaller regions. The S-band (or second window) is defined in the range 1280 to 1350 nm. The C-band (or third window) is defined in the range 1528 nm to 1565 nm. This is also subdivided into the "blue band" (1528–1545 nm) and the "red band" (1545–1561 nm). The L-band (or fourth window) is defined in the range 1561 to 1620 nm. The "new band" (or fifth window) is defined in the range 1350 to 1450 nm.

The window in the range 1450 to 1528 nm is used in single-mode fiber short-distance networks, such as LAN or MAN, that do not require EDFAs. EDFAs do not perform below 1530 nm, although other amplifier types (Raman scattering, Praseodymium-doped fiber amplifiers) may extend the applicability of this range to long-distance networks.

The S- and C-band ranges have found applications in WDM metropolitan networks. The C- and L-band ranges have found applications in ultra-high-speed (10–40 Gbps) WDM networks. The C-band is currently popular in the United States and elsewhere. It is compatible with cost-effective optical fiber amplifiers. The L-band is currently popular in Japan and elsewhere. The L-band takes advantage of the dispersion-compensating fiber that effectively extends the C-band range to 1600 nm, thus doubling the number of wavelengths better-suited in DWDM applications. Previously unavailable optical amplifiers and filters in the L-band are now becoming readily available. Moreover, to avoid four-wave mixing phenomena, a proposal to use non-uniformly spaced channels has been submitted and is under study by ITU-T (G.692).

The first window refers to the wavelength range from 820 nm and below 900 nm that is used in multimode-fiber applications. Table 3.1 summarizes the frequency utilization.

Table 3.1 Summary of Frequency Utilization for Fiber Application

Window	Label	Range (nm)	Fiber Type	Applications
First	—	820–900	MMF	LAN-type
Second	S	1280–1350	SMF	Single-λ
Third	C	1528–1561	SMF	DWDM[1]
Fourth	L	1561–1620	DSF	DWDM
Fifth	—	1350–1450	SMF AllWave™	DWDM
Fifth	—	1450–1528	SMF	DWDM/MAN[2]

[1] DWDM may also include single wavelength applications.

[2] Currently, EDFAs do not perform below the range of 1530 nm.

3.20   FIBER BIREFRINGENCE AND POLARIZATION

An ideal single-mode fiber would support two orthogonally polarized modes, one along the x-axis and one along the y-axis. However, because ideal fibers cannot be manufactured for lengths of many kilometers, actual fibers exhibit some birefringence.

The *degree of birefringence* is defined by $B = |n_x - n_y|$, where n_x and n_y are indices for the polarized fiber modes. Fiber birefringence leads to a power exchange between the two polarization components in a continuous manner, changing the polarization from linear to elliptical, to circular, and finally back to linear. The length of birefringent fiber through which polarized light undergoes a complete revolution of polarization is defined as *beat length*. The various phases of polarization within the beat length are illustrated in Figure 3.17. The beat length is given by $L_B = \lambda/B$. For $\lambda = 1550$ nm and $B \sim 10^{-7}$, $L_B \sim 15$ m.

In optical communications where a receiver detects directly total intensity, fiber birefringence is not a serious problem. However, it becomes a concern in coherent communications systems where a given direction of polarization is expected, or when polarization-sensitive components are used. To ameliorate fiber birefringence, polarization-preserving fibers have been designed and manufactured. Polarization-preserving fibers exhibit a very strong degree of birefringence $(B \sim 10^{-4})$ such that birefringence induced by core variations, comparatively, becomes negligible.

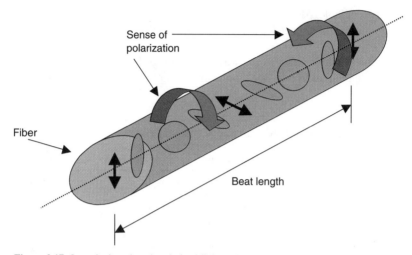

Figure 3.17 Over the beat length polarized light undergoes a complete revolution of polarization.

3.21   NONLINEAR PHENOMENA

When light enters matter, photons and atoms interact and, under certain circumstances, photons may be absorbed by atoms and excite them to higher energy levels. Many atoms, when excited to a higher state, are not stable. New photons may trigger them to come down to their initial, lower energy level by releasing energy, *photons* and/or *phonons* (the acoustic quantum equivalent of light). The photon–atom interaction causes photons to propagate through matter at a velocity that depends on their energy, $E = h\nu$. Thus, different wavelengths travel at different speeds.

In addition to photon–atom interaction, there are also photon–photon and photon–atom–photon interactions that result in some complex phenomena, some of them not well understood yet. These interactions, known as nonlinear phenomena, are best described by quantum theory, and thus, we only provide a quantitative description. They are distinguished in *forward scattering* and in *backward scattering* (Raman and Brillouin scattering) as well as in *four-wave (or four-photon) mixing*. The direction (forward and backward) is with respect to the direction of the excitation light. Backward scattering may take place due to reflected light at the end face (or other discontinuities) of the fiber.

In optical systems, nonlinear phenomena are viewed as both advantageous and as degrading:

- *Advantageous,* because they are the basis of lasers, optical amplifiers, and dispersion compensation.

- *Degrading,* because they cause signal losses, noise, cross-talk, and pulse broadening.

In general, the input–output relationship of a system is expressed by

$$O = k^1 \cdot I + k^2 \cdot I \cdot I + k^3 \cdot I \cdot I \cdot I + \cdots$$

where k^n is a higher-order system coefficient, O the output, and I the input vector. The first term ($n = 1$) describes the linear behavior of the system whereas other terms ($n > 1$) describe higher-order nonlinear behavior.

The response of any dielectric (such as glass fiber) to optical power is nonlinear; the behavior of dielectric to optical power is like a dipole. It is the dipole nature of dielectric that interacts harmonically with electromagnetic waves such as light.

When the optical power is low, it results in small oscillations and the first term of the series approximates the photon-fiber system behavior (i.e., a linear system). However, when the optical power is large, the oscillations are such that higher-order terms (nonlinear behavior) become significant.

Similarly, the polarization of an electromagnetic wave, P, induced in the electric dipoles of a medium by an electric field, E, is proportional to *susceptibility*, $\varkappa$:

$$P = e_o \left[\varkappa^1 \cdot E + \varkappa^2 \cdot E \cdot E + \varkappa^3 \cdot E \cdot E \cdot E + \cdots \right]$$

where e_o is the permittivity in vacuum. Here, again, the first term ($n = 1$) describes the linear behavior of the system whereas other terms ($n > 1$) describe higher-order nonlinear behavior.

For an *isotropic* medium the second-order (e.g., silica fiber) is orthogonal. Thus, it vanishes (or it is negligible). However, the third order results in nonlinear effects that can be significant. Among the nonlinearities, in the following section, we examine stimulated Raman scattering, stimulated Brillouin scattering, and four-wave mixing.

3.21.1 Stimulated Raman Scattering

Consider two light sources, one of a short wavelength and the other of a longer wavelength propagating within the same medium. The short wavelength source excites atoms to a high energy level. Then, due to the nonlinear properties of the medium, excited atoms are triggered by other photons and "drop" to an intermediate energy level by releasing optical energy of a longer wavelength; this longer wavelength depends on the medium. If the other source is of the same "longer wavelength" with the released wavelength, then optical energy from both "longer wavelength" light (the original one and the one generated) mix together. Eventually, all atoms at the intermediate level will "drop" to their initially low (or ground) energy level by releasing the remaining energy (Figure 3.18). This is known as *stimulated Raman scattering* (SRS). Raman scattering is dominant when the source is broadband and it may equally occur in both directions in a fiber, forward and backward.

In general, the photon frequency that is emitted when an ion falls from an energy level E_{high} to an energy level E_{low} is determined by the relationship $E = h\nu$:

$$\nu = [E_{high} - E_{low}]/h$$

In optical transmission systems with more than one wavelength in the same fiber, SRS is undesirable because it may result in signal cross-talk and it thus re-

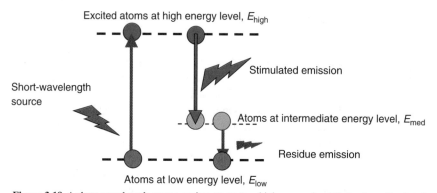

Figure 3.18 A short-wavelength source excites atoms to a high-energy level that, when stimulated, release light energy of a longer wavelength.

stricts the launched power per channel in the fiber. However, for SRS to become a significant cross-talk contributor, the transferred energy must exceed a certain threshold level, which depends on the medium.

SRS is advantageously used to optically amplify a signal. In the latter case, the short wavelength source acts like a "pump" that transfers energy from it to a modulated weak signal of a longer wavelength.

Example (see Nosu)

For a 10-channel system at 1.5 μm with channel separation $\Delta\lambda = 10$ nm (or, $\Delta f = 1.3 \times 10^3$ Ghz), the maximum allowable launched power per channel is 3 mW.   ∎

3.21.2   Stimulated Brillouin Scattering

Stimulated Brillouin scattering (SBS) is the nonlinear phenomenon by which, in contrast to SRS, a signal causes stimulated emission that propagates in the direction opposite to the signal, if a threshold power level is reached. In this case, the stimulated light is at a shorter wavelength (downshifted by 11 Ghz at 1550). Stimulated emission is in both directions. However, the part that is in the same direction as the original signal is scattered as acoustic phonons, and the part that is in the opposite direction is guided by the fiber. Now, if another optical signal at the downshifted wavelength propagates in the direction opposite to the original signal, it will be mixed with the transferred energy thus increasing signal cross-talk.

It has been experimentally determined that SBS is dominant when the spectral power (brightness) of the source is large, and it abruptly increases when the launched power reaches a threshold value. Factors that determine the threshold value of launched power, include the material of the fiber, the line-width of the pump light, the fiber length, the effective cross-section area of the fiber-core, and the bit rate of the signal.

Threshold values for SBS in fiber systems are in the 5 to 10 mW range of launched power (for externally modulated narrow line widths) and 20 to 30 mW for directly modulated lasers (ITU-T G.663).

SBS, like SRS, restricts the launched power per channel. However, SBS may also be advantageously used in optical amplification, where the backward signal may be the pump and the forward signal the one to be amplified.

3.21.3   Four-Wave Mixing

Consider three lightwave frequencies, f_1, f_2, and f_3 closely spaced (in terms of wavelength). Then, from the interaction of the three, a fourth lightwave frequency is generated, f_{fwm}, such that $f_{fwm} = f_1 + f_2 - f_3$. This is known as *four-wave mixing* (FWM, or four-photon mixing). The order of lightwave frequencies is f_1, f_{fwm}, f_3 and f_2 (Figure 3.19).

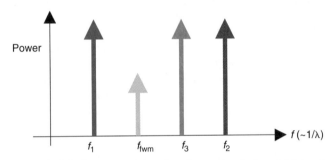

Figure 3.19 In four-wave mixing, three frequencies, f_1, f_2, and f_3 interact to produce a fourth frequency, $f_{fwm}, f_{fwm} = f_1 + f_2 - f_3$.

The output power of the f_{fwm} and the efficiency of four-wave mixing depend on several factors:

- Wavelength mismatch or channel spacing, D_b, or Δf
- Power intensity of the contributing frequencies f_1, f_2, and f_3
- Chromatic dispersion of the fiber
- Refractive index
- Fiber length
- Higher-order polarization properties of the material (nonlinear Kerr coefficient)

FWM may also occur with two signals at different wavelengths, if their intensity and wavelengths are in a specific relationship. In such a case, the fiber refractive index is modulated at the beat frequency of the two wavelengths. The phase modulation in this case creates two sidebands (at frequencies given by this difference), the intensity of which is weak as compared with the intensity of the mixing products from three signals.

The effect of FWM on optical transmission is signal-to-noise degradation and cross-talk. As the signal input power of f_1, f_2, and f_3 increases, or as the channel spacing decreases, the FWM mixing output term, f_{fwm}, increases. It has been experimentally verified that at 200-Ghz channel-spacing FWM effects are drastically decreased compared with 100-Ghz spacing.

FWM requires strong phase matching (as opposed to SRS, which does not) of coincident energy from all three wavelengths. However, both chromatic dispersion and length of fiber reduce the intensity of the FWM product. In general, FWM limits the channel capacity of a fiber system.

3.21.4   Temporal FWM, Near End and Far End

Consider a narrow light pulse at a wavelength traveling along a fiber segment. Think of the light pulse as a sliding window with constant speed along the fiber. As the light pulse slides along the fiber, it influences the electric dipoles of the fiber segment for as long as they are in it. If at the same time, there are two more pulses on adjacent wavelength channels, overlapping in time, then in this segment FWM occurs. Because the signal power at the *near end* of the fiber (close to the source) is at its maximum, the FWM product is also at its highest intensity.

Similarly, when the three light pulses arrive at a *far end* segment of a several kilometers long fiber, due to attenuation of the pulses, the FWM product at that segment is at its lowest intensity. Figure 3.20 illustrates qualitatively the contribution of FWM at the near end and at the far end of a fiber. Clearly, FWM occurs in a time continuous manner, and although at the near end it has a maximum effect, its strength is diminishing as the pulses travel along the fiber. The study of FWM in the time domain is termed *temporal FWM* (tFWM).

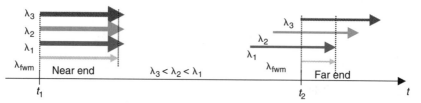

Figure 3.20 FWM of synchronized channels has a maximum effect at the near end, but due to attenuation and uneven propagation delays its effect is diminished at the far end.

3.22   SPECTRAL BROADENING

The refractive index of many materials depends on the amplitude of the electrical field. Thus, as the electrical field changes, so does the refractive index. However, refractive index variations impact the transmission characteristics of the signal itself.

As an almost monochromatic light-pulse travels through a fiber, its amplitude variation causes *phase change* and *spectral broadening*. The *phase change* is given by

$$\Delta\Phi = [2\pi(\Delta n)L]/\lambda$$

where L is the fiber length, and

$$\Delta n = n(\lambda,E) - n_1(\lambda)$$

Phase variations are equivalent to frequency modulation, or to "chirping." The *spectral broadening* is given by

$$\delta\omega = -d(\Delta\Phi)/dt$$

For a *Gaussian*-shaped pulse, spectral broadening is

$$\delta\omega = 0.86\Delta\omega\Delta\Phi_m$$

where $\Delta\omega$ is the spectral width and $\Delta\Phi_m$ is the maximum phase shift in radians.

Spectral broadening appears as if half of the pulse is frequency downshifted (known as *red shift*) and as if the other half is frequency upshifted (known as *blue shift*). Such shifts are also expected in pulses that consist of a narrow range of wavelengths that are centered around the zero-dispersion wavelength. Below the zero-dispersion point, *wavelength dispersion is negative; above it, positive.* Significant spectral broadening is observed when $\Delta\Phi_m$ is greater than or equal to 2.

3.23   SELF-PHASE MODULATION

The dynamic characteristics of a propagating light pulse in a fiber result in modulation of its own phase, due to the Kerr effect of the fiber medium. According to this phenomenon, known as *self-phase modulation (SPM)*, spectral broadening takes place (Figure 3.21).

If the wavelength of the pulse is below the zero-dispersion point (known as *normal dispersion regime*), then spectral broadening causes temporal broadening of the pulse as it propagates. If on the other hand, the wavelength is above the zero-dispersion wavelength of the fiber (the *anomalous dispersion regime*) then chromatic dispersion and self-phase modulation compensate for each other, thus reducing temporal broadening. Figure 3.21 illustrates temporal broadening.

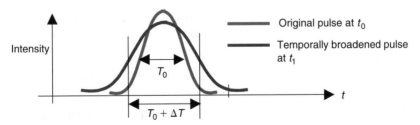

Figure 3.21 The dynamic characteristics of a propagating light-pulse in a fiber result in modulation of its own phase that results in spectral broadening.

3.24   SELF-MODULATION OR MODULATION INSTABILITY

When a single pulse of an almost monochromatic light has a wavelength above the zero-dispersion wavelength of the fiber (known as the anomalous dispersion regime) another phenomenon occurs that degrades the width of the pulse. According to this, two side lobe pulses are symmetrically generated at either side of the original pulse (Figure 3.22). This is known as *self-modulation* or *modulation instability*. Modulation instability affects the signal-to-noise ratio and is considered a special FWM case. Modulation instability is reduced by operating at low energy levels and/or at wavelengths below the zero-dispersion wavelength.

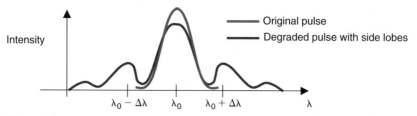

Figure 3.22 Two side lobe pulses are symmetrically generated the wavelength of a pulse is above the zero-dispersion of the fiber, a phenomenon known as self-modulation or modulation instability.

3.25   IMPACT OF FWM ON DWDM TRANSMISSION SYSTEMS

As the density of wavelengths (channels) in DWDM systems increases, it is clear that cross-talk becomes an important issue.

- If the optical-power of each channel is increased, FWM becomes more intense.

- If the launched optical power of each channel is lowered, then the actual fiber length is decreased to assure that the arriving signal can be detected reliably. This may necessitate optical amplification (optical amplification increases the cost) to extend the fiber path.

- If the channel (wavelength) density increases, or if the channel spacing decreases, FWM becomes more intense.

- If the channels are spaced further apart, then fewer wavelength channels can be used in the fiber.

3.26   COUNTERMEASURES TO REDUCE FWM

FWM in fiber transmission systems is a phenomenon that cannot be eliminated. However, several countermeasures and design approaches may help to suppress the FWM product.

- Channels are spaced unevenly, to avoid FWM.

- The channel spacing is increased to reduce FWM.

- Launched power into the fiber is reduced to reduce the FWM effect.

- Segments of fibers with opposing non-zero dispersion characteristics after long spans of standard single-mode fiber cable to maintain a near-zero net chromatic dispersion may be used.

3.27   SOLITONS

It has been implied that the contribution of the self-modulation effect (red and blue shift) depends on the pulse shape. Under specific conditions (very short pulses with a specific power spectrum), the spectral broadening due to self-modulation can be compensated for by the dispersion effect of the fiber. In this case, the pulse preserves its input shape and it is stable over the entire length of the fiber. Pulses that preserve their shape are known as *solitons*, and the condition for generation and sustained propagation is known as the *soliton regime.*

A theoretical analysis of soliton generation and propagation entails solving a homogeneous Schroedinger-type equation; it is thus beyond our purpose here. However, it should be pointed out that the *soliton regime* involves parameters such as "input optical power" (derived from a *hyperbolic secant* function), "cross-section of the fiber core," the "dielectric constant" of the vacuum ($\epsilon_0 = 8.854 \cdot 10^{-12}$ F/m), and the fiber type.

For a typical single-mode fiber, any real pulse within an area of $A = \sqrt{1.6\ W^{1/2}}$ psec ($\pm 50\%$) can reach the soliton regime; that is, it can generate one soliton. Typical solitons are about 50 psec wide (Figure 3.23). Because of the required pulse narrowness, return-to-zero (RZ) modulation is suitable in solitons (see Chapter 12 for modulation and coding techniques).

3.27.1   A Qualitative Interpretation of Solitons

As soon as a very narrow pulse is launched into the fiber, its initial pulse shape oscillates temporarily as two competing effects act on it—spectral broadening and compensation by dispersion effects. Finally, this oscillation, at some time later and after some fiber length, reaches an equilibrium compensating state and the soliton takes a shape very close to its initial. However, there are more effects that may af-

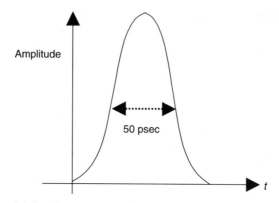

Figure 3.23 Self-modulation of very narrow pulses can be compensated for by the dispersion effect of the fiber thus preserving the pulse shape; such pulses are known as solitons.

fect the shape of the soliton. Third-order dispersion effects may cause the soliton to change its velocity and thus its shape, and fiber losses will cause the soliton to broaden its width; for example, 15-km travel in single-mode fiber will double the width of the soliton. Therefore, a low-loss single mode with low third-order dispersion characteristics fiber will enable solitons to be transmitted at very long distances and very high bit rates (due to narrowness of the pulses) without amplification.

When solitons are used in WDM systems, one undesirable event may occur— collision among solitons that belong to different channels. Collision takes place over a distance in which solitons overlap. The length of fiber over which solitons of different channels overlap is known as the *collision length*, L_{coll}. The collision length depends on fiber parameters, channel spacing, and the actual bit rate of the colliding channels. Depending on parameter value, the collision length may be 10 km or even 100 km. It has been shown that during soliton collision an exchange of energy takes place. As a result of this, the soliton frequency and the phase shift causing some residual effects.

At the receiver, because of the *collision-induced temporal shift* and because 1 s and 0 s in the bit stream are random, *timing jitter* is induced (a string of ones would cause the same shift from bit to bit, and thus no jitter). When the collision length becomes comparable to the amplifier spacing, the residual shift (jitter) may become as high as ~0.1 Ghz, which is an unacceptable value because jitter is cumulative from amplifier to amplifier.

Clearly, the soliton technique in optical transmission systems is difficult to use, due to optical nonlinearities and the high transmitted optical power. However, solitons and dispersion managed fibers, when used properly, promise an optical transmission technology that exhibits reduced nonlinear effects, high spectral efficiency, RZ modulation, ultra-high bit rates, and fiber spans at very long lengths (hundreds of kilometers) without regeneration or amplification. The latter makes soliton technology particularly attractive to long-haul and transoceanic optical transmission. Short-haul applications of soliton technology is, for the time being, cost prohibitive.

3.28 FIBER CONNECTORS

Copper wire may be installed in segments, each segment being connected with another by simply bringing the two ends in physical contact (e.g., by twisting the two ends). Consequently, no special treatment of the two copper ends is required.

Unlike copper wire, fiber requires specialized treatment. Two fiber ends placed one next to the other constitute a material discontinuity. Because photons travel from one fiber to the other, they have to overcome this discontinuity. Consequently, certain special precautions must be taken to minimize power loss as photons travel through it.

- The two fiber ends to be connected should be treated so that the end faces are flat, perpendicular to the fiber longitudinal axis, and highly polished (or form a spherical lens).

- The two end faces should be treated with antireflective coatings.

- The two fiber cores should be in perfect alignment.

- The two end faces should be brought into close proximity.

The first two are related to the treatment of fiber ends and are accomplished with specialized abrasive materials and coatings. The third is related to how well the fiber has been manufactured (i.e., so that the core is exactly at the center of the circular fiber), and how well interconnecting devices align the cores. The concentricity error of single-mode fiber (based on ITU-T G.652) should be less than 1 μm. The cores are accurately aligned with biconical self-aligned connectors or aligned grooves. Finally, the last item is related to the flatness and perpendicularity of the two end surfaces and on the accuracy of the connectors.

In any case, connector optical power loss is taken into serious account when estimating the overall power loss of an optical link. Because of the stringent power loss budget, fibers are installed preferably in long (many km) segments to minimize the number of interconnecting devices.

3.29 CONCLUSION

The quest for a fiber cable that introduces the least optical loss across a wide spectrum of wavelengths, the least dispersion, and almost no nonlinear effects still challenges fiberoptic designers and manufacturers.

However, although the transmission characteristics of fiber cable have been greatly improved, older fibers are still being used. In addition, there is a large variation in fiber specifications among both fiber cables and manufacturers. Clearly, this adds another level of complexity to the design challenges of optical systems, which must be compatible with all types of fibers and vendor equipment. Cost effectiveness is another important consideration.

Fiber cable as a transmission medium has many overwhelming qualities. Thus, many telecommunications companies, new and old, install fiber by the many thousands of kilometers each year in the ground, along bridges and highways, through sky-risers, through natural-gas-pipes, along rivers, by train rails and under the oceans, interconnecting continents, countries, cities, and homes. Thus, one can deduct conclusively that the future of fiber is truly very bright.

EXERCISES

1. Consider a fiber, 1 km long, with a refractive index $n = 1.5$. Consider also a source with a data rate at 10 Gbps. Calculate the number of bits at any time in the fiber, or the fiber bit capacity. (Approximate the group velocity by $v = c/n$.)

2. Why is the critical cone important in optical communications?

3. In a step index fiber, the core has $n_1 = 1.48$ and the cladding $n_2 = 1.46$. Calculate the numerical aperture (NA) or the critical cone for the fiber.

4. Comment on the cone angle of single-mode versus multiple-mode fiber. Which must be very small?

5. A pulse starts with a width of 30 psec and by the time it travels over 10 km of fiber, it is 60 psec. For $k = 3$ calculate the maximum bit rate.

6. The OH radical absorbs light energy about 1385 nm. In your judgment, why does OH absorb selectively this wavelength?

7. An optical link consists of 3 fiber segments, the first 10 km long, the second 30 km, and the third 20 km. The fiber attenuation is 0.1 dB/km. The segments are connected with connectors at 0.1 dB loss each. Calculate the total loss due to fiber and connectors over the link.

8. Is it true that, as the channel spacing increases, so does the FWM contribution?

4

OPTICAL SPECTRAL FILTERS AND GRATINGS

4.1 INTRODUCTION

The function of an electronic or passive (L-R-C) filter is to recognize a narrow band of electrical frequencies from a multiplicity and either pass it or reject it. Similarly, optical spectral filters function the same way, and they are key components in optical transmission systems. Optical spectral filters are based on *interference, diffraction,* or *absorption,* and they are distinguished in *fixed* and in *tunable* filters.

In this chapter, we examine the following filters:

- The Fabry-Perot interferometer
- The Bragg reflector
- Dielectric thin film interference
- The acousto-optic tunable filter
- The absorption filter
- The hybrid filter

4.2 FABRY-PEROT INTERFEROMETER

The Fabry-Perot interferometer is based on the interference of multiple reflections of a light beam by two surfaces of a thin plate (Figure 4.1). The condition for interference maxima for each wavelength is $2d \sin \Theta = n\lambda$, where n is an integer and d is the thickness of the plate. Clearly, this condition is satisfied by a number of wavelengths that are multiples of 2π, and at the maxima points the intensity is $I_{max} = E^2$.

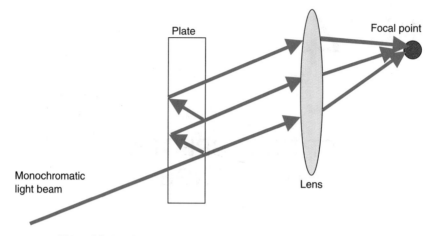

Figure 4.1 A typical example of a simple interferometer is the Fabry-Perot.

If the reflectivity of the plate surfaces is R, then the intensity between maxima is $I = (1 - R)^2/(1 + R)^2$. As the reflectivity of the surface increases, the intensity between maxima decreases, thus increasing the sharpness of the interferometer (Figure 4.2).

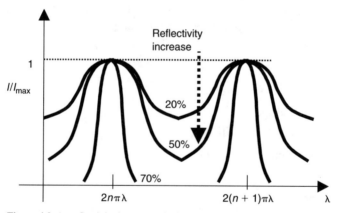

Figure 4.2 As reflectivity increases, the intensity between maxima decreases, thus increasing the sharpness of the interferometer.

4.2.1   Fabry-Perot Resonator

The *Fabry-Perot resonator* is an arrangement of two parallel plates that reflect light back and forth. To examine how this functions, consider the following (Figure 4.3):

- Let two plane parallel semi-transparent reflectors (half-mirrors) be separated by d.
- Let there be a medium with attenuation α_s and gain g.

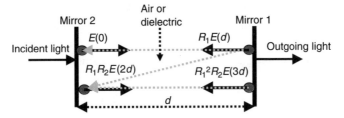

Figure 4.3 A Fabry-Perot interferometer with fixed parallel plates is known
as an *etalon*, and adjustable with a micrometer is known as an
interferometer.

- Let R_1 and R_2 be reflector #1 and #2 *power-reflected coefficient.*
- Let a pulse of photons $E(t,x)$ enter reflector 2, $E(t = 0, x = 0)$.

Then,

$$E(t,x) = A^{\{-\alpha_s x/2[j(\omega t - \beta x)]\}}$$

where α_s is the intensity attenuation coefficient, β is the propagation constant, and ω
is the light frequency. A typical Fabry-Perot interferometer may have the plates fixed,
known as an *etalon*, or adjustable with a micrometer, known as an *interferometer.*

The key question in this arrangement is: *what is the condition for resonance?*
The field at mirror #2 ($x = 0$), after been reflected by mirrors #1 and #2, is

$$E(t,0) = R_1 R_2 A^{[(g-\alpha_s)d][j(\omega t - 2\beta d)]}$$

where g is the intensity gain coefficient, the first exponent is the propagation component and the second is the phase component.

For steady-state oscillations, the amplitude of the initial light pulse ($t = 0$, $x = 0$), must be equal to the amplitude after it has been reflected back and forth. This
leads to two conditions: The amplitude condition

$$R_1 R_2 A^{[(g-\alpha_s)d]} = A$$

and the phase condition

$$\exp(-j2\beta d) = 1$$

The phase condition is satisfied only if

$$2\beta d = 2\pi m; \ \beta = (2\pi n)/\lambda$$

where m is an integer, n is the refractive index, β is the propagation constant, and λ
is the wavelength in vacuum.

The values of λ that satisfy the relationship

$$\lambda = (2dn)/m$$

provide the *resonant wavelengths* or *modes* of the Fabry-Perot resonator.

Example
For $m = 1$ and $n = 1$, then $\lambda = 2d$; for $m = 2$ and $n = 1$, then $\lambda = d$. ∎

The frequency spacing Δf between consecutive (longitudinal) modes is obtained from:

$$m - (m - 1) = (2dn/c)f_m - (2dn/c)f_{m-1}$$

or

$$1 = (2dn/c)\Delta f$$

from which one derives

$$\Delta f = c/2dn \text{ and } \Delta\lambda = \lambda^2/2dn$$

The latter indicates that a multiplicity of frequencies (wavelengths) is transmitted through the Fabry-Perot resonator. A typical transmittance profile is shown in Figure 4.4.

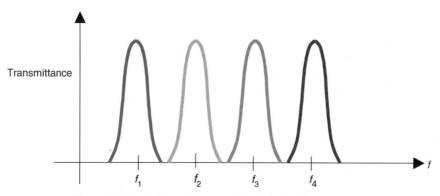

Figure 4.4 A typical transmittance profile of a Fabry-Perot resonator.

4.2.2 Finesse

An indication of how many wavelength (or frequency) channels can simultaneously pass without severe interference among them is known as the *finesse* of the Fabry-Perot resonator. The finesse is a measure of the energy of wavelengths within the cavity relative to the energy lost per cycle. Thus, the higher the finesse, the narrower the resonant line width. The finesse is the equivalent to the Q-factor of electrical filters.

Cavity losses due to imperfections of mirrors (e.g., flatness), and angle of incidence of the light beam impact the finesse value. Usually, the finesse is dominated by mirror losses due to power that flows in and out as a result of the semitransparency of the mirrors. Clearly, if the mirrors were fully reflective, they would not allow light in or out, and if they were a little reflective, the cavity would not sustain an adequate amount of light power in it.

Assuming the same reflectivity R for both mirrors, the finesse, F, is expressed by

$$F = (\pi R)/[2(1 - R)]$$

Finesse values of 20 to 100 have been achieved.

4.2.3   Spectral Width, Line Width, and Line Spacing

Spectral width is defined as the band of frequencies that a filter will pass through (Figure 4.5). The spectral width is characterized by an upper and lower frequency (wavelength) threshold. In addition, it is characterized by a gain curve that is a measure of the degree of flatness over the spectral width.

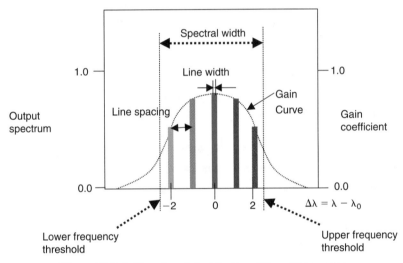

Figure 4.5 Definition of spectral width, line width, and line spacing.

Line width or *channel width* is defined as the width of the frequency channel. An ideal channel would be monochromatic; that is, a single wavelength. However, this is not possible, and thus the line width is a measure of how close to an ideal channel is, as well as an indication of the spectral content of the channel.

Line spacing is defined as the distance in wavelength units (nm) or in frequency units (Ghz) between two channels.

These definitions are important in optical system design. They determine the number of channels that the system can support, as well as the distance for error-free communication over a dispersive fiber.

4.2.4   The Fabry-Perot Filter

The Fabry-Perot filter consists of two high-reflectance multilayers separated by a $\lambda/2$ space layer (Figure 4.6). Multiple interference in the space layer causes the filter output spectral characteristic to peak sharply over a narrow band of wavelengths that

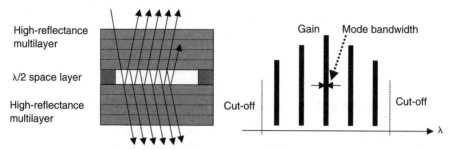

Figure 4.6 The Fabry-Perot interference filter as a band-pass filter.

are multiples of the $\lambda/2$ spacer layer. Thus, the Fabry-Perot interference filter is used exclusively as a band-pass filter.

4.3 BRAGG GRATING

Bragg grating is an arrangement of parallel semireflecting plates. To examine how this functions, consider the following (Figure 4.7):

- Let N (periodic) plane parallel semireflectors be separated by d (*Bragg spacing*).
- Let there be a medium with attenuation α_s, and gain g.
- Let R be the *power-reflected coefficient,* such that $R \ll 1$, and T the *power-transmitted coefficient,* such that $T \sim 1$.
- Let a pulse of photons $E(t,x)$ enter through mirror 1, $E(t = 0, x = 0)$

Then

$$E(t,x) = A^{(-\alpha_s x/2)[j(\omega t - \beta x)]}$$

where α_s is the intensity attenuation coefficient, β is the propagation constant, and ω is the light frequency. The key question in this arrangement is: *what is the condition for strong reflection of a particular frequency?*

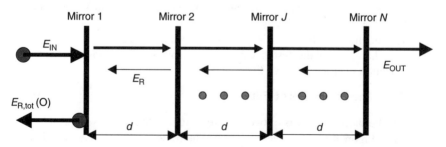

Figure 4.7 A Bragg grating with N (periodic) plane parallel semireflectors.

Let the first light-pulse at the first mirror be E_{IN}. The reflected part of E_{IN} by the first semitransparent mirror is $E_{R1}(0) = E_{IN}(0)R$ and the transmitted part is $E_{T1}(0) = E_{IN}(0)T$. R and T are the reflection and transmission coefficients, respectively.

The transmitted portion $E_{T1}(0)$ is partially reflected $[E_{R2}(d) = E_{T1}(0)\,Re^{-j\beta d}]$ and partially transmitted $[E_{T2}(d) = E_{T1}(0)Te^{-j\beta d}]$ by the second mirror, and so on. The reflected part at the Nth mirror is

$$E_{RN}[(N-1)d] = E_{T(N-1)}[(N-2)d]\,Re^{-j\beta d}$$

and the transmitted part is

$$E_{TN}[(N-1)d] = E_{T(N-1)}[(N-2)d]Te^{-j\beta d}$$

The reflected part (by the Nth mirror) arrives back to the first mirror. Taking into account the propagation constant, this is

$$E_{RN}[(N)d] = E_{T(N-1)}[(N-1)d]\,R^{N-1}\,e^{(N-1)j\beta d}$$

4.3.1 Bragg Reflector

To derive the condition for total reflection, one examines the sum of all reflected components at the first mirror. The sum yields a geometric series from which the relationship is obtained:

$$E_{R,tot}(0) = E_{IN}(0)\ R(1-M^N)/(1-M)$$

where $M = T^2\,e^{-2j\beta d}$. That is, if N is sufficiently large, then the total reflected energy at the first mirror approximates the incident energy, even if R is small.

4.3.2 Bragg Condition

In the previous relationship, the phase angle of waves at each mirror was arbitrary. If the phase angle could be a multiple of 2π, then a condition for strong reflection could be obtained; that is,

$$\arg(M) = 2\arg T - 2\beta d = 2\arg T - 2(2\pi/\lambda)d = 2\pi n$$

where n is an arbitrary number.

For simplicity, when phase $= 0$ or setting $\arg(.) = 0$, then $-(2\pi/\lambda)d = n\pi$, from which the *condition for strong reflection* or *Bragg condition* is

$$d = -n\lambda_B/2$$

That is, the Bragg spacing (or grating period) should be an integer multiple of the half wavelength. The negative sign denotes reflection, and n denotes the order of the Bragg grating. When $n = 1$ (first order) then $d = \lambda/2$, and when $n = 2$ (second order) then $d = \lambda$.

4.4 FIBER BRAGG GRATINGS

A *fiber Bragg grating* (FBG) consists of a fiber segment whose index of refraction varies periodically along its length. Variations of the refractive index constitute discontinuities that emulate a Bragg structure. A periodic variation of the refractive index is formed by exposing the germano-silicate core of the fiber to an intense ultraviolet (UV) optical interference pattern that has a periodicity equal to the periodicity of the grating to be formed. When the fiber is exposed to the intense UV pattern, structural defects are formed and thus a permanent variation of the refractive index having the same periodicity with the UV pattern. Figure 4.8a illustrates an FBG using the UV method and Figure 4.8b illustrates a monolithically made FBG with a corrugated $In_xGa_{1-x}As_yP_{1-y}$ over an InP substrate. A fiber Bragg grating incorporated in-line with a transmitting fiber is also called "in-fiber Bragg grating."

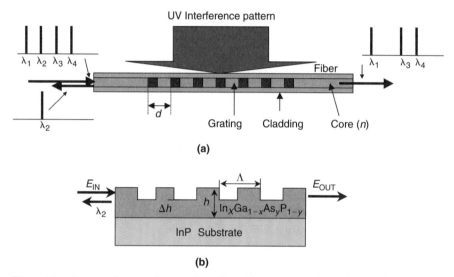

Figure 4.8 A Bragg grating made by exposing a fiber with a UV pattern (a), and a monolithic one (b).

The interference pattern has a periodicity that depends on the wavelength band the FBG is designed to operate in. For near-infrared wavelengths of about 1.55 μm, the grating is made with a periodicity, d, of 1 to 10 μm.

The UV pattern is formed with one of several optical methods (diffraction or interferometry) that generate an interference pattern of alternating minima and maxima of light intensity. Regardless of the method used, the interference pattern must be of high quality with uniform periodicity, high contrast, and sharp edges.

The UV source is provided by an excimer laser that operates at a wavelength in the 157 nm to 351 nm range. The peak absorption is at 240 nm and thus this wavelength is the most efficient. Excimer lasers may produce hundreds of milijoules in a 10- to 40-nsec pulse, and can create the grating pattern in a fiber in a single high energy shot, as the fiber is drawn (see Section 3.2.1). Continuous wave (CW) laser sources at 1-watt output may also be used.

Applying periodic pressure along the fiber may also form an FBG. Pressure also alters the structure of the fiber and the refractive index, thus creating an FBG.

There are many uses for FBGs: An FBG placed at the output of a circulator reflects back only the wavelength it is designed for, thus constructing a bandstop filter. Placed at the output of a laser, the FBG reflects back portion of the transmitted power to be monitored by a light-emitting diode (LED). When the laser ceases to function, the LED detects it and sends a message to the system.

A similar Bragg grating reflector, based on a stacked-dielectric structure is composed of quarter-wavelength thick layers, known as a *photonic lattice*, each with different refractive index. Photonic lattice reflectors have been found to reflect wavelengths over all possible angles of incidence and they do not absorb incident energy, as mirror-based reflectors do.

Fiber Bragg gratings with a linearly variable pitch may compensate for chromatic dispersion, known as chirped-FBGs (Figure 4.9). In this case, because of the linearly varying pitch (or chirp), wavelengths within a channel are reflected back at different depths of the grating, thus compensating for the travel time variation (see Section 3.12) of wavelengths in a channel. Thus, chirped-FBGs perform chromatic compression on a chromatically dispersed pulse.

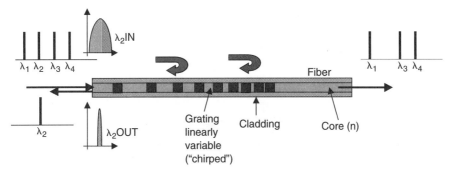

Figure 4.9 A fiber Bragg chirped-grating reflects dispersed wavelengths of a channel at different depths, thus compensating for the spectrally dispersed width.

4.5 TUNABLE BRAGG GRATINGS

The wavelength at which the reflection is maximal is given by the Bragg condition:

$$\lambda_B = 2 \, d/n$$

To make the Bragg grating tunable (i.e., to control the reflected wavelength), the Bragg spacing (grating period) must be controllable. This is achieved by one of several methods. For example, application of a stretching force elongates the fiber and thus it changes its period (*mechanical tuning*). Application of heat elongates the fiber and thus it changes its period (*thermal tuning*).

FBGs fino applications in fiber dispersion compensation, gain flattening of erbium-doped fiber amplifiers (EDFAs), and in add-drop multiplexers/demultiplexers.

However, the fiber used to make an FBG should be free of imperfections as well as of microscopic variations of the refractive index.

4.6   DIELECTRIC THIN FILM

Dielectric thin film (DTF) interference filters consist of alternate layers of high refractive index and low refractive index, each layer being λ/4 thick.

Light reflected within the layers of high index does not shift its phase whereas those within the low index shift by 180°. Taking into account the travel difference (in multiples of 2 × λ/4), the successive reflections recombine constructively at the front face producing a highly reflected beam with wavelengths within a narrow range (Figure 4.10). Outside this range the output wavelengths drop abruptly.

The primary considerations in DTF design are:

- Low-pass band loss (less than 0.3 dB).
- Good channel spacing (better than 10 nm).
- Low interchannel cross-talk (better than −28 dB).

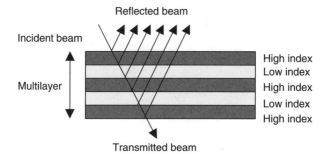

Figure 4.10   A dielectric thin film interference filter made with alternate layers of high and low refractive index, each layer λ/4 thick.

The wavelength range at the output of the λ/4 stack depends on the ratio high to low refractive index. Thus, a DTF can be used as a high-pass filter, a low-pass filter, or a high-reflectance layer.

4.7   POLARIZING BEAM SPLITTERS

Polarizing beam splitters, in general, consist of two prisms connected with a polarizing film. An incident circularly polarized beam of light is separated in two linearly polarized beams in one reflected and another refracted one in terminal equipment (TE) and the other in terminal multiplexer (TM) mode (Figure 4.11).

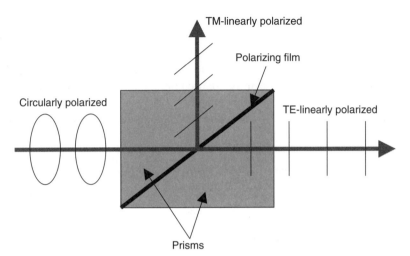

Figure 4.11 A polarizing beam splitter consisting of two prisms and a polarizing film.

4.8 TUNABLE OPTICAL FILTERS

Tunable optical filters (TOF) may be constructed with passive or active optical components. The salient characteristic of TOFs is their ability to select the range of filtered wavelengths. However, to be useful in optical communication systems they must satisfy certain requirements:

- Wide tuning range
- Constant gain
- Narrow bandwidth
- Fast tuning
- Insensitivity to temperature (no frequency drift with temperature variations)

In the following sections, we examine some TOFs.

4.9 ACOUSTO-OPTIC TUNABLE FILTERS

Acousto-optic tunable optical filters (AOTF) are based on the Bragg principle, according to which only those wavelengths pass through the filter that comply with the Bragg condition. The index of refraction is made to fluctuate periodically by applying a radio frequency (RF) acoustical signal to an optically transparent waveguide. The applied acoustical frequency (vibrations) on the waveguide disturbs its molecular structure with a periodicity, which determines the periodicity of the index of refraction. The polarization of the optical wavelength that complies with the Bragg condition is also rotated from TE to TM.

An AOTF consists of an acousto-optic TE-to-TM converter (a surface acoustic wave device [SAW], on which the acoustic signal is applied), two crossed polarizers, and two optical waveguides in very close proximity, such that light may be coupled from one waveguide to the other (Figure 4.12).

The selected λ is related to the applied acoustic frequency f_a (in Mhz) by

$$\lambda = (\Delta n)V_a/f_a$$

where Δn is the medium birefringence for the selected λ, and V_a is the acoustic velocity in the waveguide medium. Similarly,

$$\lambda = \Lambda(\Delta n)$$

where Λ is the wavelength of the acoustic wave.

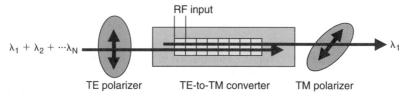

Figure 4.12 A conceptual acousto-optic tunable filter.

The acoustic power P_a for 100% polarization rotation of the selected λ is

$$P_a = (\lambda^2 A)/(2L^2 M_2) \quad (\text{mW})$$

where A is the acoustic transducer area, L is the transducer width, and M_2 the acoustic figure of merit of the medium. P_a is expressed in hundreds of milliwatts.

The filter pass-band $\Delta\lambda$ is approximated by

$$\Delta\lambda = (0.8\lambda^2)/(L\Delta n) \quad (\mu\text{m})$$

The access time τ is estimated by

$$\tau = L/V_a \quad (\mu\text{s})$$

The TE-to-TM converter of an AOTF filter is constructed with Ti:LiNbO$_3$ on which the remaining components may also be integrated to produce a single and compact component.

AOTFs are either *collinear* or *non-collinear.* Collinear AOTFs are those in which the optical signal propagates and interacts collinearly with the acoustic wave. Otherwise, they are non-collinear.

AOTFs may also be *polarization independent.* This device consists of complex acousto-optic structure that selects a wavelength regardless of its polarization state.

The salient characteristics of AOTF filters (typically of the collinear type) are:

- Broad tuning range, from 1.2 to 1.6 μm
- Narrow filter bandwidth, less than 1 nm
- Fast tunability, about 10 μs
- Acceptable insertion loss, less than 5 dB
- Low cross-talk, less than -20 dB
- One to many wavelengths selection
- Possible wavelength broadcast
- Easy wavelength registration and stabilization

AOTFs are used as:

- Single-wavelength tunable receivers
- Multi-wavelength tunable receivers
- Wavelength selective space-switch (demultiplexers)

A disadvantage of typical AOTFs is the misalignment of the polarization state of incoming light. Although the direction of the polarizer is known, the polarization state of incoming light is hard to maintain in a single-mode fiber and thus hard to control. Polarization mismatch results in coupling loss.

Another disadvantage of typical AOTFs is the frequency shift of light by an amount equal to the acoustical frequency due to Doppler effect. However, devices have been constructed that counterbalance the Doppler effect.

4.10   THE MACH-ZEHNDER FILTER

The *Mach-Zehnder* filter is based on the interference of two coherent monochromatic sources that are based on the length difference, and thus the phase difference, of two paths (see Interference), thus contributing positively or negatively.

In fiberoptic systems, a phase difference between two optical paths may be artificially constructed. Consider an input fiber with two wavelengths, λ_1 and λ_2. The optical power of both wavelengths is equally split (directional coupler #1) and each half is coupled into two waveguides of unequal length (ΔL). The two halves arrive at a second directional coupler at different phase, and based on the phase variation and the position of the output fiber, each wavelength interferes constructively on one of the two output fibers and destructively on the other. That is, wavelength λ_1 inter-feres constructively on the first fiber and wavelength λ_2 on the second (Figure 4.13).

This arrangement is used to construct an integrated device that functions as a fil-ter or as a wavelength separator, known as a *Mach-Zehnder filter*, according to which two frequencies at its input port are separated and appear at two output ports. A more detailed description of the Mach-Zehnder filter follows.

A mix of two wavelengths arrives at coupler #1. Coupler #1 equally distributes the power of wavelengths λ_1 and λ_2 into two waveguides having an optical path dif-ference ΔL. Because of the path difference, the two waves arrive at coupler #2 with a phase difference

$$\Delta\Phi = 2\pi f(\Delta L)n/c$$

where n is the refractive index of the waveguide. At coupler #2, the two waves re-combine and are directed to two output ports. However, each output port supports the one of the two wavelengths that satisfies a certain phase condition.

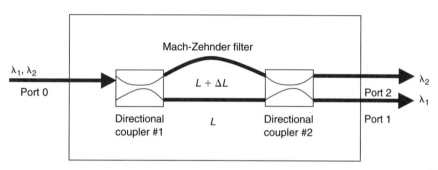

Figure 4.13 The principle of a Mach-Zehnder filter.

Wavelength, λ_1, is obtained at output port 1 if the phase difference at the end of L satisfies the conditions

$$\Delta\Phi_1 = (2m - 1)\pi$$

that is, where λ_1 contributes maximally. Wavelength, λ_2, is obtained at port 2 if the phase difference satisfies the condition:

$$\Delta\Phi_2 = 2m\pi$$

that is, where λ_2 contributes maximally; m is a positive integer. Then

$$2\pi f_1 \Delta Ln/c = (2m - 1)\pi, \text{ and } 2\pi f_2 \Delta Ln/c = 2m\pi.$$

The above relationships are satisfied for a number of m values. Thus, this filter exhibits periodic pass bands.

From the last two relations, the optical channel spacing, Δf, is derived:

$$\Delta f = c/[2n(\Delta L)]$$

4.10.1   Tunability of the Mach-Zehnder Filter

If the quantity ΔL can be adjusted at will, it is clear that the Mach-Zehnder filter can be tuned. The purpose of the quantity ΔL is to introduce the desired phase shift at the entry point of directional coupler #2. Thus, the phase shift is controlled by controlling the propagation delay of the path $L + \Delta L$ with respect to path L. This is accomplished either by altering the refractive index of the path (and thus the effective optical path) or by altering its physical length, or both.

The phase may be controlled by one of several methods (Figure 4.14):

- Mechanical compression, by means of a piezo-electric crystal, alters the physical length of the waveguide segment and its refractive index.

- Certain optical materials alter their refractive index when exposed to heat; a thin film thermoelectric heater placed on the longer path would control the refractive index of the path. A polymer material known to change its refractive index when exposed to heat is per-fluoro-cyclo-butane (PFCB).

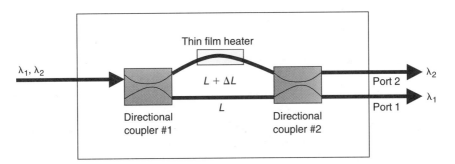

Figure 4.14 A Mach-Zehnder filter can be tuned by controlling the temperature of the $L + \Delta L$ path.

Thus, by controlling the refractive index of the path, the phase on the effective optical path $L + \Delta L$ is controlled and the wavelength selectability of the device is accomplished making the Mach-Zehnder filter a tunable *optical frequency discriminator* (OFD).

The Mach-Zehnder filter may also be cascaded to construct a multilevel filter (Figure 4.15). For example, eight wavelengths, λ_1 to λ_8, are separated by one filter into two groups, $\lambda_1, \lambda_3, \lambda_5, \lambda_7$ and $\lambda_2, \lambda_4, \lambda_6, \lambda_8$. Each group is separated by two more filters into four subgroups (λ_1, λ_5), (λ_3, λ_7), (λ_2, λ_6), and (λ_4, λ_8), and so on, until all eight wavelengths are separated.

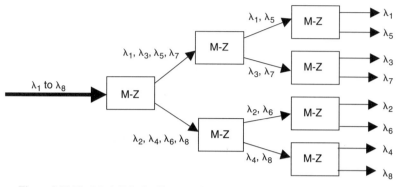

Figure 4.15 The Mach-Zehnder filter may be cascaded to construct a multilevel filter.

4.11 ABSORPTION FILTERS

Absorption filters consist of a thin film made of a material (e.g., germanium) that exhibits high absorption at a specific wavelength region. Their operation depends heavily on material properties and thus there is little flexibility in making the absorption edges of the material very sharp.

However, when absorption materials are used in combination with interference filters (DTF, Fabry-Perot), then a filter is produced that combines both sharp-rejection edges and interference filter flexibility.

4.12 BIREFRINGENCE FILTERS

The properties of birefringent crystals may be used to construct optical tunable filters. Consider two quarter-wave birefringent disks positioned in parallel and such that the first disk has its fast axis at $+45°$ and the second at $-45°$ (Figure 4.16a).

Based on this, the retardation to a monochromatic beam propagating in the z-axis is summed up to zero because one disk accelerates as much as the other decelerates. If one of the two disks is rotated by an angle $45° + \rho$, then an acceleration or a deceleration that is proportional to the angle ρ is introduced, and a phase-controlling mechanism is constructed. However, in this two-disk structure, as one of the two disks rotates, it also rotates the polarization of the beam. This is rectified by having the two $45°$ disks fixed and between them a disk that can rotate (Figure 4.16b). This arrangement constructs a single tuning stage.

Now, if the beam prior to entering the first disk has been split by a birefringent crystal in two (the ordinary and extraordinary rays), then each ray is controlled differently than the other and, as they recombine at the output, a wave-tuning mechanism or a tunable filter is constructed. This type of filter has been expanded to include more levels of tuning stages.

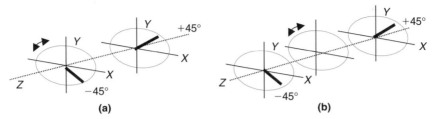

Figure 4.16 Birefringent plates may be used to construct fixed optical filters (a), or tunable filters (b).

4.13 HYBRID FILTERS

Hybrid filters consist of a structure that combines different filter types and other optical components, such as, a DTF, and a grating. Hybrid filters take advantage of the grating filter's ability to separate closely spaced optical wavelengths, and of the DTF filter's ability to separate widely spaced optical wavelengths.

4.14 TUNABLE FILTERS—COMPARISON

Each tunable filter has its own performance characteristics. Therefore, depending on the application, a filter type that best matches the performance requirements should be used.

If a *large number of channels* (~100) is required, then Fabry-Perot and acousto-optic filters are better suited, as compared with electro-optic and semiconductor filters that can process fewer channels (~10).

If *fast tuning* (~nsec) is required, then electro-optic and semiconductor filters are better suited, as opposed to acousto-optic devices (~μs) and Fabry-Perot (msec), although Fabry-Perot filters that use liquid crystals may also tune fast (in the microsecond range).

Mechanical tuning is slow (1 –10 msec) but it has a wide tuning range (~500 nm), as compared with acousto-optic tuners (tuning range of about 250 nm) and the electro-optic tuners (tuning range of about 16 nm).

If *low loss* is required, then semiconductor filters exhibit negligible loss, as compared with other types that exhibit a loss in the order of 3 to 5 dB.

Based on this, the selection of the filter type in communications depends on the application and service the system is designed for. In applications with a large number of channels but relatively slow switching speeds (e.g., video broadcasting), the Fabry-Perot seems to be better suited. In applications with few but very fast switching times (circuit-switch of few channels), the electro-optic or semiconductor type are better suited. In addition, the tuning range and the cost of each type should also be taken into account, particularly in systems that require a large number of components or are cost sensitive.

4.15   DIFFRACTION GRATINGS

Diffraction grating is an arrayed slit device that takes advantage of the diffraction property of light and it reflects light in a direction that depends on the angle of incident light, the wavelength, and the grating constant (Figure 4.17). That is, a diffraction grating reflects wavelengths in different directions when a mixed-wavelength beam impinges on it (see also 2.3.7 and Figure 2.7).

The blaze angle and the number of slits per unit length characterize a diffraction grating. For a given center wavelength λ the blaze angle θ_B is set at

$$\theta_B = \sin^{-1}(\lambda/2d)$$

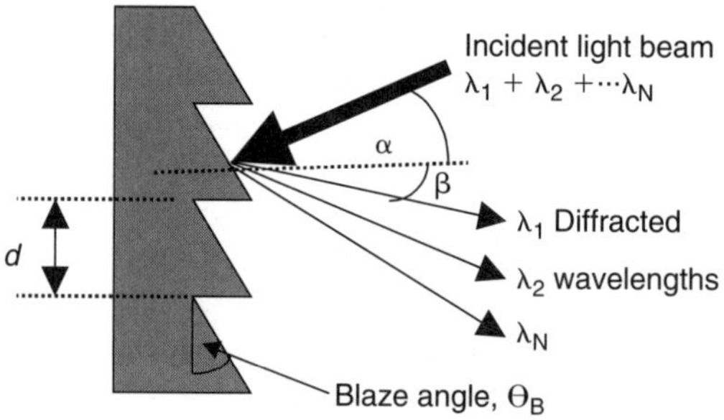

Figure 4.17   A diffraction grating is characterized by the blaze
angle and the number of slits per unit length.

When the reflected light has a path difference equal to $m\lambda$, where m is an integer and λ the wavelength, then reflected wavelengths interfere with each other and each wavelength component is diffracted at different angles, according to

$$d(\sin \alpha + \sin \beta) = m\lambda$$

where α is the angle of incidence and β the angle of diffraction. Then, the angular dispersion is

$$d\beta/d\lambda = m/(d \cos \beta)$$

Diffraction gratings operate as follows: When a polychromatic light beam impinges on a diffraction grating, each wavelength component is diffracted at different angle. Knowing the wavelengths, the angle of incidence, and the specifications of the grating, the angle of diffraction for each wavelength is calculated and at the focal points receiving fibers are placed, a fiber for each wavelength (Figure 4.18). Focusing the diffracted wavelengths may be achieved with a lens system or with a diffraction grating in a concave form.

Typically, diffraction gratings are produced by etching single silicon crystals.

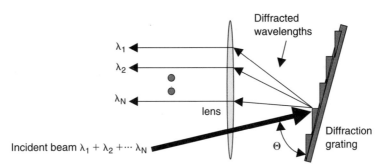

Figure 4.18 Operation of a diffraction grating.

EXERCISES

1. A Fabry-Perot interferometer has a refractive index $n = 1$. For $m = 1$, what should be the spacing to resonate at 1400 nm?
2. Calculate the finesse of a Fabry-Perot interferometer if the reflectivity is
    (a) $R = 0.9$.
    (b) $R = 0.3$.
3. The Bragg spacing is 5 times 750 nm. What is the order of the Bragg grating for a wavelength 1300 nm?
4. A Bragg grating has a grating constant $d = 700$ nm. For what wavelength value is the first-order reflection maximal?

CHAPTER 5

OPTICAL DEMULTIPLEXERS

5.1 INTRODUCTION

The main function of an optical demultiplexer is to receive from a fiber a beam consisting of multiple optical frequencies and separate it into its frequency components, which are coupled in individual fibers, as many as the frequencies. An optical multiplexer functions exactly in the opposite manner. It receives many optical wavelengths from many fibers and it converges them into one beam that is coupled into a single fiber. There are two classifications of optical demultiplexer devices, *passive* and *active*. Passive demultiplexers are based on prisms, diffraction gratings, and spectral (frequency) filters. Active demultiplexers are based on a combination of passive components and tunable detectors, each detector tuned to a specific frequency.

5.2 PRISMS

When a collimated (parallel) beam of polychromatic light impinges on one of the prism surfaces (AB), each frequency component is refracted differently (Figure 5.1). The output light from the other surface of the prism (AC) consists of the frequency components separated from each other by a small angle. A lens focuses each wavelength at a different point where receiving fibers are placed, one fiber for each wavelength channel.

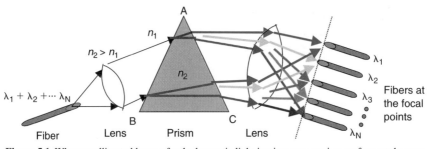

Figure 5.1 When a collimated beam of polychromatic light impinges on a prism surface, each wavelength component is refracted differently.

5.3   DIFFRACTION GRATINGS

When a polychromatic light beam impinges on a diffraction grating, each wavelength component is diffracted and directed to a different point in space. A fiber is placed at the focal points of each wavelength. Focusing the diffracted wavelengths may be achieved with a lens system or with a concave diffraction grating. The result is an $N \times 1$ wavelength demultiplexer (Figure 5.2).

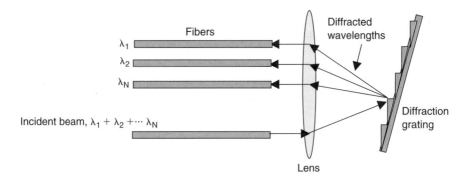

Figure 5.2 When a collimated polychromatic light beam impinges on a diffraction grating, each wavelength component is diffracted and directed to a different point in space.

5.4   ARRAYED WAVEGUIDE GRATING

Arrayed waveguide gratings (AWG) are based on the principle of interferometry. Consider a fiber, F, carrying a multiplicity of wavelengths, λ_1, λ_2, ..., λ_N. Let the light of all wavelengths from F shine in cavity S_1, which is coupled to an array of waveguides, w_1, ..., w_N. The optical length difference of each waveguide introduces wavelength-dependent phase delays in cavity S_2 where an array of fibers is coupled.

The phase difference of each wavelength interferes in such a manner that each wavelength contributes maximally at one of the output fibers (Figure 5.3).

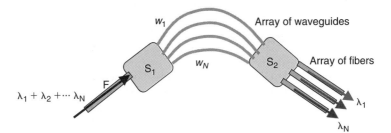

Figure 5.3 Arrayed waveguide gratings (AWG) are based on the principle of interferometry.

The salient characteristics of AWGs are:

- AWGs are polarization-dependent, but means to overcome this dependency have been reported.

- AWGs are temperature sensitive. To eliminate thermal drift, thermoelectric coolers have been used as well as SiO_2 AWGs that use silicon adhesives with a negative thermal coefficient.

- AWGs operating in the wide temperature range 0° to 85°C have been reported.

- AWGs exhibit good flat spectral response; this eases wavelength control.

- Insertion loss is in the range of <3 dB and cross-talk level is better than −35 dB.

- AWGs are suitable for integration with photodetectors.

SiO_2 AWGs for 128 channels (wavelengths) with 250-Ghz channel-spacing have been reported as well as InP AWGs for 64 channels with 50-Ghz channel-spacing. AWG devices belong to the category of phased-array gratings (PHASARS) and waveguide grating routers (WGRs).

5.5   MACH-ZEHNDER INTERFEROMETER

This interferometer is based on the interferometric properties of light and the Mach-Zehnder method. When two coherent light sources consist of more than one wavelength, the regions of maxima and minima differ for each wavelength. These regions for each wavelength may be calculated if the wavelengths, phase of signals, and the index of refraction are known. Thus, a mix of wavelengths may be separated to its component wavelengths.

Mach-Zehnder interferometers have been integrated on Silica substrates along with other components. One method for achieving integration is to combine flame hydrolysis deposition and conventional photolithography followed by ion etching. AWG and WGR filters are of the Mach-Zehnder types.

5.6   SPECTRAL FILTERS

Spectral filters positioned in the optical path can also be used to sort out wavelengths and thus can be used as demultiplexers. Two such applications are illustrated: One (Figure 5.4a) uses a filter sandwiched on the cleaved surface of a fiber, and the other (Figure 5.4b) uses a filter embedded in a graded index rod (GRIN-rod).

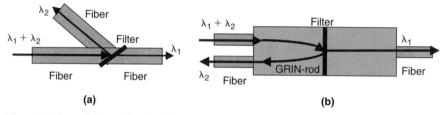

(a)   **(b)**

Figure 5.4   Spectral filters: (a) with a filter sandwiched on the cleaved surface of a fiber, and (b) with a
filter embedded in a GRIN.

5.7   ACOUSTO-OPTIC FILTER PLUS POLARIZING
BEAM SPLITTER

A combination of an all-pass polarizer, a (tunable) acousto-optic filter (AOF), and a polarizing beam splitter may be used to isolate a wavelength from a mix. This arrangement is based on the principle that beam splitters reflect a polarization mode and refract another. It is also based on the principle that AOFs rotate the polarization mode of a specific wavelength from transverse electric (TE) to transverse magnetic (TM). The operation of this demultiplexer is shown in Figure 5.5.

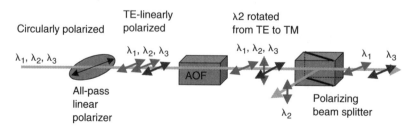

Figure 5.5   A combination of an all-pass polarizer, an acousto-optic filter, and a polarizing
beam splitter isolates a wavelength (λ_2) from a mix.

5.8   OPTICAL MULTIPLEXERS

In general, passive optical multiplexers consist of a multiplicity of input fibers, each carrying an optical signal at different wavelength. All wavelengths are focused on the same focal point and are coupled into one output fiber. Most optical passive de-multiplexers may also be used as optical multiplexers. In this category are prisms, Figure 5.6 and gratings, Figure 5.7.

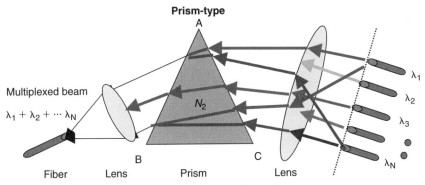

Figure 5.6 A prism as an optical multiplexer.

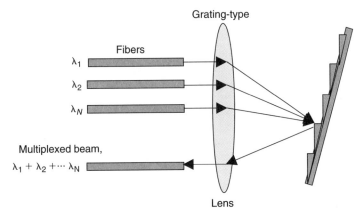

Figure 5.7 A grating as an optical multiplexer.

EXERCISES

1. How many classifications of optical demultiplexer devices are there?
2. Could a prism be considered an optical demultiplexer? If yes, then what type is it?
3. Is it true or false that a diffraction grating is an optical device that converts optical frequencies?
4. Is it true or false that an AWG is based on the principle of interferometry?
5. A Mach-Zehnder interferometer receives two coherent light sources, one at wavelength λ_1 and the other at λ_2. Is it possible to guide each wavelength to a different output?
6. Is it true that an AOF requires a specific radio frequency (RF) signal to operate?
7. What is the fundamental principle of AOFs?
8. If a polarizer, an AOF and a polarizing beam splitter are combined in cascade, what can be potentially constructed?

CHAPTER 6

LIGHT SOURCES

6.1 INTRODUCTION

There are many types of light sources. The sun and light from burning torches were the first light sources used to study optics. As a matter of fact, light emanating from certain (exited) matter still provides reference points in the optical spectrum, such as iodine, chlorine, mercury, and so on.

One of the key components in optical communication is the monochromatic light source. In optical communications, light sources must be compact, monochromatic, stable, and long lasting (many years). In practice, there are no monochromatic light sources; there are merely light sources that generate light within a very narrow band of wavelengths. Light sources used in spectrography are neither practical nor economical in communications. Stability of a light source implies constant intensity level (over time and temperature variations) and constant wavelength (no drifts).

Solid-state technology has made it possible to have such optical sources of light. There are two different types of light sources. The first type transmits a *continuous wave* (CW). Continuous emitting lasers- and light-emitting diodes (LEDs) are examples of CW light sources. This type of light source requires an external modulator at its optical output. In this arrangement, an electrical signal representing a data stream acts on the modulator that modulates the light passing through. The second type transmits *modulated light*; that is, no external modulator is necessary. This type receives an electrical data stream that directly modulates the light source. Lasers and LEDs are examples of modulated light sources.

In this chapter, we examine two popular light sources, *light-emitting diodes* and *semiconductor lasers*.

6.2   LIGHT-EMITTING DIODES

In certain semiconductors, during the recombination process of electrons with holes at the junction of n-doped and p-doped semiconductors, energy is released in the form of light. The recombination may be spontaneous or stimulated by an external stimulus such as another photon or a potential difference (voltage).

An LED is a monolithically integrated p–n semiconductor device (a diode) that emits light when voltage is applied across its two terminals. LEDs that are used in communications have a structure such that light emerges from the device edge (Figure 6.1). This facilitates coupling the LED light with a fiber. However, LEDs transmit light within a relatively wide cone that limits their application in optical transmission. Currently, sophisticated doping structures are used to increase the switching speed and narrow the optical spectrum of the LED.

Figure 6.1 An LED is a p–n semiconductor device that emits light when a voltage is applied across its two terminals.

6.2.1   Switching Speed and Output Power

The *switching speed* of an LED depends on the recombination rate, R, expressed by

$$R = J/(de) \qquad (6.1)$$

where J is the current density (A/m^2), d is the thickness of the recombination region, and e is the electron charge.

The *output power* of an LED is expressed by

$$P_{out} = \{(\eta hc)/(e\lambda)\}I \qquad (6.2)$$

where I is the LED drive current (A), η is the quantum efficiency (relative recombination/total recombination), h is Planck's constant, e is the electron charge, and λ is the wavelength of light.

6.2.2   Output Optical Spectrum

The output optical spectrum of LEDs is the range of emitted wavelengths. This depends on the absolute junction temperature (i.e., the range widens as temperature increases) and on the emission wavelength λ:

$$\Delta\lambda = 3.3(kT/h)(\lambda^2/c) \qquad (6.3)$$

where T is the absolute temperature at the junction, c is the speed of light, k is Boltzmann's constant, and h is Planck's constant.

Temperature has an adverse effect on the stability of an LED device. As temperature rises, its spectrum shifts and its intensity decreases as shown in Figure 6.2.

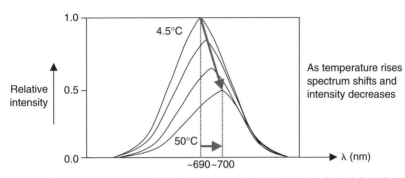

Figure 6.2 The spectral output of LEDs in the range of emitted wavelengths and depends on the absolute junction temperature.

6.2.3   Input–Output Response

An LED, being a diode, behaves like it and its I–V characteristic has a similar profile. Because its output optical power depends on the current density, which depends on the applied voltage and electron concentration, a similar response should be expected. Indeed, this is the case. However, a threshold is defined, below which the optical power is negligible (Figure 6.3).

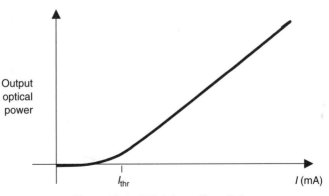

Figure 6.3 An LED behaves like a diode.

6.2.4   Modulation Response

The modulated current density J is expressed by

$$J = J_0 + J_0 m_j e^{j\omega t} \tag{6.4}$$

where J_0 is the steady-state current density, m_j is the modulation depth, and ω is the modulation frequency. This current modulates the electron density difference through the junction, $\Delta n = n - n_0$ (n_0 is the electron density at equilibrium with no bias current) as

$$\Delta n = N_0 \{ 1 + M_N e^{j(\omega t - \theta)} \} \tag{6.5}$$

where N_0 is the electron density at steady state, M_N is the electron modulation depth, and θ is the phase shift.

From the differential $d(\Delta n)/dt$ the output power modulation index, I_M, is derived in terms of the output modulation response, M_N:

$$I_M = M_N e^{-j\theta} = m_j/(1 + j\omega\tau_r) \tag{6.6}$$

where τ_r is the electron–hole recombination time. Comparing the modulation response with a first-order low-pass filter (LPF), it is concluded that their transfer functions are identical. Thus, the modulation response may be studied like an LPF, from which the 3-dB modulation bandwidth is derived:

$$\omega_{3dB} = 1/\tau_r \tag{6.7}$$

6.2.5   Conclusions

- The LED bandwidth depends on device material.
- The LED amplitude depends on the current density (i.e., on the operating V–I point).
- The LED amplitude and spectrum depend on temperature.
- LEDs are relatively slow devices (<1 Gbps).
- LEDs exhibit a relatively wide spectral range.
- LEDs are inexpensive.
- LEDs transmit light in a relatively wide cone.
- LEDs are suitable sources for multimode fiber communications.

6.3   LASERS

Laser stands for light amplification by stimulated emission radiation. It has been found that some elements in gaseous state (e.g., He–Ne) and others in crystals (e.g., ruby with 0.05% chromium) absorb electromagnetic energy (light) and remain in a semi-stable, high-energy excited state.

Lasers take advantage of stimulated emission. Some photons traveling through the excited medium interact with electrons and holes in the recombination region. A cascaded and rapid process is thus triggered, by which excited atoms drop from their high-energy state to a low-energy state by releasing energy in the form of light; that is, a single photon causes many. Emitted photons enter a region known as the cavity. The emitted photons are (in phase) reflected back and forth in the cavity to form a strong *coherent* monochromatic beam; photons traveling in other directions are eventually lost through the walls of the cavity.

The back and forth reflection of photons within a frequency-selective mechanism, such as a cavity with specific dimensions or a *grating*, results in an optical output with a narrow spectrum and a large positive gain. This is explained as follows. As energy is pumped in, the lost photons are replenished, optical feedback creates resonance, the optical gain reaches a threshold and the lasing process starts. However, the dimensions of the cavity structure (that has a dielectric constant greater than air) must be precise in wavelength multiples. Remember that, due to the dielectric constant, an imprecision of few Angstroms of semiconductor material in the cavity is equivalent to millimeters in an air cavity.

Typically, the large positive gain of lasers depends on semiconductor materials and their composition, semiconductor structure, pumped energy and feedback mechanism. Taking advantage of stimulated emission, and keeping the gas or crystal continuously in a high energy state by pumping photonic energy in it (or applying a voltage), a continuous or a pulsating coherent light amplification mechanism is achieved (see Section 6.3.1). Lasers that support a *single transversal mode* are known as *single-mode lasers* (whether they oscillate in a single or multiple longitudinal mode). Those that support both a *single transversal mode* and a *single longitudinal mode* are known as *single-frequency lasers*. If they oscillate at *several frequencies simultaneously,* longitudinal or transversal, then they are called *multifrequency lasers.*

A laser oscillates at frequencies that have sufficient gain (or amplitude) to satisfy the *amplitude* and *phase condition.*

6.3.1   The Ruby Laser

The ruby laser (Figure 6.4) is a characteristic example. It consists of a rubidium rod that contains 0.05% chromium, which is wrapped around with a flash tube. The ruby and flash tube assembly is enclosed in a cylindrical reflector having a window at one end. Both ends of the ruby rod are cut parallel and polished. One end-face is fully reflecting while the other is partially reflecting. Part of the green-blue light from the flash tube excites the chromium atoms. Initially, spontaneous emission in the ruby radiates in all directions but shortly, after 0.5 msec, coherent radiation emerges through the window that may reach peak power at several kilowatts. The wavelength

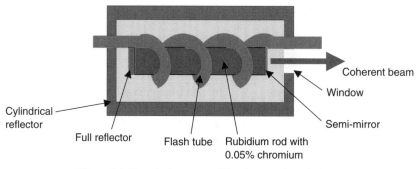

Cylindrical reflector

Full reflector

Flash tube

Rubidium rod with 0.05% chromium

Coherent beam

Window

Semi-mirror

Figure 6.4 The ruby laser exemplifies the operation of a laser.

of this coherent light is about 694 nm, but its exact value depends on the length of the ruby rod (the recombination cavity) and the temperature of the rod.

6.3.2   Semiconductor Lasers

Besides gases and rubidium, they are solid materials that exhibit the same behavior such as AlGaAs and InGaAsP. AlGaAs and InGaAsP are suitable because they can be cost-effectively manufactured, they generate light at wavelengths compatible with silica fiber, and they can be monolithically integrated with other optical components.

Semiconductor lasers are diodes constructed with the planar method; that is, by growing several thin layers of crystals with controlled consistency and doping on top of an InP substrate. The active layer of this structure, such as a straight channel of InGaAsP, is sandwiched between n- and p-type layers of InP, also known as cladding layers. When bias is applied, holes and electrons in the active region are excited. When they recombine, energy is released in the form of light. The wavelength of light depends on the energy band-gap of the active material. The active layer has a much higher refractive index than the cladding layers and thus the cladding layers confine the electron holes and the photons in the active region.

Semiconductor lasers transmit coherent light within a very narrow cone and thus the beam is more efficiently coupled to a fiber. In addition, they are directly modulated and thus better suited to high bit rates and long fiber spans as compared with LEDs. However, direct modulation at very high bit rates (~10 Gbps) may cause the laser to optically chirp, which is a form of wavelength jitter and noise. This occurs because the refractive index of the laser cavity depends on the drive current. Thus, as the drive current changes from a logic ONE to a logic ZERO and vice versa, the refractive index changes dynamically (effectively changing the resonant cavity characteristics), which causes a dynamic change in the wavelength, hence *optical chirping*. Optical chirping may be viewed as a spectral line that jitters about the central wavelength. Chirping is avoided, if external modulation is used. In this case, the laser emits a continuous wave (CW) thus avoiding the broadening of the line width. Because lasers and modulators can be made with In + Ga + As + P, both laser and modulator can be monolithically integrated on an InP substrate to yield a compact device.

The semiconductor laser designer is challenged to integrate key optical elements (cavity, filter, excitation region, reflectors, and so on) in a very small monolithic, efficient, almost monochromatic, and stable device.

Wavelength and signal amplitude stability of semiconductor lasers are important to efficient and reliable transmission. Stability depends on materials, bias voltage, and temperature. Frequency stabilization is usually established using thermoelectric cooling techniques that keep the temperature stable within a fraction of a degree centigrade. However, this adds to the cost structure and power consumption of the device, and efforts are made to design "cooler" devices.

Monolithic laser devices have been manufactured for a wide range of applications. Depending on usage, device efficiency, and cost, semiconductor lasers are designed for specific wavelength ranges, and for specific modulation rates, such as low-cost broadband transmitters in the range 45 to 622 Mbps, and ultra-fast transmitters that are modulated to rates greater than 20 Gbps. Moreover, there are two major laser categories, the *fixed frequency* and the *tunable* laser.

Semiconductor lasers have at minimum:

- an optical waveguide (to limit light in a single direction).

- an active region (where stimulated emission takes place).

- optical feedback (a cavity in which light bounces back and forth for gain and filtering purposes).

In the following sections, we examine these components.

6.4   MONOLITHIC FABRY-PEROT LASERS

Monolithic semiconductor lasers with a resonance mechanism (or optical feedback) based on the Fabry-Perot principles are constructed with the planar method; that is, growing three-dimensional (3-D) layers of crystals with controlled consistency and doping. A simplified structure of a semiconductor laser source based on the Fabry-Perot principle is shown in Figure 6.5. This structure combines a semiconductor material in the form of a straight channel (p-type AlGaAs), which is both the active region (for stimulated emission) and the optical waveguide (to guide photons in one direction). Both ends of the channel are carefully cleaved to act as mirrors with a reflectivity:

$$R = \{(n - 1)/(n + 1)\}^2$$

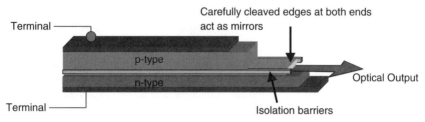

Figure 6.5 Laser structure based on the Fabry-Perot principle.

where *n* is the refractive index of the active medium. The actual produced laser structure is very complex and has many layers (typically, more than 10); in this structure, a Fabry-Perot etalon is incorporated.

By controlling 3-D geometry, semiconductor composition, and doping, the desired optical gain, optical feedback (resonance), and filtering are obtained.

The exact structure of the Fabry-Perot lasers varies among manufacturers. A complete description of these lasers is beyond our purpose.

Fabry-Perot lasers can generate several longitudinal frequencies (modes) at once. The semiconductor laser material, the frequency spacing, and the Fabry-Perot laser length determine the range of frequencies. The bias current determines the threshold frequency.

6.5   MONOLITHIC BRAGG LASERS

Cleaved edges in the Fabry-Perot structure (Figure 6.5) resulted in laser light with a line-width not as narrow as needed. Narrower line widths may be accomplished by employing Bragg gratings to act as reflectors. Bragg grating is achieved by periodically varying the index of refraction (or the doping of the material–dark/light blue regions; Figure 6.6). Such lasers are called distributed Bragg reflector (DBR). The simplified diagram illustrates the applicability of the Bragg grating (for feedback) at either sides of a laser cavity (active region) and the optical waveguide.

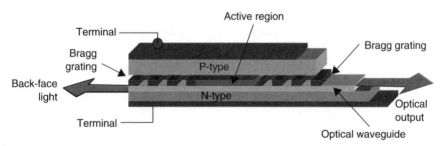

Figure 6.6 Bragg gratings may be used as frequency selective reflectors in semiconductor lasers.

6.6   DISTRIBUTED FEEDBACK LASERS

Distributed feedback (DFB) lasers are monolithic devices that have an internal structure based on InGaAsP waveguide technology and an internal grating (typically at the interface n-InP substrate and n-InGaAsP layers) to provide feedback at a fixed wavelength that is determined by the grating pitch. DFBs are an extension of the electro-absorption–modulated lasers and take their name from their structure. The DFB structure may be combined with multiple quantum well (MQW) structures to improve the linewidth of the produced laser light (as narrow as few hundred kHz). MQWs have a structure similar to the diode structure, but the active junction is few atomic layers thin—see Section 6.7). The resonant cavity may be of the Mack-Zehnder or Fabry-Perot type.

DFB lasers are reliable sources with center frequencies in the region around 1310 nm, and also in the 1520 to 1565 nm range; the latter makes them compatible with erbium-doped fiber amplifiers (EDFA) and excellent sources in dense wavelength division multiplexing (DWDM) applications.

A complete DFB laser device contains other components necessary to stabilize the center frequency and maintain a constant uniform amplitude. For example, a photodiode monitors the laser output; a thermoelectric cooler (TEC) or heatpump and a heatsink control the junction temperature of the laser chip; and feedback circuitry controls its output to constant level and frequency. A complete DFB laser packaged device may contain more components, which are necessary to stabilize the center frequency and maintain constant amplitude. For example, a device may include a 5% power reflector in conjunction with a photodiode (a positive intrinsic negative photodiode [PIN] or an avalanche photodetector [APD]) to monitor the laser output and a feedback circuit to control the output power. Another device may include a thermoelectric cooler and heater (TEC), and a heatsink to control the temperature constant to 25°C over the package temperature range -20 to 65°C. However, the internal package structure and components is not a standard; it varies from manufacturer to manufacturer.

6.7   SEMICONDUCTOR QUANTUM WELL LASERS

Semiconductor QWLs are diode lasers (see Figure 6.1) with a very thin active junction layer (50 to 100 Angstroms or 7 to 10 atomic layers) as compared to conventional diode lasers that have a tenfold or larger active layer. The active region is a GaAs (quantum well) layer sandwiched between a p-type $Al_xGa_{1-x}As$ layer and n-type $Al_yGa_{1-y}As$ layer. Very thin layers are typically grown with the molecular beam epitaxy (MBE) and metal organic chemical vapor deposition (MOCVD) methods. To visualize this device, think of a thick n-type GaAs substrate with a stack of 40 alternating p- or n-type AlGaAs and quantum well GaAs structures, topped by a last p-type GaAs thick layer. That is, GaAs*/n-AlGaAs/GaAs/p-AlGaAs/GaAs/ . . . / p-AlGaAs/GaAs*; where GaAs* indicates thick substrate layers. This structure is again sandwiched between two metallic electrode layers where the bias voltage is applied (the ground potential is connected with the n-type GaAs*).

The extremely thin active layer of the QWL has some very interesting properties. It confines electron–hole pairs to move in an almost horizontal plane that is found in a narrow energy gap between the p- and n-layers, and the recombination properties are best studied with quantum mechanical theory (hence the name of this laser type). In addition, the narrow layer guides released photons in a similar manner to a single-mode fiber. The result is that, when a bias current excites the active region, small currents produce large amounts of coherent light within a narrow linewidth, and this is a significant advantage of the QWLs. More complex structures with multiple quantum wells produce what is termed *multiple quantum well lasers* (MQWL or MQW).

6.8   VCSEL LASERS

Fabry-Perot, DFBs, and DBRs typically require substantial amounts of current to operate, in the order of tens of milliamperes. Moreover, their output beam has an elliptical cross-section, typically an aspect ratio of 3:1 that does not match the cylindrical cross-section of the fiber core. Thus, a noncylindrical beam may require additional optics. A structure that produces a cylindrical beam is known as vertical-cavity surface-emitting laser (VCSEL). This laser consists of a vertical sandwich of a p-type multilayer, an active region, and an n-type multilayer (Figure 6.7). The p-type and n-type multilayers (40 to 60 quarter-wavelength layers) comprise Bragg reflectors (DBR) that are made with In + Ga + As + (Al or P), depending on the

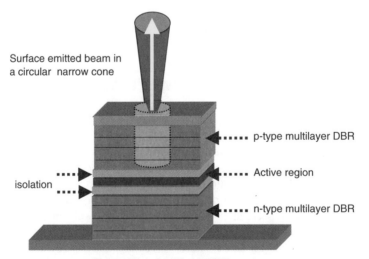

Figure 6.7 A simplified VCSEL structure.

wavelength desired. For example, In + Ga + As + P is used for lasers in the wavelength window from 1300 nm to 1550 nm. These layers are made with epitaxial growth followed by planar processing. Clearly, the above description is very general; the exact process and consistency of the multilayers and the overall device is manufacturer dependent (and proprietary).

The VCSEL structure is very compact and it can easily incorporate MQWs, since the latter is made with the same elements and with a similar (multilayer) structure, thus increasing the efficiency of the laser device. VCSEL devices may be made to form a matrix of lasers, each at different wavelength. Such a device, combined with other optical components and detectors in a matrix configuration opens the possibility of some interesting devices, such as space optical switches.

6.9   MONOLITHIC TUNABLE LASERS

Tunable lasers enable a device to emit light at specific selectable wavelengths. In wavelength division multiplexing (WDM), this represents a desirable feature if wavelength selectability is accomplished at a low cost. Tunable lasers have numerous other applications in medicine, environmental monitoring, and agriculture.

There are two categories of monolithic tunable lasers, *single-frequency* lasers and *multifrequency* lasers. Tunability may be accomplished electrically, mechanically (by trimming), or by controlling the temperature (a change of a few degrees is sufficient to tune the laser to another wavelength channel).

6.9.1   Single-Frequency Lasers

Single-frequency lasers are tuned by controlling the refractive index. In this case, the index of refraction in the lasing cavity is varied so that the peak transmissivity of the intra-cavity filter shifts to vary the wavelength. Changing the refractive index is equivalent to increasing the length of a free-space cavity.

The DBR tunable lasers are in this category.

6.9.2   Multifrequency Lasers

Multifrequency lasers are classified as *integrated cavity lasers* or as *arrayed lasers.* *Integrated cavity lasers* have an integrated cavity that serves both as a filter and as a multiport optical power combiner (multiplexer). The laser is also integrated with optical amplifiers.

Arrayed lasers are integrated arrays of individually tuned frequency lasers. The outputs are combined to produce a range of desired frequencies. The distributed feedback (DFB) arrays are in this category. An array of DFB lasers may also be used as a wavelength selectable device. In this case, several DFB lasers are monolithically integrated, each generating a different wavelength. Then, one of the DFBs is selected that generates the wavelength of interest. If each DFB has its own modulator, then a multi-wavelength source is generated.

6.10   OPTICAL COMB GENERATORS

An optical comb generator is a device that generates a predetermined range of $2K +$ 1 distinct wavelengths with a predetermined spacing Ω when an angle modulated optical signal $Y(t)$ is applied, described by

$$Y(t) = A_S \cos(\omega t + m \sin \Omega t) \tag{6.8}$$

where A_S is the signal amplitude, ω is the optical frequency, m is the modulation index, and Ω is the modulation frequency. This relationship indicates that the power of the applied signal $Y(t)$ spreads among a spectrum of several frequencies that consist of the fundamental frequency and sidebands.

The total number of components depends on the value of m. For example, for $m = 3$ there are seven terms; one fundamental and three sidebands on each side.

The output spectrum of a comb is described by

$$S(f) = \Sigma A_k \delta(f - k\Omega), -K < k < K \tag{6.9}$$

where A_k is the amplitude of the kth component and $\delta(f - k\Omega)$ is the frequency member of the comb represented by a delta function. Ideally, all A_k values should be identical; in reality, they are not due to an amplitude modulation (filtering) effect. Multifrequency tunable lasers are comb generators (see Figure 6.8).

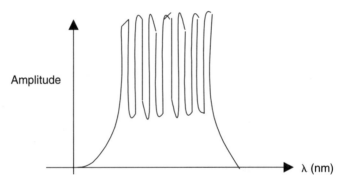

Figure 6.8 Comb generators have an output spectrum that looks like a comb.

6.11   CHIRPED-PULSE LASER SOURCES

The chirped-pulse wavelength-division multiplexing (CPWDM) method is another category of lasers that generates many wavelengths. Consider a very narrow pulse (femptoseconds wide) coupled in a dispersive fiber. Due to dispersion, the pulse is broadened to nanoseconds while spreading the spectral frequency content of the light, similar to Fourier process that generates many frequency components from an impulse; the narrower the impulse the more frequency components. This method is known as "chirping" (as in bird chirping). Now, consider a mode-locked laser source that emits a sequence of ultrashort pulses. Each pulse generates a set of pulsed frequencies in the time–spectrum continuum; each pulse is referred to as a *slice*. Now, time-division multiplexed data (via a fast modulator) modulate the bits of every slice and thus each frequency channel is modulated with different data.

6.12   MULTIFREQUENCY CAVITY LASERS

Multifrequency cavity lasers (MFL) are complex devices that consist of a K-input, N-output port (K × N) waveguide grating router (WGR) that may be integrated with several multiplexed wavelengths at each input port, and optical amplifiers at each output port. The WGR is a generalized Mach-Zehnder interferometer that consists of an array of N input waveguides, an array of N output waveguides, a waveguide grating, and two free-space regions (Figure 6.9).

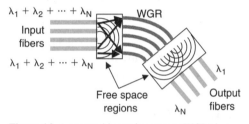

Figure 6.9 A waveguide grating router (WGR) is a
generalized Mach-Zehnder Interferometer.

An NXN WGR functions as follows: Optical signals consisting of many wavelengths at each input port are coupled via the first free-space region into the waveguide grating. The waveguide grating consists of waveguides each of different length and/or index of refraction. The optical path difference between neighboring waveguides ΔL causes a wavelength-dependent linear phase shift between them. It turns out that (because of interference) light of a certain wavelength will couple to only one output port.

The number of ports N and the free spectral range (FSR) determine the optical channel spacing (CS):

$$CS = FSR/N \qquad (6.10)$$

where the FSR is determined by (n_g is the group index of refraction and λ is the wavelength):

$$FSR = \lambda^2/(n_g\Delta L) \qquad (6.11)$$

However, the actual number of channels is constrained by the optical device technology (fiber type, resolution of transmitters and receivers, filter and amplifier characteristics), the maximum bit rate, and the optical power budget.

6.12.1   Advantages of WGRs

- Optical channel spacing is extremely accurate.

- There is low insertion loss.
- There is simultaneous operation of all wavelengths.
- They are fast tuned (<3 nsec).
- WGRs are scalable (NXN).
- Temperature variation shifts all wavelengths (entire comb), but CS remains the same.
- They have broadcast capability.

6.12.2 Disadvantages of WGRs

- WGRs are not fiber based.
- They have a relatively large physical size.
- Electrical cross-talk increases due to proximity of integrated amplifiers.
- As the number of channels increases, the optical channel spacing should be decreased, and thus, the size of the MFL increases, the intra-cavity loss increases, and device performance decreases.

6.13 MONOLITHIC DFB ARRAYS

To produce a range of desired wavelengths with small devices, DFB tuned laser arrays have been integrated in monolithic devices. In this arrangement, an independent filter, rather than a cavity with a waveguide grating, determines the wavelength of each individual DFB laser. All laser outputs have then been multiplexed and launched into the fiber.

6.13.1 Advantages of DFBs

- Integration yields small devices.
- Each DFB is modulated at very high speeds (short cavity) independently.
- Temperature variability is the same for all lasers in the device.

6.13.2 Disadvantages of DFBs

- Difficult to obtain precise channel spacing due to variability of individual filters.
- Frequency shifts of lasers do not track each other and they may drift into each other.
- Difficult to integrate many channels due to intrinsic losses.
- DFBs require a fine period grating.
- Electrical cross-talk is increased due to close proximity of integrated amplifiers.

6.14   MODULATORS

Optical modulators are integrated components designed to control the amount of continuous optical power transmitted in an optical waveguide. Thus, they are external modulators that are positioned in line with a CW laser source.

There are several semiconductor-type modulators (Figure 6.10). Among them is the integrated Mach-Zehnder (M-Z), the electro-absorption MQW and the electro-refraction modulator. The M-Z type consists of a Y-splitter junction, two phase-modulators (typically made with InGaAsP), and a Y-combiner junction (Figure 6.10a). Thus, incoming optical power is split by the first Y-junction into two equal parts. One of the two parts is phase adjusted (by controlling the refractive index), and then the two parts recombine. Based on the phase-delay, light destructively or constructively interferes at the recombining Y-junction and an on or off signal is obtained at the output. They actually function as on-off switches with the application of an on-off voltage.

MQW directional couplers operate on light-absorption properties and are based on MQW semiconductor structures (Figure 6.10b). Light is absorbed when voltage is applied. Thus, electro-absorptive devices act as fast shutters and, when combined with DFB laser sources, form elegant integrated modulators.

The electro-refraction modulator directly controls the phase of an optical wave through it when a voltage is applied (Figure 6.10c).

The major benefit of external modulators is that they have negligible chirp (phase jitter), as compared with direct modulation. Chirp and fiber dispersion effects limit the transmission distance between source-detector. In addition, external modulators can modulate high optical power CW beams with depth greater than 20 dB.

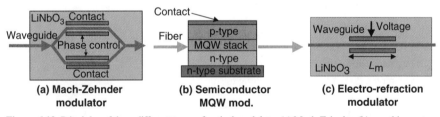

| (a) Mach-Zehnder modulator | (b) Semiconductor MQW mod. | (c) Electro-refraction modulator |

Figure 6.10 Principles of three different types of optical modulator (a) Mach-Zehnder, (b) a multi-quantum well (MQW), and (c) an electro-refraction modulator.

6.15   LASER MODULES

Laser modules are hermetically sealed packages that may contain several individual devices required to stabilize the frequency and power amplitude over a wide range of temperatures and over time (device aging). The components in a laser module are

- A laser device (e.g., MQW, DFB), a Fabry-Perot etalon, or a Bragg filter (it may also be part of the laser device structure).

- A modulator device (internal to the laser or an external lithium-niobate device).

- An internal optical isolator to suppress reflections of laser light at the inter-face (optical feedback) back into the laser device.

- A thermoelectric cooler TEC, and a heatsink; the thermistor of the TEC mon-itors the temperature that is controlled with a microprocessor acquisition cir-cuit, which adjusts the temperature to a constant level, typically 25°C.

- A monitoring photodiode (PIN or APD) that monitors the emission of laser light at the backface and controls the forward output optical power via an electronic circuit.

- A connectorized fiber pigtail that guides the laser output outside the hermeti-cally sealed package to be coupled with the transmitting fiber; the pigtail may (or may not) be of the polarization-maintaining fiber (PMF) type.

- A semiconductor optical amplifier (SOA).

The actual internal structure of the laser module and its specifications vary with manufacturer and type, and on the intended application.

In general, laser modules may operate in one of the wavelength ranges (e.g., about 1310 nm, or 1555 nm, etc.) and over the temperature range −40 to 65°C, at bit rates up to 10 Gbps (or higher). They may have an optical power up to 40 mW or higher, and they require a single voltage (+5 V), or one voltage for the laser (+3.7 V), another for the modulator (depends on the type), and yet another for the thermoelectric heat pump (+5 V). The physical size of these modules, depending on type, is approximately $50 \times 15 \times 5$ mm^3; for larger assemblies the footprint may be approximately 120×100 mm^2. Laser users should avoid direct exposure to the laser beam, as this may cause eye damage.

EXERCISES

1. How many different types of light sources are there?
2. Which type does a laser source belong to?
3. Could an LED be classified as a diode device?
4. What is the effect of temperature on the stability of LED devices?
5. What fiber network applications are LEDs most suitable for?
6. Why must a laser cavity structure with a dielectric be precise in wavelength multiples?
7. What are the basic elements of a semiconductor laser?
8. A laser source needs to be modified with the minimum amount of chirping. What type of modulation should be used?
9. Name two different resonant cavity types used in monolithic semiconductor lasers.
10. What is the basic difference of a semiconductor QWL as compared with a conventional semiconductor laser?
11. Name four advantages of the WGR devices.
12. Is it true that EDFAs perform best in the 1350 nm range?

CHAPTER 7

PHOTODETECTORS

7.1 INTRODUCTION

Photodetectors (or photosensors) are transducers that alter one of their characteristics when light energy impinges on them. In this category, *photoresistors* alter their Ohmic resistance, *rods* and *cones* of the retina neurons of the eye alter their electrochemical response, and chlorophyll in plant leaves alters the rate of converting CO_2 to O_2. Some other photodetectors alter the flow of electrical current or the potential difference across their terminals.

Photodetectors with sufficiently fast response that provide a measurable output for a small amount of light, that are easily reproducible, and that are economical, are worth investigating for applications in high-speed optical communications. This category includes avalanche photodiodes (APD) and positive intrinsic negative photodiodes (PIN).

7.2 PHOTODETECTOR CHARACTERISTICS

Photodetectors are characterized by certain key parameters. Among them are *spectral response, photosensitivity, quantum efficiency, dark current, forward biased noise, noise equivalent power, terminal capacitance, timing response* (rise time and fall time), *frequency bandwidth,* and *cut-off frequency.*

- Spectral response relates the amount of current produced with wavelength, assuming all wavelengths are at the same level of light.

- Photosensitivity is the ratio of light energy (in watts) incident on the device to the resulting current (in amperes).

- Quantum efficiency is the number of generated electron-holes (i.e., current) divided by the number of photons.

- Dark current is the amount of current that flows through the photodiode at the absence of any light (dark), when the diode is reverse biased. This is a source of noise when the diode is reversed biased.

- Forward biased noise is a (current) source of noise that is related to the shunt resistance of the device. The shunt resistance is defined as the ratio voltage (near 0 V) over the amount of current generated. This is also called *shunt resistance* noise.

- Noise equivalent power is defined as the amount of light (of a given wavelength) that is equivalent to the noise level of the device.

- Terminal capacitance is the capacitance from the p-n junction of the diode to the connectors of the device; it limits the response of the photodetector.

- Timing response of the photodetector is defined as the time lapsed for the output signal to reach from 10% to 90% its amplitude (rise time) and from 90% to 10% (fall time).

- Frequency bandwidth is defined as the frequency (or wavelength) range in which the photodetector is sensitive.

- Cut-off frequency is the highest frequency (wavelength) at which the photodetector is sensitive.

In the following, we examine the PIN and the APD photodiodes.

7.3   THE PIN PHOTODIODE

The PIN photodiode is a semiconductor device that consists of an intrinsic (lightly doped) region that is sandwiched between a p-type and an n-type. When this device is reverse biased, it exhibits an almost infinite internal impedance (i.e., like an open circuit) with an output current that is proportional to the input optical power.

The input–output relationship defines a *responsivity*, R, and a *quantum efficiency*, η, as follows:

$$R = (\text{output current } I)/(\text{input optical power } P) \text{ (amperes/watts)} \tag{7.1}$$

$$\eta = (\text{Number of output electrons})/(\text{Number of input photons}) \tag{7.2}$$

R and η are related through the relationship:

$$R = (e\eta)/(hv) \tag{7.3}$$

where e is the electron charge, η is the efficiency, h is Planck's constant, and v is the light frequency.

When a photon creates an electron–hole pair, the device produces a current pulse with duration and shape that depends on the response time of the device.

The R-C time constant determines the frequency response of the PIN device. The capacitance of the reverse-biased PIN photodiode is a limiting factor to its response (and switching speed). As the switching speed increases to very high frequencies, parasitic inductance becomes significant and causes "shot noise," which is estimated as

$$2e(I_s + I_{dark}) \tag{7.4}$$

where I_s is the signal current and I_{dark} the current that flows at the absence of signal, or *dark current*.

7.4   THE APD PHOTODIODE

The APD is a semiconductor device which, when reverse biased, creates strong fields in the junction region. When a photon causes an electron–hole pair, the pair flows through the junction. Because of the strong fields in the junction, the electron gains enough energy to cause secondary electron–hole pairs, which in turn cause more. Thus, a multiplication (or avalanche) process takes place (hence its name) and a substantial current is generated from few initial photons.

The gain, M, of an APD is expressed by

$$M = I_{APD}/I_{primary} \tag{7.5}$$

where I_{APD} is the APD output current and $I_{primary}$ is the current due to photon–electrons conversion. However, during this multiplication process, shot-noise is multiplied as well, and is estimated as:

$$2eIM^2F \tag{7.6}$$

where F is the APD noise factor.

If τ is the effective transit time through the avalanche region, the APD bandwidth is approximated as:

$$B_{APD} = 1/(2pM\tau) \tag{7.7}$$

EXERCISES

1. Name two natural and two artificial photosensors.
2. What is the switching-speed-limiting factor of a PIN diode?
3. An APD diode has very little gain; true or false?

CHAPTER 8

LIGHT AMPLIFIERS

8.1 INTRODUCTION

As the optical signal travels in a fiber waveguide it suffers attenuation (loss of power). For very long fiber spans, the optical signal may be attenuated to the degree that it becomes very weak to excite reliably the (receiving) photodetector, so that the signal may be detected at an expected low bit error rate ($\sim 10^{-9}$ to $\sim 10^{-11}$).

To reach destinations that are hundreds of kilometers away, the optical power level of the signal must be periodically conditioned. Optical amplifiers are key devices that reconstitute the attenuated optical signal, thus expanding the effective fiber span between the data source and the destination.

Some key characteristics of amplifiers are *gain, gain efficiency, gain bandwidth, gain saturation,* and *noise.* Optical amplifiers are also characterized by polarization sensitivity.

- *Gain* is the ratio of output power to input power (measured in dB).

- *Gain efficiency* is the gain as a function of input power (dB/mW).

- Bandwidth is a function of frequency, and as such *gain bandwidth* is the range of frequencies over which the amplifier is effective.

- *Gain saturation* is the maximum output power of the amplifier, beyond which it cannot increase despite the input power increase.

- *Noise* is an inherent characteristic of amplifiers. In electronic amplifiers noise is due to (random) spontaneous recombination of electron–hole pairs that produces an undesired signal added to the information signal to be amplified. In

115

optical amplifiers, it is due to spontaneous light emission of excited ions, which we will further explore.

- *Polarization sensitivity* is the gain dependence of optical amplifiers on the polarization of the signal.

In optical communications networks, there are two distinct amplification methods: the *regenerator* and the *optical amplifier.*

8.2   REGENERATORS

A regenerator receives a modulated optical signal (at a high bit rate), transforms it to an electronic signal of the same bit rate, amplifies it, and then converts the electronic signal back to optical signal of the same modulation and bit rate.

Thus, a regenerator consists of three major components: an optical receiver, an electronic amplifier, and an optical transmitter (Figure 8.1). Additional functions, such as timing, error recovery, and pulse shaping may also be incorporated. Regenerators are classified as 2R or 3R amplifiers—2R if they amplify and reshape and 3R if they amplify, reshape, and retime. An all optical amplifier is classified as 1R (amplify only).

Regenerators amplify a single wavelength and are maintenance intensive. In a multi-wavelength system, an equal number of regenerators is needed. Thus, considering that in an optical link there are several regenerators (typically spaced every 40 km), in a multi-wavelength fiber system the maintenance cost is significant.

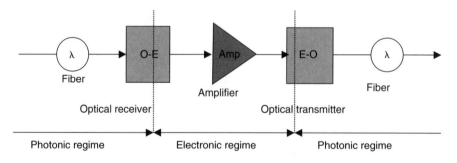

O-E=Optical to electronic
E-O=Electronic to optical
Amp = Amplifier

Figure 8.1 A regenerator consists of three major functions: the optical receiver, the electronic amplifier, and the optical transmitter.

8.3   OPTICAL AMPLIFIERS

Optical amplifiers (OAs) are devices based on conventional laser principles. They receive one or more optical signals, each within a window of optical frequencies, and simultaneously amplify all wavelengths. That is, they coherently release more photons at each wavelength. This is a significant advantage of multi-wavelength fiber systems over regenerators, because one device replaces many. OAs are 1R amplifiers (as compared to 2R and 3R regenerators); that is, they only amplify directly an optical signal.

There are two types of OAs, semiconductor optical laser-type amplifiers (SOA) and fiber-type amplifier (erbium-doped [EDFA] or praseodymium-doped [PDFA]). In addition, there are other amplifying devices that depend on the nonlinear properties of optical materials, such as the Raman and Brillouin. Optical amplifiers require electrical or optical energy to excite (pump-up) the state of electron–hole pairs. Energy is typically provided by injecting electrical current (in SOA; Figure 8.2) or optical light in the UV range (in EDFA).

To reduce optical signal losses at the couplings, antireflective (AR) coatings are used at the interface optical fiber-to-device.

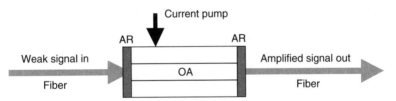

Figure 8.2 Optical amplifier (OA) are devices that are based on conventional laser principles.

Amplifiers are characterized by gain, bandwidth, gain over the bandwidth, maximum output power, dynamic range, cross-talk, noise figure, output saturation power, physical size, and so on. The output saturation power is defined as the output power level at which the gain has dropped by 3 dB.

OAs, based on their structure, are distinguished as follows:

- Traveling wave laser amplifiers
- Fabry-Perot laser amplifiers
- Injection current distributed feedback (DFB) laser amplifiers
- Stimulated Raman
- Stimulated Brillouin
- EDFA
- PDFA

Depending on the application, each structure has its own advantages and disadvantages.

8.4   SEMICONDUCTOR OPTICAL AMPLIFIERS

The most important advantage of SOAs is that they are made with InGaAsP and are thus small, compact, and may be integrated with other semiconductor and optical components. The SOA salient characteristics are:

- They are polarization dependent, and thus require a polarization-maintaining fiber.
- They have relatively high gain (20 dB).
- Their output saturation power is in the range of 5 to 10 dBm.
- They have a large bandwidth.
- They operate at the wavelength regions of 0.8, 1.3, and 1.5 μm.
- They are compact semiconductors easily integrable with other devices.
- Several SOAs may be integrated into an array.

However, SOAs have a high noise figure and high cross-talk level due to nonlinear phenomena (four-wave mixing).

8.5   ERBIUM-DOPED FIBER AMPLIFIERS

One attractive fiber optic amplifier (FOA) in optical communications systems, and particularly in DWDM systems, is the EDFA. The EDFA is a fiber segment a few meters long heavily doped with the rare earth element erbium (and also co-doped with Al and Ge). The erbium ions may be excited by a number of optical frequencies—514 nm, 532 nm, 667 nm, 800 nm, 980 nm, and 1480 nm. The shortest wavelength, 514 nm, excites erbium ions to the highest possible energy level. From this level, it may drop to one of four intermediate metastable levels, radiating phonons (the acoustical quantum equivalent of photon). From the lowest metastable level, it finally drops to the initial (ground) level, emitting photons of wavelength around 1550 nm. Similar activity takes place with the remaining wavelengths, although the number of metastable levels decreases as the wavelength becomes longer. Finally, the longest wavelength, 1480 nm, excites ions to the lowest metastable level from which it drops directly to the ground level. Figure 8.3 illustrates the two lowest and most important energy excitations and spontaneous emission for erbium; erbium has more energy levels, which for simplicity are not shown.

The two most convenient excitation wavelengths are 980 nm and 1480 nm. When a 980-nm or 1480-nm source propagates through an EDFA fiber, erbium ions

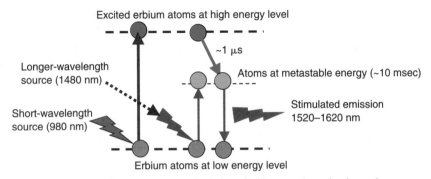

Figure 8.3 Principles of spontaneous emission of erbium; two lower levels are shown.

are excited and stimulated emission takes place releasing photonic energy in the wavelength range 1520 to 1620 nm. EDFAs that perform best within the C-band are known as C-band EDFAs and those in the L-band as L-band EDFAs (see also Table 3.1). When EDFA ions are excited by a 980-nm source, after approximately 1 μsec the excited ions fall on the metastable energy level from which, if triggered, they drop to the ground energy level and emit light at the wavelength of the triggering photon. If they are not triggered, then after approximately 10 msec (known as *spontaneous lifetime*), they spontaneously drop from the metastable level emitting light in the range around 1550 nm (Figure 8.3). In communications, the bit rate is very high (Gbps) and the bit period is very short (psec), as compared to the long lifetime (msec); thus it does not cause inter-symbol interference. However, at the absence of fast bits, the spontaneous emission adds to noise.

The EDFA amplifier consists of a coupling device, an erbium-doped fiber, and two isolators (one per EDFA end) (Figure 8.4). The fiber carrying the signal is connected via the isolator that suppresses light reflections into the incoming fiber. The isolator at the output of the EDFA suppresses the reflections by the outgoing fiber (Figure 8.4). The EDFA is stimulated by a higher optical frequency (in the UV range) laser source, known as the *pump*. Laser light from the pump (980 nm or 1480 nm or both) is also coupled in the EDFA. The pump excites the fiber additives that directly amplify a passing through optical signal at a wavelength in the 1550 nm region.

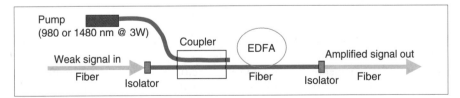

Figure 8.4 An EDFA amplifier consists of an erbium-doped silica fiber, an optical pump, a coupler and isolators at both ends.

The pump laser is specifically designed for EDFA applications. Pump lasers are enclosed in a small package (approximately $20 \times 15 \times 8$ mm^3) with a connectorized single-mode fiber pigtail that can be coupled with the EDFA (fiber). Typical pumps have a wavelength of 980 nm or 1480 nm and an output power from under 100 mW to about 250 mW.

8.5.1   Advantages of EFDAs

- A high-power transfer efficiency from pump to signal ($>$50%).

- Directly and simultaneously amplify a wide wavelength region (in the region of 1550 nm) with a relatively flat gain ($>$20 dB), which is suitable to WDM systems.

- Saturation output is greater than 1 mW (10 to 25 dBm).

- Gain time constant is long ($>$100 msec) to overcome patterning effects and inter-modulation distortions (low noise).

- Large dynamic range.

- Low noise figure.

- Polarization independent (thus reducing coupling loss to transmission fiber).

- Suitable for long-haul applications.

8.5.2   Disadvantages of EFDAs

- They are not small devices (they are kilometer-long fibers) and cannot be integrated with other semiconductor devices.

- EDFAs exhibit amplified spontaneous light emission (ASE). That is, even if no incoming signal is present, there is always some output signal as a result of some excited ions in the fiber; this output is termed *spontaneous noise*.

- There is cross-talk.

- There is gain saturation.

EDFAs have found applications in long-haul as well as in wavelength division multiplexing (WDM) transport systems. A fiber span (hundreds of kilometers long) consists of fiber segments (tens of kilometers each). Optical amplifiers are placed at the interconnecting points to restore the attenuated optical signal. Thus, there may be several EDFAs along the fiber span (typically up to 8). However, three issues become important: (a) gain flatness (all wavelengths at the EDFA output should have the same optical power); (b) dynamic gain; and (c) low noise.

All wavelengths are not amplified through EDFAs in the same way; that is, the gain is not exactly flat. This issue is addressed with gain flattening optical filters. These devices are passive in-line filters with low insertion loss, low dispersion, and stable performance over a wide range of temperatures.

The power pumped in an EDFA is shared by all wavelengths. The more the wavelengths, the less power per wavelength, and vice versa. This has an undesirable effect in optical add-dropped multiplexing (OADM) WDM with EDFAs. As wavelengths are dropped by an OADM and not added, EDFAs (in series with OADM) amplify fewer wavelengths more, and as wavelengths are added by another OADM, they are amplified less. That is, the gain does not remain at the same level from one OADM to the next. This is addressed by engineering the WDM system and dynamic gain control.

Noise is addressed differently. When engineering a fiber-optic path, it should be remembered that optical noise sources are cumulative and that the spontaneous emission of EDFAs introduces noise that degrades the S/N ratio. Thus, one may think that a strong optical signal launched into the fiber could overcome this. However, near the zero-dispersion wavelength region, four-wave mixing could become dominant and it could degrade the S/N ratio.

The selection of power (per channel) launched into the fiber becomes a puzzle: amplifier noise restricts the minimum power of the signal, and four-wave mixing limits the maximum power per channel launched into the fiber. This implies that a power level that lies between a lower and an upper limit must be selected. To determine the power level, many other parameters must be taken into account so that the required quality of signal is maintained. Some of these parameters are:

- Fiber length between amplifiers (in kilometers)
- Fiber attenuation (loss) per kilometer
- Number of amplifiers in the optical path
- Amplifier parameters (gain, noise, chromatic dispersion, bandwidth)
- Number of channels (wavelengths) per fiber
- Channel width and spacing
- Receiver (detector) specifications
- Transmitter specifications
- Polarization issues
- Optical component losses and noise (connectors, other devices)
- Quality of signal (bit error rate, S/N)
- Signal modulation method and bit rate
- Other design parameters

8.6   PRASEODYMIUM-DOPED FIBER AMPLIFIERS

PDFAs have a high gain (~30 dB), a high saturation power (20 dBm), and are suitable in the region 1280 to 1340 nm, where EDFAs are not. However, PDFAs require a non-silica fiber (fluoride) that is not very common, and a high-power (up to 300 mW) pump laser at 1017 nm (not the popular 980 nm or 1480 nm). Thus, presently PDFA technology is not popular or well developed yet.

8.7   STIMULATED RAMAN AND STIMULATED BRILLOUIN SCATTERING AMPLIFIERS

Stimulated Raman scattering (SRS) and stimulated Brillouin scattering (SBS) amplifiers are non-doped fiber amplifiers, as already described in Sections 3.20.1 and 3.20.2, that employ pump lasers to take advantage of the nonlinearity properties of the fiber. The most important feature of Raman amplifiers is that they have a wide bandwidth range that can extend over the complete useful spectrum from the 1300 nm to 1600+ nm (500 optical channels at 100-Ghz spacing) that enable a multi-Terabit transmission technology, also referred to as *Raman super-continuum*. On the negative side, Raman amplification requires very long fibers (in the order of several kilometers) and pump lasers with high optical power (>1 watt). Thermal management issues as well as safety issues are yet to be resolved.

8.8   CLASSIFICATION OF OPTICAL FIBER AMPLIFIERS

Optical fiber amplifiers (OFAs) are classified in electronic amplifiers, electronic systems, and wireless systems as *power amplifiers, pre-amplifiers,* and *line amplifiers.*

Optical fiber amplifiers should be applied properly to minimize several factors that may affect the integrity of the channel and the transmitted signal due to nonlinearities, polarization, and other effects. ITU-T has recommended parameter limits as well as applications of optical fiber amplifiers in G.662 and G.663.

8.8.1   Power Amplifiers

An OFA capable of increasing the optical power of the modulated photonic source (i.e., the optical transmitted signal) is called an *optical power amplifier.* An optical power amplifier acts like a booster. It is placed right after the source, and thus may also be integrated with it. It receives a large signal (from the laser source) with a large signal-to-noise ratio and boosts its power to levels about −10 dBm or higher.

8.8.2   Pre-Amplifiers

An OFA with very low noise that is able to increase a highly attenuated signal to a level that can be detected reliably by an optical detector is called an optical preamplifier. A pre-amplifier is placed directly before the detector and may be integrated with it.

8.8.3 Line Amplifiers

An OFA with low noise able to amplify an attenuated signal so that it can travel an additional length of fiber is called an optical line amplifier. Therefore, the line amplifier must have large gain and very low noise and it should not add noise to the already received attenuated signal.

8.8.4 Amplifier Standards

The following ITU standards deal with optical amplifiers:

(In-) line amplifier	(G.662)
Booster amplifier	(G.662)
Erbium doped fiber amplifier	(G.662)
Optical amplifier device	(G.662)
Optical amplifier subsystem	(G.662)
Optical amplifier	(G.662)
Optical fiber amplifier	(G.662)
Optical return loss	(G.957)
Optically amplified receiver	(G.662)
Optically amplified transmitter	(G.662)
Preamplifier	(G.662)
Remotely pumped amplifier	(G.973)

8.9 WAVELENGTH CONVERTERS

Wavelength conversion enables optical channels to be relocated, adding to the flexibility and efficiency of multi-wavelength systems. Wavelength conversion may be achieved by employing the nonlinearity properties of certain hetero-junction semiconductors.

SOAs are also used as wavelength converting devices. Their basic structure consists of an active layer (erbium-doped waveguide) sandwiched between a p-layer InP and an n-layer InP (Figure 8.5). Currently, various methods have been explored

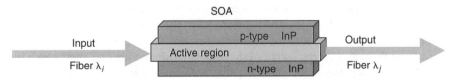

Figure 8.5 Semiconductor optical amplifiers may be used as wavelength converting devices.

that are based on *cross-gain modulation, four-wave mixing, dispersion-shifted fiber,* and other *interferometric* techniques.

8.9.1 Cross-Gain Modulation

Gain saturation in an optical amplifier occurs when high optical power is injected in the active region and the carrier concentration is depleted through stimulated emission. Then, the optical gain is reduced.

Based on this, consider two wavelengths injected in the active region of an optical amplifier. Wavelength λ_1 is modulated with binary data and wavelength λ_2, the target, is continuous (not modulated) (Figure 8.6).

When the input bit in λ_1 is a logic ONE (i.e., high power) depletion occurs, it blocks λ_2. When the bit in λ_1 is a logic ZERO (no power) depletion does not occur and λ_2 is at high power (logic ONE). Thus, a transfer of inverted data from λ_1 to λ_2 takes place. This method is known as cross-gain modulation.

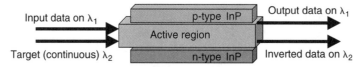

Figure 8.6 Cross-gain modulating devices transfer inverted data from one wavelength channel to another.

8.9.2 Four-Wave Mixing

We have described that four-wave mixing (FWM) is an undesirable nonlinearity. However, FWM can also be taken advantage of to produce at will an additional wavelength. Consider that a modulated wavelength λ_1 is to be converted to another, λ_2. Then λ_1 and two more wavelengths are selected, such that when all three are injected in the fiber device, due to FWM, a fourth wavelength is produced, λ_2, which is modulated as the λ_1. In series to this device, a pass-band filter is placed that passes through only the new wavelength, λ_2.

8.9.3 Optical Frequency Shifter

This method is based on the nonlinearity property of dispersion-shifted doped fibers, which produce a new wavelength when two wavelengths at high power and in close wavelength proximity interact (in the range of 1550 nm) as in FWM. Thus, by launching into a 10-km dispersion-shifted fiber a modulated wavelength, λ_1, known as the *probe signal*, and also a continuous power wavelength, λ_2, known as the *pump*, a third modulated wavelength is generated (Figure 8.7). The new wavelength, λ_3, is at λ_2 shifted by an amount equal to the difference between the original wavelength of the signal and the pump. At the output of the dispersion-shifted fiber an interference filter (IF) eliminates the probe and the pump wavelengths and allows only the frequency-shifted, λ_3, to pass through (thus acting as a band pass filter; Figure 8.8).

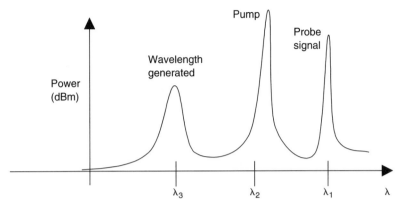

Figure 8.7 In dispersion-shifted doped fibers a third wavelength may be produced when two high-power wavelengths are in close wavelength proximity.

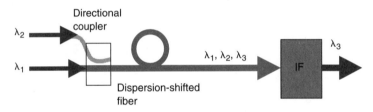

Figure 8.8 At the output of the dispersion-shifted fiber an interference filter (IF) eliminates the probe and the pump wavelengths.

EXERCISES

1. What is the main difference between a regenerator and an optical amplifier?
2. What is the difference between an SOA and an EDFA?
3. What is ASE? What is spontaneous noise?
4. For an EDFA to amplify a signal in the region of 1550 nm a strong light source is required. What is the wavelength of this light source and what is it called?
5. How are OFAs classified? Where are they placed with reference to a laser source?
6. What is a wavelength converter?
7. How can FWM be used constructively to convert one wavelength into another?
8. What is a wavelength shifter?
9. A wavelength fiber shifter requires two inputs, a probe signal and a pump source. Which is the continuous source and which is the modulated source?
10. What is required at the output of a wavelength fiber shifter to pass only the shifted frequency?

CHAPTER 9

OTHER OPTICAL COMPONENTS

9.1 INTRODUCTION

In this chapter we describe certain other optical devices, such as optical phase-locked loops, optical directional couplers, ring resonators, optical equalizers, optical isolators, polarizers, and rotators. Optical multiplexers and demultiplexers, as well as optical switches are the subject of subsequent chapters.

9.2 OPTICAL PHASE-LOCKED LOOPS

An *optical phase-locked loop* (OPLL) is a device that is based on a tunable laser source, a filter, and a photodiode bridge. Its principle of operation is similar to electronic PLLs. Ideally, the frequency from laser #1 (cos ωt) is in perfect quadrature with that from laser #2 (sin ωt). A balanced pin–diode bridge detects both frequencies. When the two frequencies are the same, the bridge is balanced at a quiescent state; otherwise, an unbalanced current is amplified and fed back through a low-pass filter to tunable laser #2 to adjust its frequency (Figure 9.1). Clearly, this arrangement assumes that both incoming light sources are at the same optical power level, and if they are not, a compensating mechanism is incorporated.

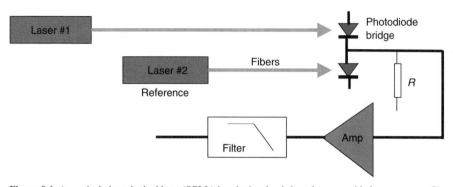

Figure 9.1 An optical phase-locked loop (OPLL) is a device that is based on a tunable laser source, a filter and a photodiode bridge.

9.3   OPTICAL DIRECTIONAL COUPLERS

Optical directional couplers are devices that transfer the maximum possible optical
power from one or more optical device(s) to another in a selected direction. Power
transfer may be from a light source into a fiber, from fiber to fiber, from fiber to a
device (such as to a filter, to a demultiplexer, etc.), and from a device to a fiber. The
making of optical directional couplers employs filters and solid-state devices.

Single-mode fiber directional couplers use the evanescent property of integrated
lightguides on a substrate to couple optical power (light) of certain wavelength from
one guide to another. Figure 9.2 illustrates two lightguides of coupling length L_0 separated by a distance d. When a voltage V_s is applied, optical power is guided through
the same guide, but with a phase change. When the applied voltage is $V = 0$, then
power is transferred through the evanescent separation region to the adjacent guide.
For maximum power transfer, certain conditions must exist:

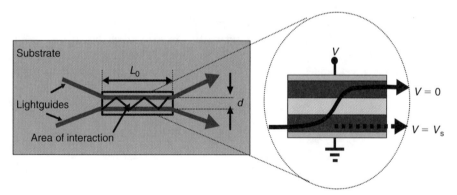

Figure 9.2 Couplers are characterized by the power coupled or lost at the coupling length, typically in
terms of power loss Γ.

- The two lightguides are in close proximity, separated by a distance d comparable to the wavelength λ to be coupled.
- The two phase velocities are in perfect synchronization.
- The refractive index of both lightguides is the same.
- The interaction (or coupling) length, L_0, is precisely equal to a coupling length (which is proportional to the exp (d/d_0)).

When the refractive index of one lightguide differs from the other, power is lost during optical power transfer. When the separation distance, d, or the equivalent optical isolation between the two guides at the coupling length L_0 increases, optical coupling decreases and at some distance d there is no coupling at all. Clearly, if the isolation between the two guides over the length L_0 is controlled, then a device with some interesting applications may be made. Such controllable devices, in addition to being used as directional couplers, may be used as power attenuators, as signal modulators, as power splitters, or as on-off switches.

Couplers are characterized by the power lost, Γ. Typically, couplers are referred to as $(1 - \Gamma)^{1/2}$ or $(\Gamma)^{1/2}$ couplers. A typical power loss in couplers is about 3 dB at 1.5 μm. Power is lost

- In the bulk of the lightguide material along the coupling length (due to scattering and absorption),
- At the sidewalls (due to structure irregularities),
- At the interface with the substrate (due to scattering, known as epitaxial interface scattering), and
- At the edges (due to reflections and fiber-coupled insertion loss).

The most desirable characteristics of optical couplers are as follows:

- High isolation
- Low coupling power loss, Γ (in dB), and thus maximum power transfer
- No signal reflectivity
- No signal absorption
- No through phase shift
- No signal distortion over the entire wavelength range of interest
- No added dispersion effects
- No added polarization effects
- No added noise, and
- Steady performance over a wide range of temperatures.

Integrated lightguides are made using a variety of compounds, such as the following:

- GaAs doped (10^{15}) over a highly doped (10^{18}) GaAs substrate
- InP doped over a highly doped InP substrate
- GaAs over AlGaAs over a GaAs substrate
- InGaAsP over a InP substrate
- Ti diffused over a lithium niobate (LiNbO$_3$) substrate, also abbreviated as Ti:LiNbO$_3$

Among them, Ti:LiNbO$_3$ has the least loss, requires a relatively low voltage, and responds quickly. Thus, these devices are also used as photonic switching devices. However, InP and GaAs devices are better suited to monolithic opto-electronic integration with laser sources or detectors.

Couplers come in different flavors. Figure 9.3 illustrates three types. Directional couplers also act as isolators and therefore a measure of goodness is the amount of power coupled in the desired direction with respect to the undesired (in dB). For maximum power transfer from a fiber, end-faces are cut perpendicular to the longitudinal axis, they are highly polished, and they are coated with anti-reflective film to prevent reflections and optical feedback that may stimulate a laser effect. Finally, the importance of fiber core alignment, due to its very small diameter (~8 μm), cannot be overemphasized.

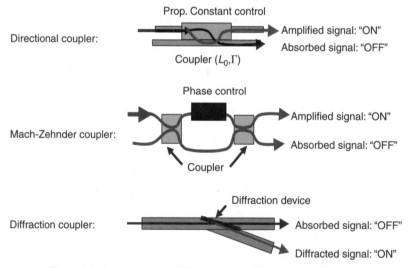

Figure 9.3 Couplers come in different types, and here three are illustrated.

9.4   RING RESONATORS

Consider a fiber ring with its core in close proximity to the transmission fiber, thus forming a coupler with a coupling length L_0 and a coupler power loss Γ at the interaction region (Figure 9.4). The coupler is a $(1 - \Gamma)^{1/2}$ type (this describes the power coupled onto the ring). The ring has a circumference length L and attenuation constant α. Now, consider a lightwave traveling through the transmission fiber.

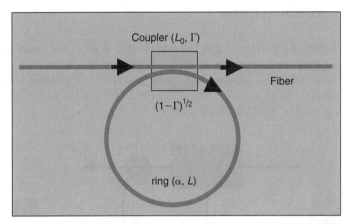

Figure 9.4 A ring resonator consists of a fiber ring with its core in close proximity to the transmission fiber.

When it reaches the coupler device, it is coupled onto the ring and travels around it. After a complete revolution around the ring, the coupled lightwave returns to the coupler with an attenuation α and a phase shift $\Phi = \beta L$ that depends on the length ring L and on the wavelength λ.

At the coupler, lightwave from the ring and lightwave from the transmitting fiber interfere constructively or destructively, depending on which condition is valid, $\Phi = 2\pi N$ or $\Phi = 2\pi(N+1/2)$, respectively, where N is an integer.

The frequency difference Δf between the maximum and minimum of the transmitted power is obtained by

$$\Delta f = c/(2n_{\text{eff}}L) \tag{9.2}$$

where n_{eff} is the effective refractive index. The effective refractive index in this case is defined as the weighted average of the refractive index of the waveguide and of the refractive index of the evanescent substrate.

The ring resonator acts like a pass-band filter with sharp cut-off characteristics and a high *finesse* (reported higher than 182). Its transmittance profile is depicted in Figure 9.5.

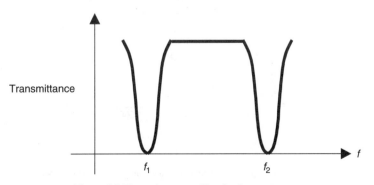

Figure 9.5 Transmittance profile of a ring resonator.

9.5   OPTICAL EQUALIZERS

The wavelengths of a generated spectral region are not all of the same amplitude. However, for proper transmission operation it is necessary to have a flat output power spectrum. Optical equalizers monitor each wavelength channel at the output and make selective amplitude adjustments to flatten the optical power of the spectrum within a band of wavelengths (Figure 9.6).

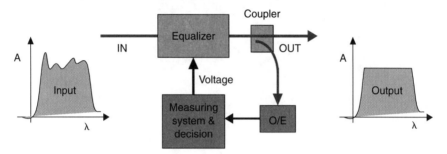

Figure 9.6 Optical equalizers flatten the optical power of a spectrum.

Their operation is as follows: at the output of each wavelength (with a given granularity) and over a wavelength range is (iteratively) measured and based on each measurement, an appropriate adjustment is performed (by the application of an appropriate voltage) on the amplitude of the measured wavelength so that a flat spectrum is achieved. Figure 9.7 illustrates a typical output in the wavelength range 1530 to 1565 nm with and without equalization.

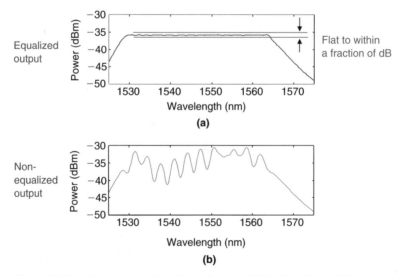

Figure 9.7 Typical power output (a) with equalization and (b) without (bandwidth granularity is 0.5 nm).

Optical equalizers that perform equalization on a dynamic basis are also called dynamic wavelength equalizers (DWEs). Currently, optical equalizers are opto-electronic feedback control subsystems. A compact, all-optical equalizer with fast dynamic range is a device of the future.

The desirable characteristics of optical equalizers are

- Large wavelength range
- Low ripple of the spectrum amplitude (small peak-to-peak variation)
- High dynamic range
- Low loss
- Polarization independent
- Fast acquisition

9.6   OPTICAL ISOLATORS

Optical isolators are devices that transmit optical power (of a band of wavelengths) in one direction more than the other direction (Figure 9.8). Optical isolator devices are characterized by *insertion loss, L,* or the loss of optical power through it, and by *isolation, I,* or the ratio of transmitted power in one direction over the other direction. Ideally, it should allow transmission of all power in one direction and no power in the other direction; that is, $L = 0$ and $I =$ infinite.

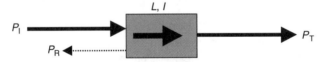

Figure 9.8 Optical isolators transmit optical power (of a band of wave-lengths) in one direction more than the other.

The quantities L and I are expressed by

$$L \text{ (dB)} = P_I \text{ (dB)} - P_T \text{(dB)} \tag{9.2}$$

and

$$I \text{ (dB)} = P_I \text{ (dB)} - P_R \text{(dB)} \tag{9.3}$$

where P_I, P_T, and P_R are the incident power, the transmitted power, and the reflected power, respectively, all expressed in decibel units.

9.7   POLARIZERS, ROTATORS, AND CIRCULATORS

Optical isolator devices are made with certain materials (formed in parallel plates or prisms) that allow one polarization direction of nonpolarized light to propagate through it. These devices are called *polarizers*. Birefringent materials can be used as polarizers.

Other materials rotate the polarization direction by an angle, and they are called *rotators*. Rotators are based on the Faraday effect. Rotators can be made with fibers doped with elements or compounds that have a large Verdet constant, such as terbium (Tb), YIG ($Y_3Fe_5O_{12}$)-yttrium-iron-garnet, and TbBiIG ($Tb_{3-x}Bi_xFe_5O_{12}$)-bismuth-substituted terbium-iron-garnet. Some, such as the YIGs, may require a strong magnetic field.

Polarizers and rotators can be combined to form isolators. Isolation is accomplished using polarizers and $\pi/4$ rotators in cascade, as shown in Figure 9.9.

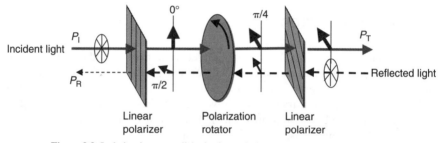

Figure 9.9 Isolation is accomplished using polarizers and $\pi/4$ rotators in cascade.

Isolators may be viewed as two port devices that allow unidirectional energy to flow from one terminal to the other. Now, if using a structure made with more than one isolator, then a three-terminal device is constructed that permits unidirectional energy to flow from terminal 1 to 2, from 2 to 3, and from 3 to 1. This device is known as a circulator. Four-terminal circulators are also available.

In fiber-optic communications systems, compactness of optical devices is a highly desirable feature. Thus, devices with large Verdet value and strong magnetic fields would result in short lengths for a desirable angle of rotation.

For example, for 45° polarization shift (rotation) at λ = 633 nm, a terbium-doped glass fiber would be around 108 mm long [for H = 1,000 Oe (Oersted) and a Verdet constant of V = 0.25 min/cm-Oe]. On the other hand, for 45° polarization shift at λ = 1300 nm, YIG devices placed in a strong (saturated) magnetic field are about 2 mm long. TbBiIG devices have also been used in the λ = 1500 nm range.

EXERCISES

1. What are the main components of an OPLL?

2. List five of the most desirable characteristics of optical couplers.

3. What is the fundamental principle on which a ring resonator operates?

4. What is an optical isolator?

5. What is a rotator?

6. Could a rotator be used to construct an isolator?

CHAPTER 10

OPTICAL CROSS-CONNECTS

10.1 INTRODUCTION

Channel cross-connecting is a key function in most communications systems. In electronic systems, the electronic cross-connecting fabric is constructed with massively integrated circuitry and is capable of interconnecting thousands of inputs with thousands of outputs. The same interconnection function is also required in many optical communications systems. Optical (channel) cross-connect may be accomplished in two ways:

1. Convert optical data streams into electronic data, use electronic cross-connect technology, and then convert electronic data streams into optical. This is known as the *hybrid approach*.

2. Cross-connect optical channels directly in the photonic domain. This is known as *all optical switching*.

The hybrid approach is currently more popular due to existing expertise in designing high-bandwidth multi-channel ($N \times N$) non-blocking electronic cross-connect fabrics. In this case, N may be in the order of thousands.

All-optical switching is used in high-bandwidth few-channel cross-connect fabrics (such as routers). N in this case is from 2 to perhaps 32, but photonic cross-connects with N in the range of up to 1000 are in experimental and planning phases. An economically feasible and reliable 1000×1000 all-photonic non-blocking and dynamically reconfigurable switch is currently a challenge, but a promising technology.

10.2   OPTICAL CROSS-CONNECT MODEL

Optical cross-connect devices are modeled after the many-port model. That is, N input ports and N output ports, with a table that defines the connectivity between input and one or more outputs. Mathematically, this model may be represented by a matrix relationship. Figure 10.1 illustrates the model and the matrix of a cross-connecting device, where I_K is the amplitude of light at input port K, O_L is the amplitude of light at output port L, and $[T_{IJ}]$ is the transmittance matrix. In general, the transmittance terms T_{IJ} are functions of the absorption and dispersion characteristics of the connectivity path. Ideally, the T_{IJ} terms are 1 or 0 signifying connect or no connect with zero connectivity loss and zero dispersion.

All-optical cross-connect fabrics are based on at least three methods:

- Free-space optical switching (waveguide grating router [WGR], Mach-Zehnder interferometers)
- Optical solid-state devices (acousto-optic and electro-optic couplers)
- Electro-mechanical mirror-based devices

Other methods are based on the polarization properties of liquid crystals and other properties of materials.

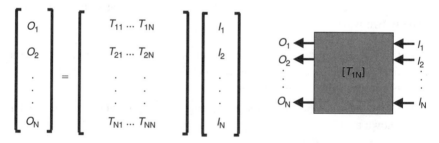

Figure 10.1 Modeling an optical cross-connect, mathematically and symbolically.

10.3   FREE-SPACE OPTICAL SWITCHING

Among the most promising switches with many input ports to many output ports is the generalized Mach-Zehnder WGR. In this device, a given wavelength at any input port appears at a specified output port (Figure 10.2). Thus, an input-to-output connectivity map is constructed; that is, a switch. This type of free-space optical switching is also known as *wavelength routing*.

Another type of free space optical switching is to mechanically steer a laser beam to one of many fibers. If we consider a matrix of beams facing a matrix of fibers, then, steering one of the source beams and a receiving fiber (so that they face

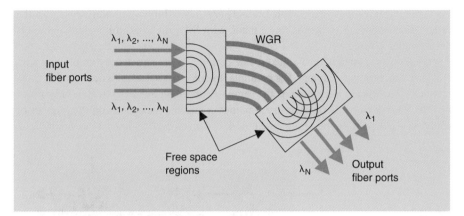

Figure 10.2 Free-space optical switching based on the generalized Mach-Zehnder waveguide grating router.

each other) achieve connectivity in space. Re-directing the source (by a small degree) to face another fiber space switching is accomplished.

10.4   SOLID-STATE CROSS-CONNECTS

Solid-state optical cross-connect devices are semiconductor directional couplers. These devices can selectively change one of their optical properties on a path upon the application of a control signal (Figure 10.3). The optical property may be polarization, propagation constant, absorption, or index of refraction. Depending on the type of material, the optical property may change by applying heat, light, mechanical pressure, electric current, or an electric field (voltage).

As an example, current injection controls the refractive index of a semiconductor waveguide, whereas electric field application controls the index of refraction of ferroelectric $LiNbO_3$ crystals. Thin film heaters may also be applied to control the refractive index.

The material type, the controlling mechanism, and the controlled property impact the switching speed of the device as well as the number of ports of the switch.

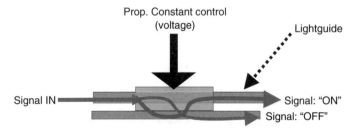

Figure 10.3 A solid-state optical cross-connect based on the principles of directional couplers.

For example, switches made with $LiNbO_3$ crystals exhibit switching speeds in the order of nanoseconds, whereas those made with SiO_2 on Si exhibit speeds in the order of under 1 msec.

A multi-port switch, also called a *star-coupler*, is constructed by employing several 2 × 2 directional couplers. For example, to construct a 4 × 4 switch, six 2 × 2 directional couplers are integrated on the same substrate (Figure 10.4). It should be noted that the total power loss of each input–output connectivity depends on the number of couplers in the path. In the arrangement of 4 × 4, each path includes three couplers.

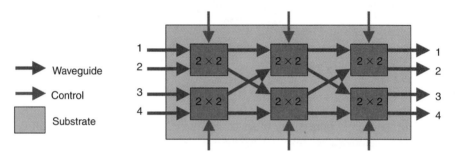

Figure 10.4   A star-coupler multiport switch using several 2 × 2 LINbO$_3$ directional couplers.

Although the number of ports can be large (e.g., 128 × 128), due to cumulative losses, practical switches have a rather limited number of ports, for example, 16 × 16 and perhaps 32 × 32. Solid-state optical cross-connects are characterized by a number of parameters. For example, (number in parenthesis refer to a typical SiO_2 on Si device):

- Switching matrix (2 × 2, 4 × 4, and so on)
- Insertion loss (typically 1 dB)
- Isolation (typically 35 dB)
- Cross-talk (typically −40 dB)
- Switching speed (in the range of msec to nsec)
- Polarization-dependent loss (fraction of dB)
- Spectral flatness (typically ± 1 dB)
- Operating temperature (0 to 70°C)
- Operating voltage (typically +5 V)
- Number of inputs and outputs (e.g., 2 × 2)
- Whether they block an input or not

In addition, the package type (e.g., hermetically sealed), type of fiber connector, and physical dimensions are important parameters. For an example, a 2 × 2 optical cross-connect is a rather large device (~100 × 10 × 10 mm).

10.5 MICRO-ELECTRO-MECHANICAL SWITCHES: REFLECTOR-TYPE

An optical cross-connect technology has employed a technology known as nano-technology to micro-machine tiny mirrors on a substrate that can be used to switch by reflecting optical beams. This technology, also known as micro-electro-mechanical systems (MEMS), uses an outgrowth of semiconductor processing, which is an already proven technology (this technology is expected to become as simple as a merely rubber-stamp to create nanomolds, nanoparts and nanomachines that may be used in communications and in other fields as well). Using deposition, etching, and lithography, tiny machines (smaller than the human hair) are micro-machined on a substrate. Such machines may be gears, linear stepper drives, pulleys, tweezers, bending beams, screws, electric motors, polished flat plates, and so on. Thus, a highly polished (with gold) flat plate (or a mirror) is connected with an electrical actuator and is placed vertically in the gap of three intersecting waveguides. This arrangement constructs an optical switch whereby the mirror may let an optical beam pass through or reflect it in a different direction. The mirror may move to accomplish this by one of many methods, depending on the fabrication technology. It may be connected, for example, so that by rotating the mirror between two positions it directs a beam to one of two directions (Figure 10.5a). It may be pulled down (when a voltage is applied) or up (when no voltage; Figure 10.5b). Similarly, it may be linearly pulled back from or inserted in an optical waveguide gap to change the direction of a beam. In Figure 10.6 an actual micro-photograph of a MEMS (of the type in Figure 10.5b) is shown. Another structure places the mirror in an electrostatic actuator (see photo in Figure 10.8) and thus it can be tilted in specific directions, based on the value of the applied voltage (in the order of 100–200 V). With reference to Figure 10.5, when the mirror is at one orientation it lets the light beam to be coupled to waveguide #1 (and to output #1) and when at the other orientation to be coupled to waveguide #2 (and to output 2).

MEMS technology, although complex, uses well-known IC-batch processing; thus, many MEMS devices may be manufactured on the same wafer, reducing the cost per

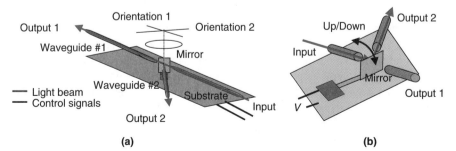

(a) **(b)**

Figure 10.5 Micro-machined mirrors can be rotated (a) or moved up/down (b) to construct optical switches.

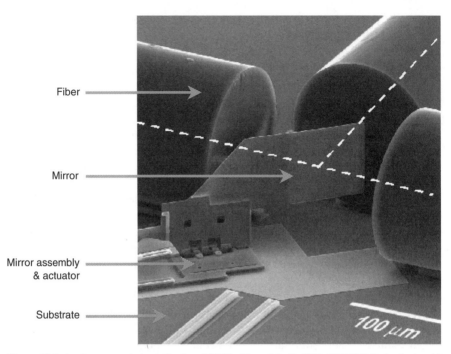

Figure 10.6 A microscope photograph of an MEMS. (*Copyright © 1999. LUCENT Technologies. All rights reserved. Reprinted with permission.*)

system. MEMS have demonstrated low-loss connectivity (fraction of a dB), on-off contrast ratio of better than 60 dB, low switching power (2 mW), compact design and, when integrated with other devices, higher density multifunctional optical switching systems. However, MEMS technology is slower ($\sim$ 10 ms) than LiNbO$_3$ solid-state switches.

10.6   ELECTRO-MECHANICAL SWITCHES: MIRROR ARRAY

MEMS technology has expanded to integrate many mirrors on the same chip, arranged in an array. Based on this technology, each mirror, connected with a micromachined electrical actuator, may be independently tilted so that an incident light beam is reflected in a desired direction. Thus, an array of N mirrors can direct N optical input signals impinging on them to N positions in space where there are positioned output waveguides. The concept of a four-mirror switching array is shown in Figure 10.7 and an actual photograph in Figure 10.8. Clearly, this technique may be extended to construct a $N \times N$ mirror matrix, where N can be potentially 1000.

MEMS technology promises low-loss connectivity, compact design, and large interconnecting matrices. However, the precision of tilting the mirrors is very critical and as they are tilted, their orientation must consistently be at exactly the correct

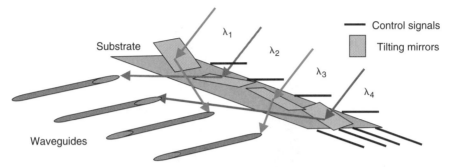

Figure 10.7 Multiple micro-machined mirrors may be arranged in an *N* array or even in a *N* × *N* matrix configuration.

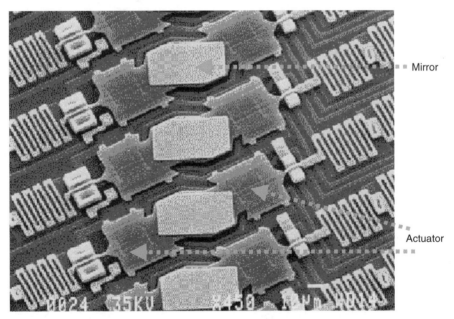

Figure 10.8 A microscope photograph of an array of micro-machined mirrors (magnified 450 times). (*Copyright © 1999. LUCENT Technologies. All rights reserved. Reprinted with permission.*)

angle; minor deviations in angle position may increase optical signal loss and increase cross-talk. Moreover, as a mirror changes position, the reflected light beam traverses the optical field of other output fibers, and thus caution should be taken so that the reflected beam is not coupled to these traversed output fibers. If it were, it could contribute to the bit error rate of the signal at that output fiber. Current designs have demonstrated negligible coupled optical power in traversed output fibers.

Figure 10.9 illustrates a conceptual application of MEMS when teamed with a grating to construct a space switch with channel drop capability (for add-drop capability see Problem 10.7).

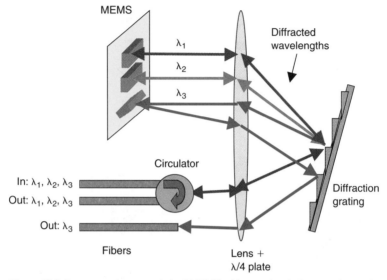

Figure 10.9 A conceptual space switch of MEMS with a grating (red arrows denote the switched channel).

10.7   SWITCHING SPEEDS

Currently, the speed of optical switching devices depends on the materials used to make the switch, the principle on which the switch operates, and on the design technology. Switching speeds vary from seconds to nanoseconds. As a note, although speed is an important parameter, there are many more parameters that one should consider in the selection of the switch type such as optical loss, dispersion, reliability, stability, switching-matrix size, external voltage (if any), temperature dependence, physical size, cost, and so on.

Switching speeds include

- Thermo-optic switching devices that are in the order of few milliseconds (~2 msec).

- Acousto-optic switching devices that are in the order of microseconds.

- Electro-optic ceramic-compound switching devices that are potentially in the order of microseconds.

- MEM switching devices that are in the order of microseconds.

- SiO_2 on Si planar devices that are in the order of milliseconds or microseconds.

- $LiNbO_3$ switching devices that are in the order of nanoseconds.

- Non-linear electro-optic devices, based on polymers such as amino-phenylene-isophorone-isoxazolone (APII), that are in the order of few picoseconds (these are still in the experimental phase).

EXERCISES

Consider the matrix relationship of Figure 10.6.

1. How many 1s can each row have?

2. What happens if a row has more than one 1?

3. How many 1s can each column have?

4. What happens if a column has more than one 1?

5. Under what circumstances could a row have more than one 1?

Consider the matrix relationship (ideal case) that describes a WDM Mach-Zehnder cross-connect.

6. Under what circumstances could a row have more than one 1?

7. What does it mean if a column has more than one 1?

8. From the various optical switches available, mention the fastest, one with medium speed and a slow one.

CHAPTER 11

OPTICAL ADD-DROP
MULTIPLEXERS

11.1 INTRODUCTION

Optical multiplexers are components specifically designed for wavelength division multiplexing (WDM) systems. The demultiplexer undoes what the multiplexer has done; it separates a multiplicity of wavelengths in a fiber and directs them to many fibers (Figure 11.1).

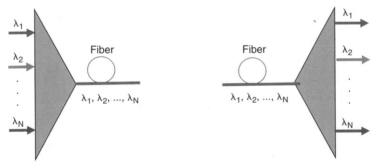

Figure 11.1 The main function of an optical multiplexer is to couple two or more wavelengths into the same fiber. The reverse takes place at a demultiplexer.

11.2 THE OADM FUNCTION

The main function of an optical multiplexer is to couple two or more wavelengths into the same fiber.

It is clear that if a demultiplexer is placed and properly aligned back-to-back with a multiplexer, then, there in the area between them the two individual wavelengths exist. This presents an opportunity for an enhanced function, one that could remove an individual wavelength and also insert an individual wavelength. Such a function would be called an *optical wavelength drop and add demultiplexer/multiplexer,* and for brevity, *optical add-drop multiplexer.* OADM is still evolving and although these components are relatively small, in the future, integration will play a key role in producing compact, monolithic and cost-effective devices.

11.3 OPTICAL ADD-DROP MULTIPLEXERS

The OADM selectively removes (drops) a wavelength from a multiplicity of wavelengths in a fiber, and thus traffic on this channel. It then adds in the same direction of data flow the same wavelength, but with different data content.

The model of an OADM, for wavelength λ_1, is schematically shown in Figure 11.2, where F_1 signifies a filter selecting wavelength λ_1 while passing through all other wavelengths, and M_1 signifies a multiplexer that multiplexes all wavelengths.

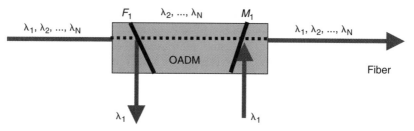

Figure 11.2 The Optical Add-Drop Multiplexer is a DWDM function.

A better view of OADM function is shown in Figure 11.3. This function is especially used in WDM ring systems as well as in long-haul with drop-add features. A possible structure of the optical add-drop function using an optical 2×2 switch is illustrated (for one wavelength) in Figure 11.4. More optical switches may be added between demultiplexer and multiplexer to support more drop-add wavelengths.

OADMs are classified as *fixed* wavelength and as *dynamically* wavelength selectable OADMs. In fixed wavelength OADM, the wavelength has been selected and remains the same until human intervention changes it. In dynamically selectable wavelength OADM, the wavelengths between the optical demultiplexer/multiplexer may be dynamically directed from the outputs of the demultiplexer to any of the inputs of the multiplexer. This may be accomplished for example with an array of micro-mirrors (see Section 10.6, Figure 10.9).

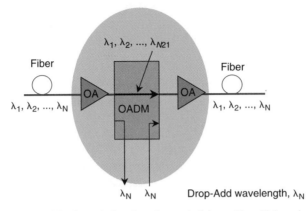

Figure 11.3 The main function of an optical drop-add multiplexer is to selectively remove a wavelength and add the same wavelength in the fiber (OAs are optional).

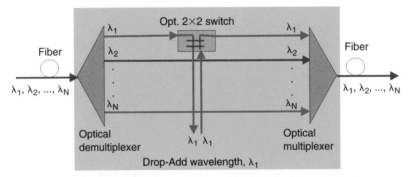

Figure 11.4 The main function of an optical drop-add multiplexer is to selectively remove a wavelength and add the same wavelength in the fiber.

EXERCISES

1. What is the main function of an optical multiplexer?
2. Could a passive optical demultiplexer be used as a multiplexer? If yes, why?
3. Name two popular demultiplexers.
4. A fiber transports a bundle of wavelengths. However, a specific wavelength needs to be dropped off at a node, whereas the remaining continue their travel in the fiber. Is this possible? If no, why? If yes, how?
5. Could a 2 × 2 optical switch be used as an OADM?
6. If a single wavelength can be dropped off and added, could more than one wavelength be dropped off and added? If no, why? If yes, how?
7. The diagram of Figure 10.9 (Chapter 10) illustrates a switch with drop capability only. What would it take to make it a space switch with add and drop capability?

REFERENCES

[1] L. Desmarais, *Applied Electro-Optics*, Prentice-Hall, 1999.

[2] R. Ramaswami, and K.N. Sivarajan, *Optical Networks*, Morgan Kaufmann Publ., San Francisco, CA, 1998.

[3] B. Mukherjee, *Optical Communication Networks*, McGraw-Hill, 1997.

[4] I.P. Kaminow, ed., and T.L. Koch, ed., *Optical Fiber Communications IIIA* and *Optical Fiber Communications IIIB*, Academic Press, 1997.

[5] J.C. Palais, *Fiber Optic Communications*, 3rd ed., Prentice-Hall, Englewood Cliffs, N.J., 1992.

[6] M.H. Freeman, *Optics*, 10th edition, Butterworths, London, 1990.

[7] W.H.A. Fincham, and M.H. Freeman, *Optics*, Butterworths, London, 1974.

[8] E.B. Brown, *Modern Optics*, Reinhold Publishing Co., New York, 1965.

[9] R.G. Hunsperger, *Integrated Optics: Theory and Technology*, Springer-Verlag, New York, 1984.

[10] S. Sudo, ed., *Optical Fiber Amplifiers: Materials, Devices, and Applications*, Artec House, Boston, 1997.

[11] K. Nassau, *The Physics and Chemistry of Color*, J. Wiley & Sons, New York, 1983.

[12] J. Hecht, *The Laser Guidebook*, 2nd ed., Tab Books, Blue Ridge Summit, PA, 1992.

[13] T. Wildi, *Units and Conversion Charts*, 2nd ed., IEEE Press, New York, 1995.

[14] D.P. Jablonowski, U.C. Paek, and L.S. Watkins, "Optical Fiber Manufacturing Techniques," *AT&T Technical Journal*, vol. 66, issue 1, Jan–Feb 1987, pp. 33–44.

[15] W.M. Flegal et al., "Making Single-Mode Preforms by the MCVD Process," *AT&T Technical Journal*, vol. 65, issue 1, Jan–Feb 1986, pp. 56–61.

[16] J.B. MacChesney, P.B. O'Connor, and H.M. Presby, "A New Technique for the Preparation of Low Los and Graded Index Optical Fibers," *Proceedings of IEEE*, vol. 62, 1974, pp. 1278–1279.

[17] D. Kalish, and L.G. Cohen, "Single-Mode Fiber: From Research and Development to Manufacturing," *AT&T Technical Journal*, vol. 66, issue 1, Jan–Feb 1987, pp. 19–32.

[18] J.E. Clements, T.I. Ejim, W.A. Gault, and E.M. Monberg, "Bulk III-V Compound Semi-conductor crystal growth," *AT&T Technical Journal*, vol. 68, no. 1, 1989, pp. 29–42.

[19] W.D. Johnston, Jr., M.A. DiGiuseppe, and D.P. Wilt, "Liquid and Vapor Phase Growth of III-V Materials for Photonic Devices," *AT&T Technical Journal*, vol. 68, no. 1, 1989, pp. 53–63.

[20] Dutta N.K., "III-V Device Technologies for Lightwave Applications," *AT&T Technical Journal*, vol. 68, no. 1, 1989, pp. 5–18.

[21] D.S. Alles, and K.J. Brady, "Packaging Technology for III-V Photonic Devices and Integrated Circuits," *AT&T Technical Journal*, vol. 68, no. 1, 1989, pp. 83–92.

[22] J.J. Refi, "Optical Fibers for Optical Networking," *Bell Labs Technical Journal*, vol. 4, no. 1, 1999, pp. 246–261.

[23] R.J. Mears, L. Reekie, I.M. Jauncey, and D.N. Payne, "Low-Noise Erbium-Doped Fiber Amplifier Operating at 1.54 µm," *Elect. Lett.*, vol. 23, no. 19, Sept. 1987, pp. 1026–1028.

[24] E. Desurvire, J.R. Simpson, and P.C. Becker, "High-Gain Erbium-Doped Traveling-Wave Fiber Amplifiers," *Optics Lett.*, vol. 12, no. 11, Nov. 1987, pp. 888–890.

[25] K-W Cheung, "Acoustooptic Tunable Filters in Narrowband WDM Networks: System Issues and Network Applications," *IEEE JSAC*, vol. 8, no. 6, August 1990, pp. 1015–1025.

[26] D.A. Smith, J.E. Baran, J.J. Johnson, and K-W Cheung, "Integrated-Optic Acoustically-Tunable Filters for WDM Networks," *IEEE JSAC*, vol. 8, no. 6, August 1990, pp. 1151–1159.

[27] S.R. Mallison, "Wavelength-selective filters for single-mode fiber WDM systems using Fabry-Perot interferometers," *Appl. Optics*, vol. 26, 1987, pp. 430–436.

[28] N. Goto, and Y. Miyazaki, "Integrated Optical Multi-/Demultiplexer Using Acoustooptic Effect for Multiwavelength Optical Communications," *IEEE JSAC*, vol. 8, no. 6, August 1990, pp. 1160–1168.

[29] N. Takato, et al., "Silica-Based Integrated Optic Mach-Zehnder Multi/Demultiplexer Family with Channel Spacing of 0.01-250 nm," *IEEE JSAC*, vol. 8, no. 6, August 1990, pp. 1120–1127

[30] R.C. Alferness, "Waveguide Electro-Optic Modulators," *IEEE Trans. Microwave Theory and Techniques*, MTT-30, 1982, pp. 1121–1137.

[31] R.C. Alferness, "Guided-Wave Devices for Optical Communication," *IEEE J. Quant. Electron.*, QE-17, 1981, pp. 946–949.

[32] R.C. Alferness, and L.L. Buhl, "Low-cross-talk waveguide polarization multiplexer/demultiplexer for $\lambda = 1.32$ μm," *Optics Lett.*, vol. 10, 1984, pp. 140–142.

[33] T.K. Findakly, "Glass Waveguides by Ion Exchange: A Review," *Optical Engineering*, vol. 24, 1985, pp. 244–255.

[34] W. Warzanskyj, F. Heisman, and R.C. Alferness, "Polarization-independent electro-acoustically tunable narrow-band wavelength filter," *Appl. Phys. Lett.*, vol. 56, 1990, pp. 209–211.

[35] J. Frangen, et al., "Integrated optical, acoustically-tunable wavelength filter," *Proc. 6th European Conf. Integrated Opt.*, Paris, SPIE, 1989, post-deadline paper.

[36] F. Heismann, L. Buhl, and R.C. Alferness, "Electrooptically tunable narrowband Ti:LiNbO3 wavelength filter," *Electron. Lett.*, vol. 23, 1987, pp. 572–573.

[37] F. Ouellette, "All-fiber for efficient dispersion compensation," *Optics Letters*, vol. 16, no. 5, March 1991, pp. 303–304.

[38] R.M. Measures, A.T. Alavie, M. LeBlanc, S. Huang, M. Ohn, R. Masskant, D. Graham, "Controlled grating chirp for variable optical dispersion compensation," Proceedings of the 13th Annual Conference on European Fiber Optic Communications and Networks, Brighton, England, 1995, pp. 38–41.

[39] G.D. Boyd, and F. Heismann, "Tunable acoustooptic reflection filters in LiNbO3 without a Doppler shift," *J. Lightwave Technol.*, vol. 7, Apr. 1989, pp. 625–631.

[40] L.G. Kazovsky, "Optical Signal Processing for Lightwave Communications Networks," *IEEE JSAC*, vol. 8, no. 6, August 1990, pp. 973–982.

[41] S.E. Miller, "Coupled-wave theory and waveguide applications," *Bell System Technical Journal*, vol. 33, 1954, pp. 661–719.

[42] A. Yariv, "Coupled mode theory for guided wave optics," *IEEE J. Quantum Electron.*, vol. QE-9, 1973, pp. 919–933.

[43] D. Sadot, and E. Boimovich, "Tunable Optical Filters for Dense WDM Networks," *IEEE Communications Mag.*, vol. 36, no. 12, Nov. 1998, pp. 50–55.

[44] M. Zirngibl, "Multifrequency Lasers and Applications in WDM Networks," *IEEE Communications Mag.*, vol. 36, no. 12, Nov. 1998, pp. 39–41.

[45] S.D. Personick, "Receiver Design for Digital Fiber Optic Communication Systems, I," *Bell Systems Technical Journal*, vol. 52, no. 6, 1973, pp. 843–874.

[46] S.D. Personick, "Receiver Design for Digital Fiber Optic Communication Systems, II," *Bell Systems Technical Journal*, vol. 52, no. 6, 1973, pp. 875–886.

[47] F. Tong, "Multiwavelength Receivers for WDM Systems," *IEEE Communications Mag.*, vol. 36, no. 12, Nov. 1998, pp. 42–49.

[48] K.A. McGreer, "Arrayed Waveguide Grating for Wavelength Routing," *IEEE Communications Mag.*, vol. 36, no. 12, Nov. 1998, pp. 62–68.

[49] A. Iocco, H.G. Limberger, and R.P. Salathe, "Bragg grating fast tunable filter," *Electr. Lett.*, vol. 33, no. 25, Dec. 1997, pp. 2147–2148.

[50] M.K. Smit, and C. van Dam, "PHASAR-based WDM-devices: principles, design and application," *IEEE J. Sel. Topics Quantum Electr.*, vol. 2, no. 2, 1996, pp. 236–250.

[51] H. Tanobe, et al., "Temperature insensitive arrayed waveguide gratings on InP substrate," *IEEE Photon Technol. Lett.*, vol. 10, no. 2, 1998, pp. 235–237.

[52] D. Nesset, T. Kelly, and D. Marcenac, "All-Optical Wavelength Conversion Using SOA Nonlinearities," *IEEE Comm. Mag.*, vol. 36, no. 12, Nov. 1998, pp. 56–61.

[53] J.M. Senior, and S.D. Cusworth, "Devices for wavelength multiplexing and demultiplexing," *Proceedings of IEEE*, vol. 136, no. 3, June 1989, pp. 183–202.

[54] Y.K. Chen, and C.C. Lee, "Fiber Bragg Grating-Based Large Nonblocking Multiwavelength Cross-Connects," *J. Lightwave Techn.*, vol. 16, no. 10, 1998, pp. 1746–1756.

[55] C.R. Doerr, "Proposed WDM Cross Connect Using a Planar Arrangement of Waveguide Grating Routers and Phase Shifts," *IEEE Photon. Technol. Lett.*, vol. 10, April 1998, pp. 528–530.

[56] J.E. Ford, V.A. Aksyuk, D.J. Bishop, and J.A. Walker, "Wavelength Add/Drop Switching Using Tilting Micromirrors," *J. Lightwave Technol.*, vol. 17, no. 5, May 1999, pp. 904–911.

[57] J.R. Thompson, and R. Roy, "Multiple four-wave mixing process in an optical fiber," *Optics Letters*, vol. 16, no. 8, April 1991, pp. 557–559.

[58] K. Inoue, "Experimental Study on Channel Crosstalk Due to Fiber Four-Wave Mixing Around the Zero-Dispersion Wavelength," *IEEE J. Lightwave Technology*, vol. LT-12, no. 6, June 1994, pp. 1023–1028.

[59] C.A. Brackett, "Dense Wavelength Division Multiplexing Networks: Principles and Applications," *IEEE JSAC*, vol. 8, no. 6, Aug. 1990, pp. 948–964.

[60] C.R. Giles, and M. Spector, "The Wavelength Add/Drop Multiplexer for Lightwave Communication Networks," *Bell Labs Technical Journal*, vol. 4, no. 1, 1999, pp. 207–229.

[61] U. Koren, et al., "Wavelength division multiplexing light sources with integrated quantum well tunable lasers and optical amplification," *Appl. Phys. Lett.*, vol. 54, 1989, pp. 2056–2058.

[62] G. Coquin, K.W. Cheung, and M. Choy, "Single- and multiple-wavelength operation of acousto-optically tuned lasers at 1.3 microns," *Proc. 11th IEEE Int. Semiconductor Laser Conf.*, Boston, MA, 1988, pp. 130–131.

[63] H. Kobrinski, and K.W. Cheung, "Wavelength-tunable optical filters: Applications and technologies," *IEEE Commun. Mag.*, vol. 27, Oct. 1989, pp. 53–63.

[64] S. Suzuki, et al., "A photonic wavelength-division switching system using tunable laser diode filters," *ICC'89 Conference Records*, Boston, MA, 1989, paper 23.1.

[65] C. Dragone, "Efficient NXN star couplers using Fourier optics," *J. Lightwave Technol.*, vol. 7, 1989, pp. 479–489.

[66] C.M. Ragdale, D. Reid, D.J. Robbins, and J. Buus, "Narrowband Fiber Grating Filters," *IEEE JSAC*, vol. 8, no. 6, Aug. 1990, pp. 1146–1150.

[67] Y. Sun, A.K. Srivastava, J. Zhou, and J.W. Sulhoff, "Optical Fiber Amplifiers for WDM Optical Networks," *Bell Labs Technical Journal*, vol. 4, no. 1, 1999, pp. 187–206.

[68] M.J. Adams, "Theory of twin-guide Fabry-Perot laser amplifiers," *Proceedings of IEEE*, vol. 136, no. 5, Oct. 1989, pp. 287–292.

[69] G.J. Cannell, A. Robertson, and R. Worthington, "Practical Realization of a High Density Diode-Coupled Wavelength Demultiplexer," *IEEE JSAC*, vol. 8, no. 6, Aug. 1990, pp. 1141–1145.

[70] A.J. Lowery, "Computer-aided photonics design," *IEEE Spectrum*, vol. 34, no. 4, April 1997, pp. 26–31.

[71] K.S. Giboney, L.A. Aronson, and B.E. Lemoff, "The ideal light source for datanets," *IEEE Spectrum*, vol. 35, no. 2, Febr. 1998, pp. 43–53.

[72] M-C. Amann, and W. Thulke, "Continuously Tunable Laser Diodes: Longitudinal versus Transverse Tuning Scheme," *IEEE JSAC*, vol. 8, no. 6, Aug. 1990, pp. 1169–1177.

[73] K. Kobayashi, and I. Mito, "Single frequency and tunable laser diodes," *J. Lightwave Technol.*, vol. 6, Nov. 1988, pp. 1623–1633.

[74] L.A. Coldren, and S.W. Corzine, "Continuously tunable single frequency semiconductor lasers," *IEEE J. Quantum Electron.*, vol. QE-23, June 1987, pp. 903–908.

[75] M. Okuda, and K. Onaka, "Tunability of distributed Bragg reflector laser by modulating refractive index in corrugated waveguide," *Japan J. Appl. Phys.*, vol. 16, 1977, pp. 1501–1502.

[76] Y. Kotaki, M. Matsuda, H. Ishikawa, and H. Imai, "Tunable DBR laser with wide tuning range," *Electron. Lett.*, vol. 24, Apr. 1988, pp. 503–505.

[77] H.A. Haus, *Waves and Fields in Optoelectronics*, Prentice-Hall, Englewood Cliffs, N.J., 1984.

[78] S. Adachi, "Refractive indices of III-IV compounds: Key properties of InGaAsP relevant to device design," *J. Appl. Phys.*, vol. 53, 1982, pp. 5863–5869.

[79] J. Stone, and D. Marcuse, "Ultrahigh finesse fiber Fabry-Perot interferometers", *J. Lightwave Technol.*, vol. LT-4, no. 4, Apr. 1986, pp. 382–385.

[80] A.A.M. Saleh, and J. Stone, "Two-stage Fabry-Perot filters as demultiplexers in optical FDMA LAN's," *J. Lightwave Technol.*, vol. LT-7, 1989, pp. 323–330.

[81] S.R. Mallinson, "Wavelength selective filters for single-mode fiber WDM systems using Fabry-Perot interferometers," *Appl. Optics*, vol. 26, 1987, pp. 430–436.

[82] A.M. Hill, and D.B. Payne, "Linear crosstalk in wavelength division multiplexed optical fiber transmission systems," *J. Lightwave Technol.*, vol. LT-3, 1985, pp. 643–651.

[83] G. Hernandez, *Fabry-Perot Interferometers*, Cambridge University Press, Cambridge, 1986.

[84] F.J. Leonberger, "Applications of Guided-Wave Interferometers," *Laser Focus*, March 1982, pp. 125–129.

[85] H. Van de Stadt, and J.M. Muller, "Multimirror Fabry-Perot interferometers," *J. Opt. Soc. Amer. A*, vol. 2, 1985, pp. 1363–1370.

[86] P.A. Humblet, and W.M. Hamdy, "Crosstalk Analysis and Filter Optimization of Single- and Double-Cavity Fabry-Perot Filters," *IEEE JSAC*, vol. 8, no. 6, Aug. 1990, pp. 1095–1107.

[87] K.Y. Eng, M.A. Santoro, T.L. Koch, J. Stone, and W.W. Snell, "Star-Coupler-Based Optical Cross-Connect Switch Experiments with Tunable Receivers," *IEEE JSAC*, vol. 8, no. 6, Aug. 1990, pp. 1026–1031.

[88] H. Toba, K. Oda, K. Nosu, and N. Takato, "Factors Affecting the Design of Optical FDM Information Distribution Systems", *IEEE JSAC*, vol. 8, no. 6, Aug. 1990, pp. 965–972.

[89] Onaka, H., et al., "1.1 Tb/s WDM Transmission Over a 150 Km 1.3 Zero-Dispersion Single-Mode Fiber," OFC'96, San Jose, CA, Feb. 1996, pp. PD19:1–5.

[90] A.R. Chraplyvy, "Optical Power Limits in Multi-Channel Wavelength-Division-Multiplexed System due to Stimulated Raman Scattering," *Electron. Lett.*, vol. 20, no. 2, Jan. 1984, pp. 58–59.

[91] K. Inoue, "Four-Wave Mixing in an Optical Fiber in the Zero-Dispersion Wavelength Region," *IEEE J. Lightwave Technology*, vol. LT-10, no. 11, Nov. 1992, pp. 1553–1563.

[92] K. Inoue, "Suppression of Fiber Four-Wave Mixing in Multichannel Transmission Using Birefringent Elements," *IEICE Trans. Comm.*, vol. E76-B, no. 9, Sept. 1993, pp. 1219–1221.

[93] K. Nosu, *Optical FDM Network Technologies*, Artec House, Boston, 1997.

[94] M. Cvijetic, *Coherent and Nonlinear Lightwave Communications*, Artec House, Boston, 1996.

[95] H. Toba, and K. Nosu, "Optical Frequency Division Multiplexing System-Review of Key Technologies and Applications," *IEICE Trans. Comm.*, vol. E75-B, no. 4, Apr. 1992, pp. 243–255.

[96] D. Cotter, "Stimulated Brillouin Scattering in Monomode Optical Fiber," *J. Opt. Comm.*, vol. 4, 1983, pp. 10–16.

[97] P.S. Henry, "Lightwave Primer," *IEEE J. Quantum Electron.*, vol. QE-21, 1985, pp. 1862–1879.

[98] M. Kawasaki, "Silica Waveguides on Silicon and Their Application to Integrated Optic Components," *Opt. Quantum Electron.*, vol. 22, 1990, pp. 391–416.

[99] L. Kazovsky, S. Benedetto, and A. Willner, "Optical Fiber Communication Systems," Artec, Boston, 1996.

[100] N.A. Jackman, S.H. Patel, B.P. Mikkelsen, and S.K. Korotky, "Optical Cross Connect for Optical Networking," *Bell Labs Technical Journal*, vol. 4, no. 1, 1999, pp. 262–281.

[101] H. Takahashi, et al., "Arrayed-Waveguide Grating for Wavelength Division Multiplexing/Demultiplexing with Nanometer Resolution," *Electron. Lett.*, vol. 26, 1990, pp. 87–88.

[102] J. Minowa, and Y. Fujii, "Dielectric Multilayer Thin Film Filters for WDM Transmission," *IEEE J. of Lightwave Technology*, vol. 1, no. 1, 1983, pp. 116–121.

[103] W.K. Chen, *Passive and Active Filters*, John Wiley and Sons, New York, 1986.

[104] R. Watanabe, et al., "Optical Multi/Demultiplexers for Single-Mode Fiber Transmission," *IEEE J. of Quantum Electronics*, vol. 17, no. 6, 1981, pp. 974–951.

[105] Y. Hibino, et al., "High Reliability Silica Based PLC 1X8 Splitters on Si," *Electron. Lett.*, vol. 30, no. 8, 1994, pp. 640–641.

[106] K. Kato, et al., "Packaging of Large-Scale Integrated Optic NXN Star Couplers," *IEEE Photon. Technol. Lett.*, vol. 4, no. 33, 1993, pp. 348–351.

[107] A. Hasegawa, and Y. Kodama, "Signal Transmission by Optical Solitons in Monomode Fiber," *IRE Proc.*, vol. 69, 1981, pp. 1145–1150.

[108] R. Bullough, and P.J. Caudrey, *Solitons*, Springer-Verlag, Berlin, 1980.

[109] N. Doran, and K. Blow, "Solitons in Optical Communications," *IEEE J. Quantum Electron.*, vol. QE-19, 1983, pp. 1883–1888.

[110] L.F. Mollenauer, et al., "Experimental Observation of Picosecond Pulse Narrowing and Solitons in Optical Fibers," *Phys. Rev. Lett.*, vol. 45, 1980, pp. 1095–1096.

[111] J.P. Gordon, "Theory of Soliton Self-Frequency Shift," *Optics Lett.*, vol. 11, 1986, pp. 855–858.

[112] H. Rokugawa, et al., "Wavelength Conversion Laser Diodes Application to Wavelength-Division Photonic Cross-Connect Node with Multistage Configuration," *IEICE Trans. Comm.*, vol. E-75-B, no. 4, 1992, pp. 267–273.

[113] O. Ishida and H. Toba, "A 1.55-mm Lightwave Frequency Synthesizer," *IEICE Trans. Comm.*, vol. E75-B, no. 4, 1992, pp. 275–280.

[114] K. Vilhelmsson, "Simultaneous Forward and Backward Raman Scattering in Low-Attenuation Single-Mode Fibers," *J. Lightwave Techn.*, vol. LT-4, no. 4, 1986, pp. 400–404.

[115] H. Kobrinski, and K-W. Cheung, "Wavelength-Tunable Optical Filters: Applications and Technologies," *IEEE Comm. Mag.*, Oct. 1989, pp. 53–63.

[116] R. Tewari, and K. Thyagarajan, "Analysis of Tunable Single-Mode Fiber Directional Couplers Using Simple and Accurate Relations," *J. Lightwave Techn.*, vol. LT-4, no. 4, 1986, pp. 386–399.

[117] N. Kashima, *Passive Optical Components for Optical Fiber Transmission*, Artec, Boston, 1995.

[118] S. Kawakami, "Light Propagation Along Periodic Metal-Dielectric Layers," *Appl. Opt.*, vol. 22, 1983, p. 2426.

[119] K. Shiraishi, S. Sugayama, K. Baba, and S. Kawakami, "Microisolator," *Appl. Opt.*, vol. 25, 1986, p. 311.

[120] K. Shiraishi, S. Sugayama, and S. Kawakami, "Fiber Faraday Rotator," *Appl. Opt.*, vol. 23, 1984, p. 1103.

[121] W. Eickhoff, "In-Line Fiber-Optic Polarizer," *Electron. Lett.*, vol. 6, 1980, p. 762.

[122] T. Hosaka, H. Okamoto, and J. Noda, "Single-Mode Fiber Type Polarizer," *IEEE J. Quantum Electron.*, vol. QE-18, 1982, p. 1569.

[123] R.A. Bergh, H.C. Lefevre, and H.J. Shaw, "Single-Mode Fiber-Optic Polarizer," *Opt. Lett.*, vol. 5, 1980, p. 479.

[124] J.C. Palais, *Fiber Optic Communications*, 3rd ed., Prentice-Hall, Englewood Cliffs, N.J. 1992.

[125] M. Francon, *Optique: formation et traitment des images*, Macon & Cie, Paris, 1972.

[126] T.G. Robertazzi, ed., *Performance Evaluation of High Speed Switching Fabrics and Networks*, IEEE Press, New York, 1993.

[127] Y. Pan, C. Qiao, and Y. Yang, "Optical Multistage Interconnection Networks: New Challenges and Approaches," *IEEE Communications Magazine*, vol. 37, no. 2, Feb. 1999, pp. 50–56.

[128] J.G. Eden, "Photochemical Processing of Semiconductors: New Applications for Visible and Ultraviolet Lasers," *IEEE Circuits and Devices Magazine*, vol. 2, no. 1, Jan. 1986, pp. 18–24.

[129] R.J. von Gutfeld, "Laser-Enhanced Plating and Etching for Microelectronic Applications," *IEEE Circuits and Devices Magazine*, vol. 2, no. 1, Jan. 1986, pp. 57–60.

[130] J. Bokor, A.R. Neureuther, and W.G. Oldham, "Advanced Lithography for ULSI," *IEEE Circuits and Devices Magazine*, vol. 12, no. 1, Jan. 1996, pp. 11–15.

[131] A. Yariv, "Quantum Well Semiconductor Lasers Are Taking Over," *IEEE Circuits and Devices Magazine*, vol. 5, no. 6, Nov. 1989, pp. 25–28.

[132] J. LaCourse, "Laser Primer for Fiber-Optics Users," *IEEE Circuits and Devices Magazine*, vol. 8, no. 2, March 1992, pp. 27–32.

[133] D. Botez, and L.J. Mawst, "Phase-locked Laser Arrays Revisited," *IEEE Circuits and Devices Magazine*, vol. 12, no. 11, Nov. 1996, pp. 25–32.

[134] Z.V. Nesterova, and I.V. Aleksaandrov, "Optical-fiber sources of coherent light," *Sov. J. Opt. Technol.*, vol. 54, no. 3, March 1987, pp. 183–190.

[135] T. Komukai, et al., "Upconversion Pumped Thulium-Doped Fluoride Fiber Amplifier and Laser Operating at 1.47 µm," *IEEE Quantum Electr.*, vol. 31, 1995, pp. 1880–89.

[136] G. Eisenstein, "Semiconductor Optical Amplifiers," *IEEE Circuits and Devices Magazine*, vol. 5, no. 4, July 1989, pp. 25–30.

[137] C.F. Buhrer, "Four waveplate dual tuner for birefringent filters and multiplexers," *Applied Optics*, vol. 26, no. 17, Sept. 1987, pp. 3628–3632.

[138] J.W. Evans, "The Birefringent Filter," *J. Opt. Soc. Am.*, vol. 39, 1949, p. 229.

[139] H. Hinton, *An Introduction to Photonic Switching Fabrics*, Plenum, 1993.

[140] C. Tocci, and H.J. Caufield, *Optical Interconnection—Foundations and Applications*, Artec, 1994.

[141] A. Budman, et al., "Multi-gigabit optical packet switch for self-routing networks with subcarrier addressing," *Proc. OFC'92*, paper Tu04, San Jose, CA, Feb. 1992.

[142] C-K. Chan, L-K. Chen, and K-W. Cheung, "A Fast Channel-Tunable Optical Transmitter for Ultrahigh-Speed All-Optical Time-Division Multi-access Network," *IEEE JSAC*, vol. 14, no. 5, June 1996, pp. 1052-56.

[143] K. Padmanabhan, and A.N. Netravali, "Dilated networks for photonic switching," *IEEE Trans. Communications*, vol. 35, no. 12, Dec. 1987, pp. 1357–65.

[144] C. Qiao et al., "A time domain approach for avoiding crosstalk in optical blocking multistage interconnection networks," *J. Lightwave Techn.*, vol. 12, no. 10, Oct. 1994, pp. 1854–62.

[145] R.A. Thompson, "The dilated slipped banyan switching network architecture for use in an all-optical local-area network," *J. Lightwave Techn.*, vol. 9, no. 12, Dec. 1991, pp. 1780–87.

[146] D. Hunter and D. Smith, "New architecture for optical TDM switching," *J. Lightwave Techn.*, vol. 11, no. 3, Mar. 1993, pp. 495–511.

[147] E. Nussbaum, "Communication Network Needs and Technologies—A Place for Photonic Switching," *IEEE JSAC*, vol. 6, no. 7, August 1988, pp. 1036–1043.

[148] S.A. Cassidy, and P. Yennadhiou, "Optimum Switching Architectures Using D-Fiber Optical Space Switches," *IEEE JSAC*, vol. 6, no. 7. August 1988, pp. 1044–1051.

[149] C.J. Smith, "Nonblocking Photonic Switch Networks," *IEEE JSAC*, vol. 6, no. 7, August 1988, pp. 1052–1062.

[150] J.D. Evankow, Jr., and R.A. Thompson, "Photonic Switching Modules Designed with Laser Diode Amplifiers," *IEEE JSAC*, vol. 6, no. 7, August 1988, pp. 1087–1095.

[151] W.D. Johnston, Jr., M.A. DiGiuseppe, and D.P. Wilt, "Liquid and Vapor Phase Growth of III-V Materials for Photonic Devices," *AT&T Techn. J.*, vol. 68, no. 1, Jan./Feb. 1989, pp. 53–63.

[152] W.G. Dautremont-Smith, R.J. McCoy, and R.H. Burton, "Fabrication Technologies for III-V Compound Semiconductor Photonic and Electronic Devices," *AT&T Techn. J.*, vol. 68, no. 1, Jan./Feb. 1989, pp. 64–82.

[153] N.K. Dutta, "III-V Device Technologies for Lightwave Applications," *AT&T Techn. J.*, vol. 68, no. 1, Jan/Feb 1989, pp. 5–18.

[154] K.Y. Eng., "A Photonic Knockout Switch for High-Speed Packet Networks," *IEEE JSAC*, vol. 6, no. 7, August 1988, pp. 1107–1116.

[155] R.C. Alferness, "Waveguide Electrooptic Switch Arrays," *IEEE JSAC*, vol. 6, no. 7, August 1988, pp. 1117–1130.

[156] T. Ikegami, and H. Kawaguchi, "Semiconductor Devices in Photonic Switching," *IEEE JSAC*, vol. 6, no. 7, August 1988, pp. 1131–1140.

[157] R.I. Macdonald, "Terminology for Photonic Matrix Switches," *IEEE JSAC*, vol. 6, no. 7, August 1988, pp. 1141–1151.

[158] J.V. Wright, S.R. Mallinson, and C.A. Millar, "A Fiber-Based Crosspoint Switch Using High-Refractive Index Interlay Materials," *IEEE JSAC*, vol. 6, no. 7, August 1988, pp. 1160–1168.

[159] J. Skinner, and C.H.R. Lane, "A Low-Crosstalk Microoptic Liquid Crystal Switch," *IEEE JSAC*, vol. 6, no. 7, August 1988, pp. 1178–1185.

[160] T. Morioka, and M. Saruwatari, "Ultrafast All-Optical Switching Utilizing the Optical Kerr Effect in Polarization-Maintaining Single-Mode Fibers," *IEEE JSAC*, vol. 6, no. 7, August 1988, pp. 1186–1198.

[161] H.S. Hinton, "Architectural Considerations for Photonic Switching Networks," *IEEE JSAC*, vol. 6, no. 7, August 1988, pp. 1209–1226.

[162] H. Inoue, H. Nakamura, K. Morosawa, Y. Sasaki, T. Katsuyama, and N. Chinone, "An 8 mm Length Nonblocking 4 × 4 Optical Switch Array," *IEEE JSAC*, vol. 6, no. 7, August 1988, pp. 1262–1266.

[163] R. Driggers, P. Cox, and T. Edwards, *An Introduction to Infrared and Electro-Optical Systems*, Artech House, 1999.

[164] R. Marz, *Integrated Optics: Design and Modeling*, Artech House, 1995.

[165] J. Hecht, *Understanding Fiber Optics*, Prentice-Hall, 1999.

[166] S.V. Kartalopoulos, "A Plateau of Performance?", Guest Editorial, *IEEE Communications Mag.*, Sept. 1992, pp. 13–14.

[167] J. Nellist, "Understanding Telecommunications and Lightwave Systems," IEEE Press, 1996.

[168] W.Y. Zhou, and Y. Wu, "COFDM: An Overview," *IEEE Trans., Broadcasting*, vol. 41, no. 1, Mar. 1995, pp. 1–8.

[169] D.J. Bishop, and V.A. Aksyuk, "Optical MEMS Answer High-Speed Networking Requirements," *Electronic Design*, April 5, 1999, pp. 85–92.

[170] R. Tewari, and K. Thyagarajan, "Analysis of Tunable Single-Mode Fiber Directional Couplers Using Simple and Accurate Relations," *IEEE J. of Lightwave Technology*, vol. LT-4, no. 4, April 1986, pp. 386–390.

[171] N.A. Olsson, and J. Hegarty, "Noise Properties of a Raman Amplifier," *IEEE J. of Lightwave Technology*, vol. LT-4, no. 4, April 1986, pp. 396–399.

[172] N. Shibata, K. Nosu, K. Iwashita, and Y. Azuma, "Transmission Limitations Due to Fiber Nonlinearities in Optical FDM Systems," *IEEE J. on Selected Areas in Communications*, vol. 8, no. 6, August 1990, pp. 1068–1077.

STANDARDS

1. ANSI/IEEE 812-1984, "Definition of Terms Relating to Fiber Optics."

2. Bellcore, TR-NWT-233, "Digital Cross Connect System," November 1992.

3. Bellcore, TR-NWT-917, "Regenerator," October 1990.

4. ITU-T Recommendation G.650, "Definition and test methods for the relevant parameters of single-mode fibres," 1996.

5. ITU-T Recommendation G.652 version 4, "Characteristics of a single-mode optical fiber cable," April 1997.

6. ITU-T Recommendation G.653 version 4, "Characteristics of a dispersion-shifted single-mode optical fiber cable," April 1997.

7. ITU-T Recommendation G.655 version 10, "Characteristics of a non-zero dispersion-shifted single-mode optical fiber cable," October 1996.

8. ITU-T Recommendation G.661, "Definition and test methods for the relevant generic parameters of optical fiber amplifiers," November 1996.

9. ITU-T Recommendation G.662, "Generic characteristics of optical fiber amplifier devices and sub-systems," July 1995.

10. ITU-T Recommendation G.663, "Application related aspects of optical fiber amplifier devices and sub-systems," July 1995.

11. ITU-T Recommendation G.671, "Transmission characteristics of passive optical components," November 1996.

12. http://www.itu.int/ITU-T/index.html

OTHER SOURCES

The above references represent a short sample of publications. The interested reader may consult additional sources published by major institutes and societies in communications and in optics, in conference proceedings (OFC, SPIE, ICC, Globecom, etc.), workshop proceedings, and books. There is a vast number of sources so it is impossible to mention each one. In addition, there are courses offered by colleges as part of their continuing education program, as well as by independent educational institutions and companies.

PART III
CODING OPTICAL
INFORMATION

An optical source is a requirement for generating optical data to be transported over a fiber. The source is modulated by the data signal (see 6.14 modulators) so that when the modulated light impinges onto the receiver's photodetector, the original data is recreated. The modulation method in optical communications is very important, as it plays a key role in the signal power that is coupled into the fiber, in the reduction of non-linearity contributions (e.g., four-wave mixing, etc.), in the reduction of the overall signal-to-noise ratio, and increasing the reliability of signal detection.

Detection techniques *heterodyne* and *homodyne* that were developed for radio transmission, known as *coherent*, are also used in optical transmission. However, in optical transmission, the term "coherent" indicates that another light source is used as the local oscillator at the receiver.

In the case of digital communications systems, the phase, frequency, or amplitude of a carrier signal may be modulated. When the phase is modulated, the method is called *phase-shift keying* (PSK); when the frequency is modulated, it is called *frequency-shift keying* (FSK); when the amplitude is modulated, it is called *amplitude-shift keying* (ASK). Each modulation method has its own advantages and disadvantages. Another method by which the intensity of a light source is modulated and also detected by a photodetector is known as *intensity modulation with direct detection* (IM/DD).

The modulation technique plays an important role in the performance of fiber transmission. For example, coherent techniques improve receiver sensitivity by ~20 dB and thus longer fibers may be used (an additional 100 km at 1.55 μm). In dense wavelength division multiplexing (DWDM) systems, where many channels are used in the same fiber, the channel spacing with IM/DD is in the order of 100 Ghz whereas with coherent techniques it can be as small as 1 to 10 Ghz.

An example of coherent detection of an incoming modulated signal using a local oscillator (i.e., a light source of a frequency in the vicinity of the transmitted source) is shown in Figure III.1. However, it should be noted that coherent detection requires a local oscillator with a narrow spectral (or line) width comparable to the

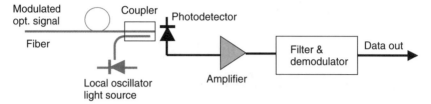

Figure III.1 Coherent detection requires a local oscillator with a narrow spectral width comparable to the source in the incoming signal.

source in the incoming signal, otherwise this method is impractical. However, local oscillators emit light spontaneously and thus they become sources of noise. Therefore, the selection of the local oscillator and its amplitude are important in receiver design. In the case of IM/DD, the incoming signal is directly coupled into the detector, thus eliminating the coupler and the local oscillator.

Part III consists of two chapters. Chapter 12 describes several coding techniques that are used in digital transmission and in digital optical transmission and Chapter 13 describes the decoding techniques.

CHAPTER 12

DIGITAL TRANSMISSION AND CODING TECHNIQUES

12.1 INTRODUCTION

A number of coding techniques are used in communications systems—electrical or optical—to transmit a signal. In this chapter, we review some of them. Keep in mind that, although in electrical transmission, voltages may swing between a negative and a positive level, in optical transmission, light may change between no-light to some light intensity level; that is, there is no negative light as there is in voltage.

12.2 RETURN TO ZERO AND NON-RETURN TO ZERO

Figure 12.1 illustrates the *return to zero* (RZ) coding and the *non-return to zero* (NRZ). With either method, the signal alternates between a positive ($+$V) and a negative ($-$V) voltage. Logic 1 is when the signal is at positive voltage and logic 0 when at negative. However, in the NRZ method, transitions from logic 0 to logic 1, and vice versa, are directly crossing the zero voltage level, whereas in the RZ method, transitions stay temporarily on the zero voltage level.

In optical communications, the terms RZ and NRZ are used differently. Because in this case there is no negative light, NRZ means that a bit of logical value 1 (a pulse of light) changes its value (light to no-light) at the boundaries of the bit period. Conversely, RZ indicates that the pulse of light is narrower than the bit period. In an optical signal, a logic 1 remains for about ⅓ of the bit period on and ⅔ off. A logic 0 remains ⅔ of the bit period off.

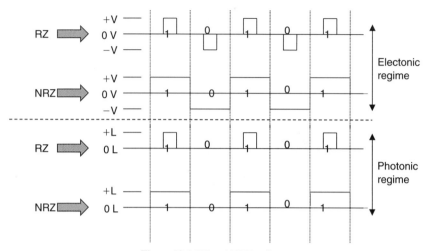

Figure 12.1 RZ and NRZ coding.

12.3 UNIPOLAR AND BIPOLAR SIGNALS

A *bipolar* signal is a three-voltage-level signal that typically swings between a positive and a negative voltage (Figure 12.2). Bipolar signals may be RZ or NRZ. In a digital bipolar signal, the ones alternate between the two voltages, positive and negative. This results in a zero-DC component on the transmission line.

A *unipolar* signal is a two-level signal that typically swings between zero and a positive level. A unipolar signal is considered an on-off signal that may be applied to either electrical or optical signals. In electrical transmission, assuming that statistically there is an equal number of 1s and 0s, then there is a DC component that may reach half the peak positive voltage. For transmission over long distances, this DC component is undesirable. In optical transmission, a unipolar signal is also known as on-off keying (see Section 12.5).

Another category is the *multilevel* signal. In this case, several voltage levels (e.g., 8) may be used, each level corresponding to one of eight codes. Although multilevel signals are attractive because of their inherent code compression properties, nevertheless they are not used for transmission in communications networks. In op-

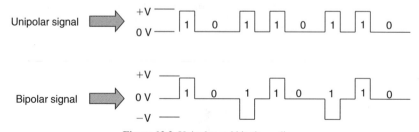

Figure 12.2 Unipolar and bipolar coding.

tical transmission, multilevel signals do not exist. However, the author has defined methods that use multi-wavelength signals.

12.4   4B/5B, 8B/10B CODING

The *4B/5B* code translates four bits into one of sixteen predetermined 5-bit codes. Thus, even if the original 4-bit code is 0000, it is translated to a 5-bit not-all-zero code. This method avoids having all zeros in any code. It may also be designed such that consecutive patterns avoid certain strings of ones. The 4B/5B implies that an initial 1Gbps bit rate, after the conversion, has been increased to 1.25 Gbps because of the added bit. That is, there is 25% overhead bandwidth penalty. Similarly, the *8B/10B* code translates eight bits into one of 256 predetermined 10-bit codes. The bandwidth penalty is also 25%.

12.5   ASK FORMAT

Amplitude-shift keying (ASK) is a technique that modulates the intensity of a light beam (the carrier) directly by an electrical bit stream (the modulating frequency). For bits having the value "1" the carrier has its maximum amplitude and for bits having the value "0" it has its minimum or zero amplitude. This, examined at the unipolar signal case (see Figures 12.1 and 12.2) is also known as *on-off keying* (OOK).

There are two ASK variations, RZ by which the signal returns to zero at every symbol (1, 0), and NRZ, by which it does not (see Figure 12.1, photonic regime).

The ASK format can be used in coherent or in IM/DD systems. However, when a semiconductor laser is directly modulated, the signal phase also shifts. In IM/DD detection phase-shift is unimportant. Coherent detection, however, requires constant phase, and thus the amplitude is externally modulated using a titanium-diffused LiNbO$_3$ waveguide in a Mach-Zehnder configuration (Figure 12.3), or a semiconductor directional coupler based on electro-absorption multi-quantum well (MQW) properties and structures (Figure 12.4).

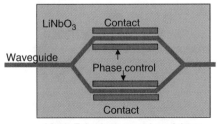

Mach-Zehnder external modulator

Figure 12.3 In coherent detection the amplitude is extremely modulated using a titanium-diffused LiNbO$_3$ Mach-Zehnder waveguide.

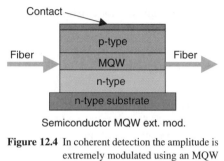

Semiconductor MQW ext. mod.

Figure 12.4 In coherent detection the amplitude is
extremely modulated using an MQW
directional coupler.

12.5 PSK FORMAT

Phase-shift keying (PSK) is a technique that modulates the phase of a light beam
(the carrier) while the frequency and amplitude remain constant during all bits, thus
appearing as a continuous light wave. For binary PSK, the phase is 0° or 180°. For
multilevel PSK, the change may be in increments of, for example, 45° (8 levels).
PSK is a coherent technique.

PSK is implemented externally by passing the light beam through a device that operates on the principle that, when a voltage is applied to it, its refractive index changes,
known as an electro-refraction modulator. Such devices are made with electro-optic
crystals with proper orientation, such as $LiNbO_3$. The phase difference is expressed by:

$$\delta\phi = (2\pi/\lambda)(\delta n)L_m \tag{12.1}$$

where the index change δn is proportional to applied voltage, V, and L_m is the length
over which the index changes by the applied voltage (Figure 12.5).

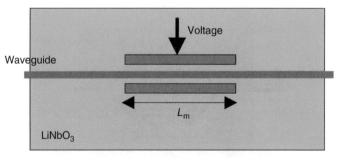

PSK external modulator

Figure 12.5 An electro-refraction modulator changes its refractive index when
a voltage is applied to it and thus the phase of a passing light beam
through it.

12.6   FSK FORMAT

Frequency-shift keying (FSK) is a technique that modulates the frequency ω of a light beam. The frequency of the lightwave changes by Δf, $f + \Delta f$ for logic "1," and $f - \Delta f$ for logic "0." FSK is a coherent two-state (on-off) FM technique. Typical frequency changes are about 1 Ghz. The total bandwidth of an FSK signal is approximated to $2\Delta f + 2B$, where B is the bit rate and Δf the frequency deviation.

- When the deviation is large, $\Delta f \gg B$, the bandwidth approaches $2\Delta f$ and this case is known as *wideband FSK*.
- When the deviation is narrow, $\Delta f \ll B$, the bandwidth approaches $2B$ and this case is known as *narrowband FSK*.

Both cases are distinguished by the frequency modulation index $\Delta f/B = \beta_{FM}$. Clearly, the frequency modulation index is $\beta_{FM} \gg 1$ or $\beta_{FM} \ll 1$.

The implementation of FSK devices is based on electro-acoustic Bragg modulators or on distributed feedback (DFB) semiconductor lasers. Semiconductor lasers exhibit a frequency shift when the operating current changes. A small change in current (~1 mA) would shift the frequency by ~1 Ghz. Because the current change is small, the intensity (amplitude) change is small, too. Thus, DFB semiconductor lasers make very good and fast coherent FSK sources with high modulation efficiency. Figure 12.6 summarizes all shift-keying modulation methods.

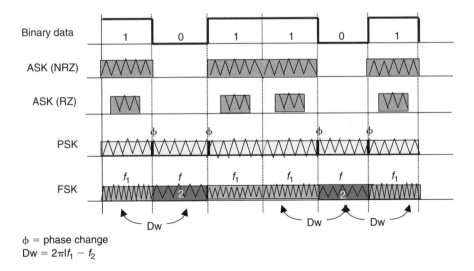

Figure 12.6 Examples of coding/decoding optical information.

EXERCISES

1. In optical coherent systems, what type is the local oscillator at the receiver?
2. What parameters may be modulated in digital transmission?
3. Consider an on-off modulator. How is this modulation method known?
4. Which modulation techniques would be better suited for long-haul applications?
5. Mention two coherent modulation techniques.
6. What is the difference between an electrical RZ signal and an optical RZ signal?
7. Are bipolar signals possible in optical transmission?
8. A signal is coded using a 8*B*/10*B* coder. If the bit rate before the coder is 2 Gbps, what is the bit rate on the fiber?

CHAPTER 13

DECODING
OPTICAL INFORMATION

13.1 INTRODUCTION

Optical decoding entails detecting an optical signal and retrieving (or demodulating) binary coded information from the received modulated lightwave based on one of the three coding techniques discussed earlier:

- Detect optical amplitude level if amplitude-shift keying (ASK) is used.
- Detect phase change (from $0°$ to $180°$) if phase-shift keying (PSK) is used.
- Detect frequency change (from $\omega - \Delta\omega$ to $\omega + \Delta\omega$) if frequency-shift keying (FSK) is used.

Because each technique is different, clearly the receiver device and design are also different.

13.2 ASK DEMODULATORS

ASK demodulators use photodetectors that directly detect incident photonic amplitude. Based on a threshold level, incident amplitude above it is interpreted as logic "1" and below it as logic "0." There may be instances when the incident amplitude is ambiguous due to photonic noise sources, and an erroneous 1 or 0 may be produced. To remove noise from the signal, the retrieved signal is low-pass filtered and sampled at the rate of the expected incoming bit rate by a local phase-locked loop (PLL).

It should be pointed out that for long fiber lengths, due to signal attenuation, the incident light at the receiver is not very strong but is counted in single-digit photons per bit (logic 1), known as the *quantum limit* of the receiver. Consequently, the incoming signal should be coupled with the receiver with no losses, the signal should be dispersion compensated, the sensitivity of the receiver should be very high.

13.3   PSK AND FSK DEMODULATORS

PSK and FSK demodulators are based on coherent (homodyne and heterodyne) principles. This means that, in addition to the received optical signal from the fiber, one or two local oscillators (optical sources) are required by the receiver to interact with the received optical signal and extract binary information. The basic principle of a homodyne PSK demodulator (without noise) is as follows (Figure 13.1).

The received optical modulated signal, ω_S, is mixed coherently with a locally generated frequency, ω_{LO}. Both frequencies are the same and they interact interferometrically. Clearly, when both frequencies are in phase, there is maximum optical contribution; otherwise, they cancel each other out. Because this arrangement is based on optical interference, phase stability is important. The mixed optical signal is detected by a photodetector that provides a logic 1 or 0 electrical output. Clearly, the demodulator becomes more complex when noise is included.

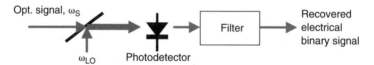

Figure 13.1   The basic principle of a homodyne PSK demodulator.

The basic principle of a homodyne FSK demodulator (without noise) is as follows (Figure 13.2). The received optical modulated signal, ω_S, is split into two equal parts. Then, each part interacts interferometrically with a locally generated frequency, one part with $\omega_1 = \omega_S - \Delta\omega$, and the other with $\omega_2 = \omega_S + \Delta\omega$. Because each local frequency coincides with the frequency of a logic 0 or a logic 1, it is obvious that if two optical filters, OF_1 and OF_2, are used, each centered at one of the two respective frequencies, then the temporal bits 1 and 0 are recognized. Recombining the two halves in the time domain, the complete data bit stream is recovered. Because this arrangement is based on optical interference, optical phase alignment and stability are important. Clearly, the demodulator becomes more complex when noise is included.

A simplified FSK demodulator is constructed if the received optical modulated signal, ω_S, is passed through a tunable filter tuned to pass the frequency $\omega_2 = \omega + \Delta\omega$. Whenever this frequency is detected, logic 1 is generated; otherwise, logic 0 is detected (Figure 13.3). The tunable filter provides the flexibility of selecting a given frequency and it acts like an FSK to ASK converter. The demodulator becomes more complex when noise is included.

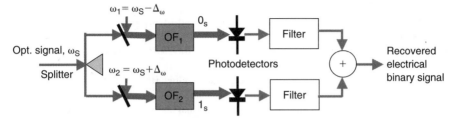

Figure 13.2 The basic principle of a homodyne FSK demodulator.

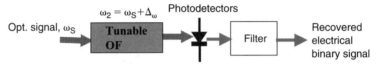

Figure 13.3 A simplified FSK demodulator.

EXERCISES

1. Could a receiver designed to detect a PSK signal detect an FSK signal?
2. A PSK modulator shifts the phase by 180° thus decoding a 1 or a 0, or two states, depending on the received phase. If we had a PSK modulator that shifts by 30°, how many states are possible?
3. A signal has traveled about 200 km of fiber without amplification. Comment on the receiver precautions for reliable signal detection.
4. Consider a PSK receiver. How do the received signal and the local oscillator interact to decode the signal?
5. Consider an FSK signal. What kind of an optical device is required to decode the signal?

REFERENCES

[1] Palais, J.C., *Fiber Optic Communications*, 3rd ed., Englewood Cliffs, N.J., Prentice-Hall, 1992.

[2] I.P. Kaminow, ed., and T.L. Koch, ed., *Optical Fiber Communications IIIA and Optical Fiber Communications IIIB*, Academic Press, 1997.

[3] R. Ramaswami, and K.N. Sivarajan, *Optical Networks*, Morgan Kaufmann Publ., San Francisco, CA, 1998.

[4] B. Mukhergie, *Optical Communications Networks*, McGraw-Hill, New York, 1997.

[5] R.A. Linke, "Optical Heterodyne Communications Systems," *IEEE Comm. Mag.*, Oct. 1989, pp. 36–41.

[6] R.A. Linke, and A.H. Gnauck, "High-Capacity Coherent Lightwave Systems," *J. of Lightwave Technology*, vol. 6, no. 11, 1988, pp. 1750–1769.

[7] R.E. Slusher, and B. Yurke, "Squeezed Light for Coherent Communications," *J. of Lightwave Technology*, vol. 8, no. 3, 1990, pp. 466–477.

[8] J.A.C. Bingham, "Multicarrier Modulation for Data Transmission: An Idea Whose Time Has Come," *IEEE Comm. Mag.*, vol. 28, no. 5, May 1990, pp. 5–14.

[9] R.D. Gitlin, J.F. Hayes, and S.B. Weinstein, *Data Communications Principles*, Plenum, New York, 1992.

[10] T. Wildi, *Units and Conversion Charts*, IEEE Press, New York, 1991.

[11] J. Nellist, "Understanding Telecommunications and Lightwave Systems," *IEEE Press*, 1996.

[12] A. Borella, G. Cancellieri, and F. Chiaraluce, *Wavelength Division Multiple Access Optical Networks*, Artec House, Boston, 1998.

[13] P. Black, and T. Meng, "A 1-Gb/s Four-state Sliding Block Viterbi Decoder," *IEEE JSSC*, vol. 32, no. 6, June 1997, pp. 797–805.

[14] D. Edforrs, et al., "An introduction to orthogonal frequency-division multiplexing," http://www.tde.lth.se/home/oes/publications.html.

[15] R.E. Matick, *Transmission Lines for Digital and Communication Networks*, IEEE Press, 1995.

[16] Members of the Technical Staff, *Transmission Systems for Communications*, Bell Telephone Laboratories, 1982.

[17] S.U.H. Qureshi, "Adaptive Equalization," *Proc. IEEE*, vol. 73, no. 9, Sept. 1985, pp. 1349–86.

STANDARDS

[1] ANSI/IEEE 812-1984, "Definition of Terms Relating to Fiber Optics."

[2] Bellcore, TR-NWT-499, "Transport Systems Generic Requirements [TSGR]: Common Requirements," issue 5, Dec. 1993.

[3] IEEE 802.3ab, 1000BaseT.

[4] IEEE 802.1 to 802.6, Local Area Networks.

[5] ITU-T draft Recommendation G.692 [ex Gsaf), "Optical Interfaces for Multichannel Systems with Optical Amplifiers," Oct. 1998.

[6] ITU-T Recommendation G.702, "Digital Hierarchy Bit Rates," 1988.

[7] ITU-T Recommendation G.741, "General Considerations on Second Order Multiplex Equipment," 1988.

[8] ITU-T Recommendation I.432, "B-ISDN User-Network Interface—Physical Layer Specification."

PART IV
DENSE WAVELENGTH
DIVISION MULTIPLEXING

Transporting SONET OC-192 (or SDH STM-64) signals at 10 Gbps over single-mode fiber has become a technology of the past. Transporting OC-768 at 40 Gbps over single-mode fiber for 100 km is an advanced technology that is becoming readily available. At 40 Gbps, half-a-million simultaneous telephone conversations can be transmitted. Transporting above 40 Gbps is the next challenge. Although such rates may seem more than adequate, combined voice and data traffic (video, Internet, etc.) may require yet more bandwidth in a single fiber. Thus, some reasonable questions are: What is the upper bandwidth limit in a fiber? At which point will opto-electronic (transmitter, receiver) devices reach their limit? Does this mean that the fiber is approaching a maximum bandwidth capacity?

Advancements in laser and opto-electronic device technology have made it possible to transmit more than one wavelength in the same fiber. This is known as *wavelength division multiplexing* (WDM). Adding wavelengths in the same fiber effectively increases the bandwidth capacity of a fiber and thus negates the immediate need to install additional fibers or increase the data bit rate to extremely high levels. That is, WDM enables transporting the equivalent bandwidth of several OC-192 (or OC-768) signals by carrying each signal on a different wavelength in the same fiber. In the full low-loss range of a single mode fiber (1200 to 1600 nm), some 1000 wavelength channels separated by 50 GHz may be used. At 40 Gbps per wavelength, a total aggregate bandwidth of 40 Tbps per fiber may be achieved. Assuming 50% utilization of a 432-fiber cable, the total aggregate bandwidth is an astonishing 8000 Tbps.

CHAPTER 14

DWDM SYSTEMS

14.1 INTRODUCTION

Current wavelength division multiplexing (WDM) systems use each wavelength as a separate channel. Each channel may transport homogeneous or heterogeneous traffic, such as synchronous optical network/synchronous digital hierarchy (SONET/SDH) over one wavelength, asynchronous transfer mode (ATM) over another, and perhaps time division multiplexing (TDM) voice, video, or Internet over another. Moreover, WDM makes it possible to transfer traffic at different bit rates. Thus, depending on the application, one wavelength (or channel) may carry traffic at OC-3, OC-12, OC-48, or up to OC-192 rate, and another wavelength possibly at a lower or even an undefined rate (a rate defined by end-user equipment).

Apart from the number of services and traffic types, there are many key questions in WDM: How many wavelengths can be multiplexed in a single fiber? How are the wavelength channels monitored, managed, protected, and provisioned? As opto-electronic technology moves forward, it is possible to have a high density of wavelengths in the same fiber. Thus, the term *dense wavelength division multiplexing* (DWDM) is used. In contrast, there are also low wavelength density WDM systems, and a lower density yet, termed *coarse WDM* (CWDM).

Conventional single-mode fibers transmit wavelengths in the 1300 and 1550 nm range and absorb wavelengths in the range 1340 to 1440 nm range. WDM systems use wavelengths in the two regions of 1310 and 1550 nm. Special fibers have made it possible to use the complete spectrum from 1310 to beyond 1600 nm. However, although new fiber technology opens up the spectrum window, not all optical components perform with the same efficiency over the complete spectrum. As an example, erbium-doped fiber amplifiers (EDFAs) perform best in the range of 1550 nm. Will other fiber amplifiers perform as well so that different amplifier types could be included?

DWDM systems take advantage of advanced optical technology (e.g., tunable lasers, narrow-band optical filters, etc.) to generate many wavelengths in the range around 1550 nm. ITU-T recommendation G.692 defines 43 wavelength channels, from 1530 to 1565 nm, with a spacing of 100 Ghz, each channel carrying an OC-192 signal at 10 Gbps. However, systems with wavelength channels of more than 43 wavelengths have been introduced, and systems with many more wavelengths are on the experimenter's workbench.

Currently, commercial systems with 16, 40, 80, and 128 channels (wavelengths) per fiber have been announced. Those with forty channels have channel-spacing of 100 Ghz, and those with 80 channels have a channel spacing at 50 Ghz. This channel separation determines the width of the spectral (wavelength) narrowness of each channel, or how close (in terms of wavelength) the channels are. Forty-channel DWDM systems can transmit over a single fiber an aggregate bandwidth of 400 Gbps (10 Gbps per channel). It is estimated that at 400 Gbps, more than 10,000 volumes of an encyclopedia can be transmitted in 1 second.

The number of channels also depends on the type of fiber. A single strand of single-mode fiber can transmit over 80 km without amplification. Placing eight optical amplifiers in cascade, the total distance is extended to over 640 km (this is typical for 80-channel systems at 10 Gbps per channel).

There is a race among companies and experimenters to break new records; longer distances, more channels, and higher bit rates frequently make the news. And this trend is expected to continue until all limits of physics for this technology have been reached and pushed back.

Although DWDM technology is still evolving and technologists and standards bodies are addressing many issues, systems are being offered with few tens of wavelengths in the same fiber. However, it is reasonable to assume that in the near future we will see DWDM systems with several hundreds of wavelengths in a single fiber. Theoretically, more than 1000 channels may be multiplexed in a fiber. DWDM technology with more than 200 wavelengths has already been demonstrated. Devices with 200 wavelengths per fiber at 40 Gbps per wavelength with an aggregate bandwidth of 8 Tbps per fiber are feasible. Eight Tbps per fiber is an aggregate bandwidth that exceeds all needs today. Nevertheless, this bandwidth may become tomorrow's norm if we extrapolate the witnessed data traffic explosion.

DWDM utilizes a large aggregate bandwidth in a single fiber by taking advantage of advanced optical technology that is able to launch and multiplex many wavelengths in one fiber, switch wavelengths optically, and at the receiving end, demultiplex and read each wavelength separately. In DWDM, each wavelength constitutes a separate channel capable of carrying traffic at a bit rate that may not be the same on all channels. Because a channel does not exactly consist of a singular wavelength but of a narrow band around a center wavelength, each band is spaced from the next by several Ghz to provide a safety zone and avoid channel–wavelength overlapping and thus cross-talk. This is necessary because laser sources and tunable filters may drift with temperature and time, optical amplifiers do not exhibit true flat gain over the wavelength range, spontaneous noise from EDFAs is cumulative, and there are often dispersion effects.

14.2 DWDM NETWORK TOPOLOGIES

Initially, DWDM started with one topology: point-to-point. However, it has come to be considered for a number of network topologies, in addition to direct point-to-point, point-to-point with add-drop capability, ring, fully mesh connected, and star. At the exception of the point-to-point, each topology may be mapped into a fiber-ring topology with many wavelengths. Depending on topology and fiber length, optical amplification may or may not be required. The need for amplification and the number of amplifiers (if any) that may be required are estimated according to distance between transmitter and receiver and to system design parameters, such as number of wavelengths (channels), channel width, channel separation, modulation technique, bit rate, fiber type, and other optical component characteristics.

Figure 14.1 illustrates a DWDM point-to-point topology with an optional amplifier. This topology is more suitable for long-haul ultra-high aggregate bandwidth transport (where each wavelength is distinguished by different color–wavelength multiplexers and demultiplexers are not shown). An optical add-drop multiplexer (OADM) may also be included on the link, if one or more wavelengths are to be dropped and added.

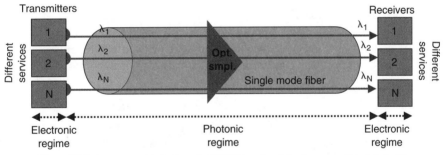

Figure 14.1 A conceptual point-to-point DWDM system (also known as "big fat pipe").

Figure 14.2 illustrates a five-node, fully connected, mesh topology DWDM mapped onto a ring (a single ring is shown for clarity), and a star network also mapped onto a ring. Each interconnecting link is shown via a separate channel (wavelength), and in the fully connected case, four wavelengths are added/dropped at each node. The hub of the star network may receive a wavelength from a node on the ring and selectively convert it to another wavelength destined to another node on the same ring. This function is also referred to as *broadcast and select*.

Notice that although we make reference to nodes, the conventional communications networks "node" may be replaced by "router" that is better suited to data networks. It should be pointed out, however, that modern networks transport a mix of

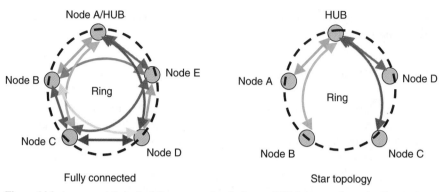

Figure 14.2 A representation of a fully connected and of a star WDM ring topology; the fiber is shown dotted line (black) and interconnecting links are shown via separate channels (colored).

TDM (digital signal level n [DSn], SONET/SDH), ATM and Internet traffic. In DWDM applications, a router that performs DSn and optical carrier level n (OC-n) grooming, optical multiplexing, switching, and provides real-time quality of service (QoS), starts looking like a traditional node. Therefore, although nodes and routers are conceptually different, herein for brevity we do not distinguish between the two. WDM networking examines and evaluates these issues in detail, but this is beyond our scope.

14.3   DWDM APPLICABILITY

DWDM systems are applicable to many network types and on all network layers (Figure 14.3). For example, they are applicable to backbone networks (networks that

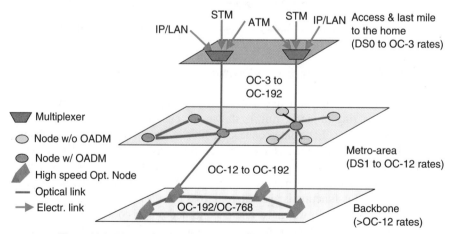

Figure 14.3 WDM is applicable to all network layers, from access to backbone.

optically transport bulk ultra-high bandwidth data at very high bit rates) that cover a large geographical area (intercontinental) or they interconnect continents (trans-oceanic). Intercontinental systems may have a point-to-point, mesh, star or ring topology, whereas transoceanic systems are predominantly point-to-point with a possible few add-drops. A possible submarine DWDM network may also be of the ring or star type interconnecting a cluster of islands. DWDM systems are applicable to metropolitan areas interconnecting many high-rise buildings, to a campus environment or within a multi-level building. Finally, they are applicable to enterprise smaller size (business) networks (with fewer nodes) where a variety of traffic types (TDM, SONET/SDH, ATM, internet protocol [IP], etc.) merge to be transported to higher level network. The ring or mesh topology is more suitable in such applications. One of the nodes is a hub providing connectivity with other networks. Notice that as we move from the access to backbone layers, bit rates increase because bandwidth is aggregated. Table 14.1 tabulates the legacy narrowband and broadband rates and Table 14.2 the SONET and SDH rates.

In DWDM applications, each node sources and terminates one (or more) wavelength(s) such that a fully interconnected mesh network or a star network is constructed with a single fiber. Depending on the number of nodes and wavelengths, a WDM system is termed DWDM if there are many wavelengths, and CWDM if there are few wavelengths, typically, there are spaced by 50–500 Ghz. Moreover, each wavelength may transport different services, such as IP, SONET/SDH, ATM, or other. As a result, practical systems are designed to handle one or more service types.

Table 14.1 Narrowband and Broadband Rates

Facility	USA	Europe	Japan
DS0	64 Kbps	64 Kbps	64 Kbps
DS1	1.544 Mbps		1.544 Mbps
E1		2.048 Mbps	
DS1c	3.152 Mbps		3.152 Mbps
DS2	6.312 Mbps		6.312 Mbps
E2		8.448 Mbps	32.064 Mbps
DS3	44.736 Mbps	34.638 Mbps	
DS3c	91.053 Mbps		
			97.728 Mbps
E3			139.264 Mbps
DS4	274.176 Mbps		
			397.2 Mbps

Table 14.2 SONET/SDH Rates

	Signal Designation		Line Rate
SONET	**SDH**	**Optical**	**(Mbps)**
STS-1	STM-0	OC-1	51.84
STS-3	STM-1	OC-3	155.52
STS-12	STM-4	OC-12	622.08
STS-48	STM-16	OC-48	2,488.32
STS-192	STM-64	OC-192	9,953.28
STS-768	STM-254	OC-768	39,813.12

As an example, a family of products offered by LUCENT Technologies, known as WaveStar™, has been designed to handle any service at any bandwidth (Figure 14.4). For example WaveStar OLS 400G multiplexes up to 80 wavelengths at OC-48 per fiber ($80 \times 2.5 = 200$ Gbps/fiber) or up to 40 wavelengths at OC-192 per fiber ($40 \times 10 = 400$ Gbps/fiber).

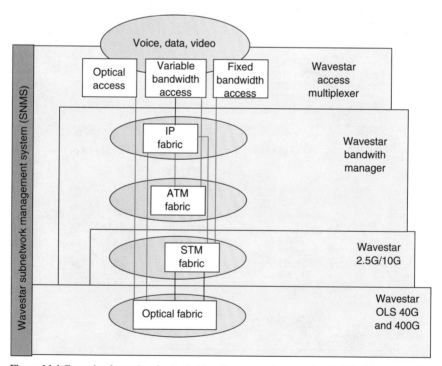

Figure 14.4 Example of a product family that handles any service at any bandwidth. (From LUCENT Technologies, *Bell Labs Technology*, vol. 2, no. 2, p. 12, Reprinted with permission.)

   Similarly, products from other well-known companies support a range of wavelength channels at various rates. Nevertheless, DWDM networks have several unre-
solved issues to address. Standards bodies are working toward drafting recommendations, but in the meantime each manufacturer offers systems with semiprivate
solutions to meet market needs and to make an early entry. For example, operations,
administration, maintenance, and provisioning (OAM&P) as well as dynamic wavelength assignment are on the drawing board. Network management may also differ
from vendor to vendor along with reliability, latency, and quality of service agree-
ments. Some use a supervisory (wavelength) channel for OAM&P (typically at
1310 nm or at about 1500 nm), but standardization of the wavelength, its bit rate,
and the protocol has not yet been accomplished. Some use proprietary methods to
enable transporting a mix of services and traffic types, although proposals have been
made to produce a standard. For example, such method is the *digital wrapper*,
which, based on TDM principle, encapsulates an optical channel and with additional
overhead. This overhead includes OAM&P functions as well as forward error correction (FEC) to extend the transported range by 4–5 dB (a practice similar to submarine applications (ITU-T recommendation G.975). Current systems support fixed
wavelength assignment for each node or are manually reconfigurable. Dynamic
wavelength assignment is another area to be standardized. Each network provider
also provides their own solution for wavelength protection. The set of wavelengths
is different from system to system, thus making interoperability almost impossible
(Figure 14.5). Based on the above, a description of DWDM standard networks becomes an impossible task for the time being. In Chapter 15 we will address these issues. Again, this is a current view and the interested designer should be mindful of
upcoming standards and recommendations.

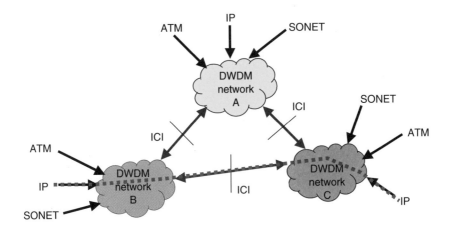

Figure 14.5 Multi-network interoperability. All networks must be compatible in order that a service must be provided end-to-end (dotted line) with the same guarantees; ICI is the
intercarrier interface.

CHAPTER **15**

ENGINEERING
DWDM SYSTEMS

15.1 INTRODUCTION

The design of DWDM systems requires the resolution of several issues. Excluding cost, several key parameters influence the design of a system and a network:

- Nominal center frequencies (wavelengths)
- Channel capacity
- Channel width
- Channel spacing or channel separation
- Channel bit rate and modulation
- Multi-channel frequency stabilization
- Channel performance
- Channel dispersion
- Power launched
- Power received
- Optical amplification
- Fiber type used as the transmission medium
- Optical power budget
- Type of services supported
- Aggregate bandwidth management
- Protocol used to transport supported services

183

- Network management protocol
- Network reliability
- Network protection and survivability strategies
- Network scalability and flexibility
- Wavelength management
- Interoperability

15.2   ITU-T NOMINAL CENTER FREQUENCIES

For wavelength division multiplexing (WDM) system interoperability, the operating center frequency (wavelength) of channels must be the same at the transmitting and at the receiving end. Presently, ITU-T (standards) recommends 81 channels (wavelengths) in the C-band starting from 1528.77 nm, and incrementing in multiples of 50 Ghz (or 0.39 nm).

Accordingly, starting with the first center frequency at 196.10 THz (or 1528.77 nm), and decrementing by 50 GHz (or incrementing by 0.39 nm), a table with all center frequencies (wavelengths) is constructed. These are the center frequencies (wavelengths) of the channels that are considered for recommendation by ITU-T G.692 (as of October 1998). Thus, the first of the 81 channels in the C-band is at frequency 196.10 GHz or wavelength 1528.77 nm, the second channel is at frequency 196.05 GHz or wavelength 1529.16 nm, and so on, and the last frequency is at 192.10 GHz or wavelength 1560.61 nm. However, as fiber technology evolves and optical components improve, more channels may be appended to this table. This may be expressed by the relationship:

$$F = 193.1 \pm m \times 0.1 \text{ THz} \qquad (15.1)$$

where 193.1 Thz is a reference frequency and m is an integer. For a channel spacing of 100 GHz, the center frequencies of the channels are those that start with the first channel in the table and continue every other one. Similarly, for channel spacing of 200 GHz or 400 GHz, one starts with the first center frequency (wavelength) and continues accordingly. Figure 15.1 illustrates a linear scale, calibrated in wavelength and frequency.

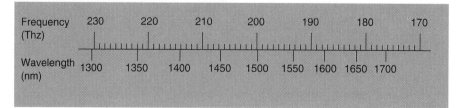

Figure 15.1 DWDM channels in frequency (Thz) and wavelength (nm) in the spectrum defined by ITU-T.

Notice that frequency (and not wavelength) is used as a reference. The reason is that certain materials emit specific well-known optical frequencies that can be used as accurate reference points. In addition, frequency remains constant, whereas wavelength is influenced by the refractive index of the material.

15.3   CHANNEL CAPACITY, WIDTH, AND SPACING

The number of channels, the channel selection (center frequency) and the frequency width of each channel, as well as the channel separation are important parameters in dense wavelength division multiplexing (DWDM) system design. Channel center frequency and width determines the number of non-overlapping channels in the spectrum. Channel width, wavelength, bit rate, type of fiber, and fiber length determine the amount of dispersion. Channel separation should allow for a frequency deviation (~2 GHz) caused by frequency drifts in the laser, filter, and amplifier devices and thus avoid interchannel interference.

15.4   CHANNEL BIT RATE AND MODULATION

The bit rate of a channel and the modulation technique are parameters that determine the limits of channel width and channel separation, as well as channel performance (e.g., bit error rate [BER], cross-talk, etc.). Dispersion and dispersion management, noise induced by amplifiers, and noise induced by other sources should be considered, as they affect the signal to noise ratio and thus the signal integrity.

15.5   WAVELENGTH MANAGEMENT

In DWDM systems where each wavelength is used as a separate channel, it is reasonable to consider the reliability of the transmitter, receiver, amplifier, and other active optical components on the optical path between transmitter-receiver. When, for example, a laser or photodetector cease to perform, a fault is declared. However, for a fault to be declared, the fault must first be detected. This implies that an optical monitoring function should exist, which in optical components is costly and not so trivial. Nevertheless, assuming that this function exists, there should be a capability to isolate the fault and restore service. In DWDM, if an optical component fails, it will affect one or more wavelengths. Thus, protection wavelengths should be allocated to replace the faulty ones.

Besides hard faults, there may be wavelength channels that perform below acceptable levels (e.g., BER $< 10^{-9}$). Monitoring optical signal performance in DWDM is more complex than a merely good/bad detection. At any rate, when the signal degrades, then it should be dynamically switched to a protection or stand-by wavelength that is known to perform better (this implies that the protection wavelength must also be continuously monitored for performance).

Either way, wavelength fault or signal degradation result in switching to another wavelength. In DWDM systems and networks, switching to another wavelength requires "wavelength management." However, the end-to-end path in DWDM, as it traverses many nodes, consists of many sections (between nodes). If a wavelength changes to another within one section, then the other sections on the path must be notified of the change, and if there are wavelength converters (or regenerators), they too must be tuned to the new wavelength.

In the case of an all-optical network, changing one wavelength to another becomes a multidimensional problem that needs further study. In certain cases, due to lack of available wavelengths, another route is found to establish end-to-end connectivity. This means that the new route does not impact the budgeted optical power of the optical path.

Currently, wavelength management is in infancy and depending on network level it is addressed in a simple deterministic manner (1:N, 1:1, 1+1, etc.). However, work is under research or in the proposal phase.

15.6   MULTICHANNEL FREQUENCY STABILIZATION

In DWDM systems with optical filters, filter detuning, or frequency offset from the center frequency, takes place. As detuning increases, interference with neighboring channels increases and so does the optical cross-talk. In addition, detuning increases insertion loss. Therefore, mechanisms that correct or compensate for detuning should be incorporated.

15.7   CHANNEL PERFORMANCE

The BER is a performance requirement that is specified by standards. DWDM systems should be designed so that signal integrity is maintained. The BER depends on interchannel interference, optical power level at the receiver with respect to the sensitivity of the receiver, modulation technique, and other noise sources (externally coupled noise, jitter, etc.).

15.8   CHANNEL DISPERSION

In DWDM systems, as wavelengths travel through fibers and various optical components (filters, amplifiers, etc.), dispersion or optical pulse widening occurs. Moreover, as light travels from one fiber to another (due to connectors and splices), it is subject to further losses and dispersion. Depending on the number of channels, the frequency distribution of each channel around the center frequencies, the channel separation, the optical path length, and the dispersion characteristics of all devices in the path (including fiber(s) and connectors), the total dispersion of each channel should be calculated. As dispersion increases, so does cross-talk (that effects signal integrity) and received power (that impacts receiver sensitivity).

15.9   POWER LAUNCHED

In DWDM systems, the *maximum allowable power per channel* launched in the fiber, or the transmitted power, is the starting point of power calculations to assure that the optical signal at the receiver has enough power to be detected without errors (or within a BER objective, e.g., $<10^{-11}$). However, the maximum allowable power per channel cannot be arbitrary, because as explained, as coupled power increases so do the nonlinear phenomena.

15.10   OPTICAL AMPLIFICATION

In DWDM systems, optical signal losses should be carefully budgeted and optical amplification (erbium-doped fiber amplifiers [EDFA]) should be used as appropriate to restore the intensity of the optical signal (if needed). However, optical amplification introduces cumulative pulse widening and cost. Conversely, if EDFAs are to be used, the number of channels and the wavelength range (1.3 vs. 1.55 nm) should be considered because EDFAs operate best in the range of 1.55 nm.

15.11   FIBER TYPE AS THE TRANSMISSION MEDIUM

We have described a number of limitations already encountered in optical transmission, such as amplifier bandwidth, amplifier spontaneous emission (ASE), and linear effects such as fiber attenuation, chromatic dispersion, and polarization mode dispersion (PMD). In addition, in DWDM there are nonlinear effects related to the refractive index and scattering that degrade system performance.

The contribution of the nonlinear effects to transmission is defined as the optical power density (power/effective area) times the length of the fiber. The *effective area* is defined as the cross-section of the light path in a fiber. Depending on the type of fiber, the effective area varies between 50 and 72 μm^2, the lowest corresponding to dispersion-shifted fiber and the highest to single-mode fiber. Clearly, the higher the optical power density and the longer the fiber, the more the nonlinear contribution.

For a fixed length of fiber, the only variable that can be manipulated to lower the nonlinear contribution is optical power. However, if the optical power is lowered, the bit rate should be lowered to maintain transmission at the expected BER.

15.12   OPTICAL POWER BUDGET

In DWDM systems, the optical power budget amounts to calculating all signal losses at every component in the optical path (couplers, filters, cross-connects, connectors, splices, mux/demux, fiber, optical patch panels, etc.) between transmitter and receiver. The main objective is to assure that the power of the optical signal at the receiver is greater than the sensitivity of the receiver.

Power gain and loss (in dB) is additive, and thus the power budget is a straight-forward addition or subtraction calculation. One typically starts with the power of the optical signal to be launched into fiber, expressed as 0 dB. Then, for each loss item, the dB loss is subtracted from it, and for optical amplifiers the gain is added to it. The remaining is compared with the receiver sensitivity. Typically, a net power margin of several dB is highly desirable.

(Margin) =
(Transmitter output power) $-$ (Receiver sensitivity) $-$ (Σ losses), (dB)   (15.2)

As an example, the total loss in a cable is calculated by the sum:

$$\Sigma\alpha_n{\cdot}L + \alpha_s{\cdot}x + \alpha_c{\cdot}y \text{ over all concatenated fiber segments}$$ (15.3)

where α_n is the loss coefficient, L is the length of the nth fiber segment, α_s is the mean splice loss, x is the number of splices, α_c is the mean loss of line connectors and y is the number of connectors (see also Section 3.17.1).

The power budget, in addition, determines the fiber length between transmitter-receiver. This length, for a given transmitter output power, depends on the sensitivity of the receiver and on the bit rate. For example, for a transmitter output 0 dBm, at OC-12 rate, and a receiver sensitivity of -35 dBm, the fiber length (for SMF) is determined to 64 km. For OC-48 and a receiver sensitivity of -29 dBm, the fiber length is determined to 51 km.

15.13   TYPE OF SERVICES SUPPORTED

Communications services are many: synchronous and asynchronous, real time and non-real time, low bandwidth and high bandwidth, circuit switched and non-circuit switched. A DWDM system is designed to support several services, thus adding to the complexity of the system and network design. A possibility is to put each different service type on a different wavelength. Another possibility is to packetize each different service type and then multiplex packets and transport them over the same wavelength.

15.14   AGGREGATE BANDWIDTH MANAGEMENT

A typical node has many inputs. That is, it may be connected, in addition to other nodes, to terminals that may support different services and at a different bit rate, constant or variable. Thus, the node should be able to support a different level of quality of service for each type of service and an aggregate bandwidth that confluences to the node. The hub, on the other hand, should be able to process the total bandwidth of all nodes connected to it. Consequently, the hub may be an advanced machine that recognizes all types of services supported by all nodes connected to it, provide bandwidth management functionality, and in many instances provide network management. In DWDM networks, the total aggregate bandwidth at the hub may be of the order exceeding the Tbps.

15.15   PROTOCOL USED TO TRANSPORT SUPPORTED SERVICES

The nodes and the hub must be able to process all protocols required by each service supported. Synchronous optical network/synchronous digital hierarchy (SONET/SDH), asynchronous transfer mode (ATM), frame relay, internet protocol (IP), video, telephony, signaling, and so on, require different protocols. For example, telephony requires call processing (TR-08 or TR-303) whereas ATM requires call admission control (CAC) and quality of service warranties. Similarly, the priority of services varies, telephony having the highest priority whereas certain packet-data services may have the lowest. Typically, all these communications protocols are transparent to many WDM networks on the optical layer; that is, the optical link between transmitter and receiver. However, the optical link layer must be compatible between the two terminating devices that must support and perform fault management, restoration, and survivability functionality.

15.16   PROTOCOL FOR NETWORK MANAGEMENT

The DWDM network communicates with the overall communications network. DWDM network health and billing information are communicated to a remote station from where the DWDM network is managed.

15.17   NETWORK RELIABILITY

The DWDM network processes many services and has a very large bandwidth throughput. As such, the reliability of the network is very important. Reliability is expressed in terms of quality of signal (BER), downtime (seconds per year without service), and traffic rerouting time (in seconds or milliseconds).

15.18   NETWORK PROTECTION AND SURVIVABILITY STRATEGIES

Many high-speed and high-bandwidth systems have incorporated into their design strategies to provide uninterrupted service when one or more links or nodes fail. Protection strategies may be at the input level (1+1, 1:N), at the service level, at the wavelength level (in DWDM systems), at the facility (fiber) level, and at the node level. The time involved to switch to a protection channel, wavelength, facility, or reroute all traffic, from the time a fault has been declared varies and is prescribed in various ITU-T and Bellcore recommendations (see also Chapter 16). In addition, the protection and the survivability strategies are service-type, system, and network-architecture dependent. In many systems/networks, they also depend on the transport protocol.

15.19   NETWORK SCALABILITY AND FLEXIBILITY

The network, as well as the network elements, must be scalable such that small incremental increases (in wavelength, hardware, and software) will accommodate increased bandwidth demand. In addition, network elements must be flexible enough to adapt to protocol upgrades and offer new services, as standards and market needs evolve. Network scalability and flexibility are highly desirable and service providers place them at the top of their list.

15.20   WAVELENGTH MANAGEMENT

The signal integrity on a wavelength assigned to a DWDM channel should be continuously monitored. This includes interference due to optical noise as well as fault location and isolation of all components in the optical channel, transmitter, receiver, amplifiers, filters, and so on. When the signal quality of a channel is degraded, then the wavelength management should be able to dynamically assign another wavelength. This means that DWDM systems have optical devices with performance monitoring, (additional) wavelengths for protection, and protocols that support dynamic wavelength assignment.

15.21   INTEROPERABILITY

Interoperability assures seamless service and data flow from one service provider network to another. Some networks have standard transport protocols and interfaces while others are private or nonstandard. In addition, systems use wavelengths that, although compliant with ITU standards, belong to a subset of them. However, each system manufacturer uses a different subset optimized for the particular application the system is designed for. Moreover, components used by one system manufacturer may not have the same frequency stability and line width with another system manufacturer, and to add to it, the fiber installed from one network to another may not be exactly of the same type. Therefore, when two dissimilar systems are connected, certain wavelengths (using wavelength converters) must be converted to others, and the signal level must be equalized to meet receiver requirements. In addition, the transport protocol must be identical, else it may make interoperability impossible. Finally, interoperability implies that network management and survivability on the end-to-end optical path have been addressed and resolved.

15.22   SINGLE-MODE POWER LOSS CALCULATIONS:
AN EXAMPLE

The following is an approximate example of power loss calculations over an optical link.

Equipment manufacturer model: "APEX, Inc." model F145XYZ
Detector type: APD
Maximum receive signal: -15 dBm
Receiver sensitivity, P_R: -35 dBm @10^{-9} BER
Bit rate: 1 Gbps
Transmitter wavelength: 1310 (±20) nm
Total fiber span length: 45 km
Fiber loss: 0.35 dB/km

1. Transmitter output power: P_T -8.0 dBm
2. Receiver sensitivity($@10^{-9}$ BER): P_R -35.0 dBm
3. Total fiber system gain (#1-#2): G 27 dB
4. Dispersion loss($@10^{-9}$ BER): P_D 1.0 dB
5. Miscellaneous losses (modal P_M 0.4 dB
   noise, connector reflections, etc.):
6. Connector losses (4 @ 1.0 dB each): L_C 4.0 dB
7. Splice losses (9 @ 0.2 dB each): L_S 1.8 dB
8. Margin for future 4 repair splices: M_R 0.8 dB
9. Margin for WDM upgrades: M_{WDM} 3.0 dB
10. Maximum allowable fiber loss: L 16.0 dB
    (#3-#4-#5-#6-#7-#8-#9)
11. Total loss due to fiber: L_F 15.75 dB
12. Receive signal level: R -34.75 dBm
    (#1-#4-#5-#6-#7-#8-#9-#11)

It can thus be concluded that the received power level is within the receiver sensitivity (-35 dBm), although there is very little margin. Consequently, no amplification is required, no attenuator at the receiver is required, and total fiber loss (15.75 dB) is within the maximum allowable fiber loss (16.0 dB).

15.23   CHANNEL CALCULATIONS IN A NETWORK: THREE EXAMPLES

1. Consider a WDM system with N wavelengths over a wavelength range BW(λ) (expressed in nm) that is supported by transmitters, filters, and receivers. In addition, consider that if the bit rate is B Gbps, $2B$ GHz of bandwidth is needed for encoding (this determines the channel width). Moreover, if the channel bit rate is B Gbps, for low cross-talk, a channel spacing of $6B$ GHz is required (as a rule of thumb). Based on the above, determine the conditions that N channels can be used in this network.

For a center frequency λ, and from the identity

$$\Delta f = c\Delta\lambda/\lambda^2 \tag{15.4}$$

the bandwidth range (in terms of frequency) is

$$\Delta f = \mathrm{BW}(f) = c\mathrm{BW}(\lambda)/\lambda^2 \tag{15.5}$$

Now, the bandwidth required over all N channels is

$$\mathrm{BW}_{req} = 2BN + 6B(N-1) \tag{15.6}$$

Assuming that BW_{req} is equal or less than $\mathrm{BW}(f)$, then

$$N = (\mathrm{BW}_{req} + 6B)/8B \tag{15.7}$$

Clearly, if BW_{req} were greater than $\mathrm{BW}(f)$, the number of channels that can be accommodated is smaller.

2. For the previous example, calculate the maximum number of channels that fit in Δf.

For a bandwidth Δf and for the same assumptions, the maximum number of channels is calculated by

$$N = (\Delta f + 6B)/8B \tag{15.8}$$

3. For the previous example, consider that the channel spacing is fixed to CS and that the channel width to CW. How many channels can fit in bandwidth Δf?

From

$$\Delta f = (CW)N + CS(N-1) \tag{15.9}$$

one obtains

$$N = (\Delta f + CS)/(CW + CS) \tag{15.10}$$

CHAPTER 16

DWDM TOPOLOGIES

16.1 INTRODUCTION

Dense wavelength division multiplexing (DWDM) networks are classified into four major topological configurations: DWDM point-to-point with or without add-drop multiplexing network, fully connected mesh network, star network, and DWDM ring network with OADM nodes and a hub. Each topology has its own requirements and, based on the application, different optical components may be involved in their design.

In addition, there are hybrid network topologies that may consist of stars and/or rings that are interconnected with point-to-point links. For example, the Metropolitan Optical NETwork project (MONET) is a WDM network that is developed for and funded by a number of private companies and by U.S. government agencies. It consists of two subnetworks, one located in New Jersey and one in the Washington, D.C. and Maryland area; the two are interconnected with a long distance point-to-point optical link.

16.2 POINT-TO-POINT TOPOLOGY

Point-to-point topology is predominantly for long-haul transport that requires ultra-high speed (10 to 40 Gbps), ultra-high aggregate bandwidth (in the order of several Tbps), high signal integrity, reliability, and fast path restoration capability. The distance between transmitter and receiver may be several hundred kilometers, and the number of amplifiers between the two endpoints is typically less than 10 (as determined by power loss and signal distortion). Point-to-point with add-drop multiplexing enables to drop and add channels along its path. Number of channels, channel spacing, type of fiber, signal modulation method, and component type selection are all important parameters in the calculation of the power budget.

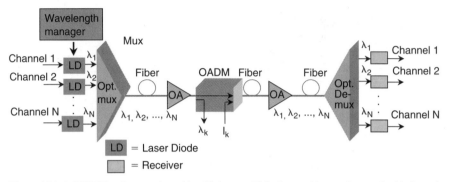

Figure 16.1 A DWDM point-to-point with add-drop multiplexing enables to drop and add channels along its path.

In DWDM, each channel is carried over a specified wavelength (λ_i) also known as "optical channel." Different channels may carry different data (e.g., voice, data, video, data packets) at different bit rates. In the transmitter-receiver optical link there are involved several optical components: fiber(s), optical amplifiers, OADM, optical filters, couplers, laser sources, and modulators and receivers. Each has its own signal-affecting characteristic, as described in Part II. An end-to-end simplistic view of a DWDM point-to-point system that includes lasers, an optical multiplexer and de-multiplexer, fibers, optical amplifiers (OA), and an optical add/drop multiplexer is shown in Figure 16.1.

16.3   RING-CONFIGURED MESH AND STAR NETWORKS

Currently, a variety of proprietary ring DWDM networks have been deployed. In general, a DWDM ring network consists of a fiber in a ring configuration that fully interconnects nodes; some systems may have two fiber rings for network protection. Such a ring may cover a local or a metropolitan area and span a few tens of kilometers. The fiber ring may contain few (4) to many wavelength channels, and few to many nodes. The bit rate per wavelength channel may be 622 Mbps or lower, or 1.25 Gbps or higher. One of the nodes on the ring is a hub station where all wavelengths are sourced, terminated, and managed, and where connectivity with other networks takes place. Each node and the hub have optical add-drop multiplexers (OADM) to drop-off and add a designated wavelength channel(s).

In DWDM ring networks, the hub station may source and terminate several types of traffic (e.g., synchronous transport module [STM], internet protocol [IP], video). The hub manages all channels (wavelengths) assigned to a path between nodes and also the traffic type. At an OADM, one (or more) optical frequency is dropped off and added, whereas the remaining frequencies pass through it transparently. However, as the number of OADMs increases, the signal is subject to

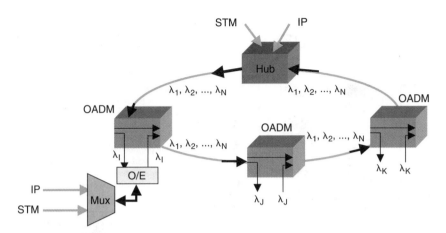

Figure 16.2 A DWDM ring network; the hub station sources and terminates several types of payloads.

losses and optical amplification may be required (not shown). The number of nodes is typically less than the number of wavelengths in the fiber. Figure 16.2 depicts a basic configuration, but does not address network survivability or ring fault avoidance.

In the ring topology, the hub station manages channel (wavelength) assignment so that a fully connected network of nodes with OADM is accomplished. The hub may also provide connectivity with other networks. In addition, an OADM node may be connected with a mux/demux where several data sources are multiplexed. A simple ring topology with a hub and two nodes, A and B, linked via wavelength λ_k is shown in Figure 16.3, where node A also multiplexes several data sources. However, being on the same channel (and same wavelength), all data sources are terminated by the corresponding OADM node (node B).

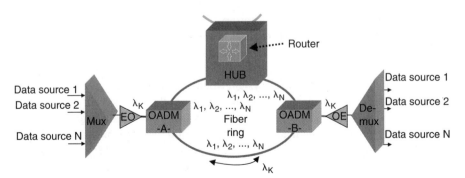

Figure 16.3 In a DWDM ring topology, channel (wavelength) assignment may be managed by the hub station.

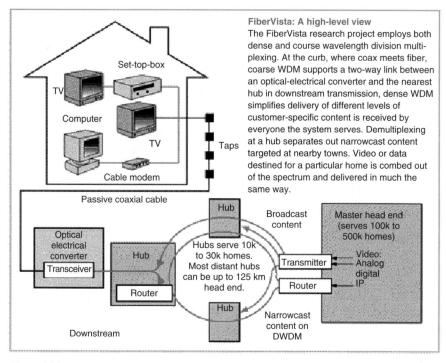

Figure 16.4 View of LUCENT Technologies' project FiberVista is illustrative of a DWDM and CWDM system that delivers all service types to the home. [From LUCENT Technologies, *Bell Labs Technology*, vol. 2, no. 2, 1998, p. 13, Reprinted with permission.]

A project that is illustrative of a coarse WDM (CWDM) system applied in the access area (residential) is illustrated in Figure 16.4. This project, dubbed FiberVista, reuses TV technology to open up the fiber capacity to residential users and offers to the home all types of services—IP, video, analog, and digital. With FiberVista, each hub on a fiber ring can serve 10,000 to 30,000 homes; hubs can be as far as 125 km. From the master-head, a transceiver (an optical/electrical converter) converts the optical signal to an electrical via a coax cable with taps that feed individual homes where cable modems and set-top boxes can select among TV, Internet, and voice services. Such a system would transmit in the upstream direction (from the home) more than 4 Mbps per home, and in the downstream direction (to the home) about 1 Gbps. At the curb, where coax meets fiber, bidirectional CWDM support (1550 nm downstream and 1300 nm upstream) links the transceiver with the hub. Similar ring architectures are also studied for metropolitan (large city) and for enterprise networks (business community, high rises).

16.4   A DWDM HUB

In this section, we attempt to provide stimulating discussion and we do not try to provide system solutions. The area of DWDM node and DWDM hub is currently evolving.

16.4.1   Transmit Direction

A hub, in general, accepts various (electrical) payloads, such as communications transport protocol/Internet protocol (TCP/IP), asynchronous transfer mode (ATM), STM, high-speed Ethernet (1 Gbps, 10 Gbps) and so on. Each traffic type (channel) is sent to its corresponding physical interface where a wavelength is assigned and is modulated at the electrical-to-optical converter. The optically modulated signals from each source is then optically multiplexed and launched into the fiber (Figure 16.5).

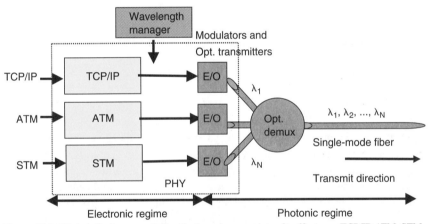

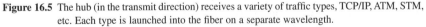

Figure 16.5 The hub (in the transmit direction) receives a variety of traffic types, TCP/IP, ATM, STM, etc. Each type is launched into the fiber on a separate wavelength.

16.4.2   Receive Direction

When a hub receives a WDM signal, it optically demultiplexes it to its component wavelengths (channels), and it converts each optically modulated signal to a digital electrical. Each digital signal then is routed to its corresponding electrical interface, TCP/IP, ATM, STM, and so on (Figure 16.6). Notice, however, that each channel re-

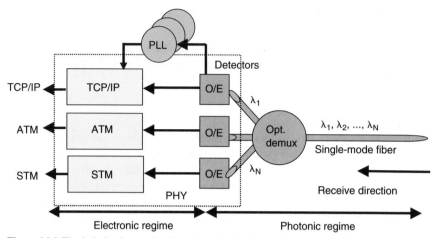

Figure 16.6 The hub (in the receive direction) demultiplexes the optical signal to its component, wavelength channels, and it converts each channel to a traffic type, TCP/IP, ATM, STM, etc.

quires its own clock recovery circuitry (only one is shown) because each one may be at a different bit rate.

16.5　FAULTS

DWDM networks must be able to detect faults on the link or on the ring (broken fiber, faulty port unit, inoperable node) and isolate a fault. The objective is to offer continuous transmission (service) or service with the minimum disruption possible, as recommended in standards. Depending on network topology and architecture, fault avoidance may be accomplished with dual counter-rotating rings (in ring networks), similar to the fiber distributed data interface (FDDI). When a fault is detected in a counter-rotating ring architecture, then the neighboring OADMs reroute traffic via a U-turn optical cross-connect avoiding the fault (Figure 16.7). When the fault recovers or is fixed, the ring network returns to its normal (prior to the fault occurrence) state.

Similarly, in point-to-point topology, detected faults will trigger a procedure to find an alternative path or it will cause alarms. In mesh architecture, faults will trigger a different path selection procedure that bypasses the fault. One of the outstanding issues that network architects have to answer is: When the fault recovers or is fixed, does the network return to the previous state or does it continue until another fault is encountered?

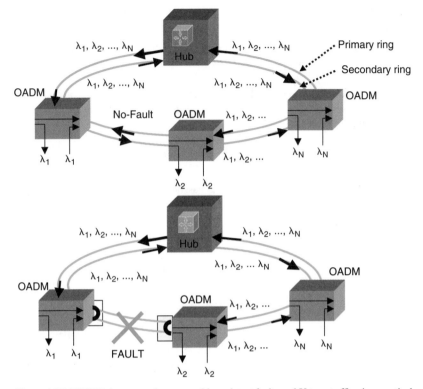

Figure 16.7 DWDM ring networks are capable to detect faults and U-turn traffic via an optical cross-connect thus avoiding the fault.

It should be pointed out that fault avoidance requires complex optical cross-connect devices that put an additional burden on the power and cost budget of the ring network. Thus, depending on the application, the burden of the protecting ring should be carefully assessed.

REFERENCES

[1] S.V. Kartalopoulos, *Understanding SONET/SDH and ATM: Communications Networks for the Next Millennium*, IEEE Press, New York, NY, 1999.

[2] B. Furht, *Handbook of Internet and Multimedia: Systems and Applications*, IEEE Press, New York, NY, 1999.

[3] L.G. Raman, *Fundamentals of Telecommunications Network Management*, IEEE Press, New York, NY, 1999.

[4] Palais, J.C., *Fiber Optic Communications*, 3rd ed., Prentice-Hall, Englewood Cliffs, NJ., 1992.

[5] A. Borella, G. Cancellieri, and F. Chiaraluce, *Wavelength Division Multiple Access Optical Networks*, Artec House, Boston, 1998.

[6] B.T. Doshi, S. Dravida, P. Harshavardhana, O. Hauser, and Y. Wang, "Optical Network Design and Restoration," *Bell Labs Technical Journal*, vol. 4, no. 1, 1999, pp. 58-84.

[7] L.Y. Lin, E. Karasan, and R.W. Tkach, "Layered Switch Architectures for High-Capacity Optical Transport Networks," *IEEE J. on Selected Areas in Communications*, vol. 16, no. 7, Sept. 1998, pp. 1074–1080.

[8] M. Koga, et al., "Large-Capacity Optical Path Cross-Connect System for WDM Photonic Transport Network," *IEEE J. on Selected Areas in Communications*, vol. 16, no. 7, Sept. 1998, pp. 1260–1269.

[9] D. Banerjee, J. Frank, and B. Mukherjee, "Passive Optical Network Architecture Based on Waveguide Grating Routers," *IEEE J. on Selected Areas in Communications*, vol. 16, no. 7, Sept. 1998, pp. 1040–1050.

[10] S. Chatterjee, and S. Pawlowski, "All-Optical Networks," *Comm. of the ACM*, vol. 47, no. 6, June 1999, pp. 74–83.

[11] S.V. Kartalopoulos, "A Manhattan Fiber Distributed Data Interface Architecture," *Globecom'90*, San Diego, December 2-5, 1990.

[12] S.V. Kartalopoulos, "Disaster Avoidance in the Manhattan Fiber Distributed Data Interface Network," *Globecom'93*, Houston, TX, December 2, 1993.

[13] S.R. Johnson, and V.L. Nichols, "Advanced Optical Networking—LUCENT's MONET Network Elements," *Bell Labs Techn. J.*, vol. 4, no. 1, 1999, pp. 145-162.

[14] L.D. Garrett, et al., "The MONET New Jersey Network Demonstration," *IEEE J. on Selected Areas in Communications*, vol. 16, no. 7, Sept. 1998, pp. 1199-1219.

[15] Y. Chen, M.T. Fatehi, H.J. LaRoche, J.Z. Larsen, and B.L. Nelson, "Metro Optical Networking," *Bell Labs Techn. J.*, vol. 4, no. 1, 1999, pp. 163-186.

[16] A.R. Chraplyvy, "High-Capacity Lightwave Transmission Experiments," *Bell Labs Techn. J.*, vol. 4, no. 1, 1999, pp. 230-245.

[17] D.B. Buchholz, et al., "Broadband Fiber Access: A Fiber-to-the-Customer Access Architecture," *Bell Labs Techn. J.*, vol. 4, no. 1, 1999, pp. 282-299.

[18] G.C. Wilson, et al., "FiberVista: An FTTH ot FTTC System Delivering Broadband Data and CATV Services," *Bell Labs Techn. J.*, vol. 4, no. 1, 1999, pp. 300-322.

[19] A. Jourdan, et al., "Key Building Blocks for High-Capacity WDM Photonic Transport Networks," *IEEE J. on Selected Areas in Communications*, vol. 16, no. 7, Sept. 1998, pp. 1286-1297.

[20] M. Berger, et al., "Pan-European Optical Networking Using Wavelength Division Multiplexing," *IEEE Com. Mag.*, vol. 35, no. 4, 1997, pp. 82-88.

[21] B. Fabianek, K. Fitchew, S. Myken, and A. Houghton, "Optical Network Research and Development in European Community Programs: From RACE to ACTS," *IEEE Com. Mag.*, vol. 35, no. 4, 1997, pp. 50-56.

[22] M.W. Chbat, et al., "Toward Wide-Scale All-Optical Transparent Networking: The ACTS Optical Pan-European Network [OPEN) Project," *IEEE J. on Selected Areas in Communications*, vol. 16, no. 7, Sept. 1998, pp. 1226-1244.

[23] P. Gambini, et al., "Transparent Optical Packet Switching: Network Architecture and Demonstrators in the KEOPS Project," *IEEE J. on Selected Areas in Communications*, vol. 16, no. 7, Sept. 1998, pp. 1245-1259.

[24] R. Gaudino, et al., "MOSAIC: A Multiwavelength Optical Subcarrier Multiplexed Controlled Network," *IEEE J. on Selected Areas in Communications*, vol. 16, no. 7, Sept. 1998, pp. 1270-1285.

[25] D. Cotter, J.K. Lcek, and D.D. Marcenac, "Ultra-High-Bit-Rate Networking: From the Transcontinental Backbone to the Desktop," *IEEE Com. Mag.*, vol. 35, no. 4, 1997, pp. 90-96.

[26] S.F. Midkiff, "Fiber Optic Backbone Boosts Local-Area Networks," *IEEE Circuits and Devices Magazine*, vol. 8, no. 1, Jan. 1992, pp. 17-21.

[27] E. Traupman, P. O'Connell, G. Minnis, M. Jadoul, and H. Mario, "The Evolution of the Existing Infrastructure," *IEEE Communications Mag.*, vol. 37, no. 6, 1999, pp. 134-139.

[28] A.G. Malis, "Reconstructing Transmission Networks Using ATM and DWDM," *IEEE Communications Mag.*, vol. 37, no. 6, 1999, pp. 140-145.

[29] R.K. Snelling, "Bringing Fiber to the Home," *IEEE Circuits and Devices Magazine*, vol. 7, no. 1, Jan. 1991, pp. 23-25.

[30] H. Toba, and K. Nosu, "Optical Frequency Division Multiplexing Systems: Review of Key Technologies and Applications," *IEICE Trans. Commun.*, vol. E75, no. 4, Apr. 1992, pp. 243-255.

[31] O.E. DeLange, "Wide-band optical communication systems: part II-frequency-division-multiplexing," *Proc. IEEE*, vol. 58, no. 10, 1970, pp. 1683-1690.

[32] D.K. Hunter, et al., "WASPNET: A Wavelength Switched Packet Network," *IEEE Comm. Magazine*, vol. 37, no. 3, March 1999, pp. 120-129.

[33] E. Modiano, "WDM-Based Packet Network," *IEEE Comm. Magazine*, vol. 37, no. 3, March 1999, pp. 130-135.

[34] H. Kobrinski, R.M. Bulley, M.S. Goodman, M.P. Vecchi, and C.A. Bracket, "Demonstration of high capacity in the LAMBDANET architecture: a multi-wavelength optical network," *Electron Lett.*, vol. 23, 1987, pp. 303-306.

[35] R. Glance, K. Pollock, C.A. Burrus, B.L. Kasper, G. Eisenstein, and L.W. Stulz, "Densely spaced WDM coherent optical star network," *Electron. Lett.*, vol. 23, no. 17, 1987, pp. 875-876.

[36] N. Takato, et al., "128-channel polarization-insensitive frequency-selection-switch using high-silica waveguides on Si," *IEEE Photon. Technol. Lett.*, vol. 2, no. 6, 1990, pp. 441-443.

[37] Y-K. M. Lin, D. Spears, and M. Yin, "Fiber-Based Local Access Network Architectures," *IEEE Comm. Mag.*, Oct. 1989, pp. 64-73.

[38] R.A. Linke, "Optical Heterodyne Communications Systems," *IEEE Comm. Mag.*, Oct. 1989, pp. 36-41.

[39] B. Ramamurthy, and B. Mukerjee, "Wavelength Conversion in WDM Networking," *IEEE J. on Selected Areas in Communications*, vol. 16, no. 7, Sept. 1998, pp. 1061-1073.

STANDARDS

[1] ANSI/IEEE 812-1984, "Definition of Terms Relating to Fiber Optics."

[2] ANSI T1X1.5/99-002, "A Proposal for Providing Channel-Associated Optical Channel Overhead in the OTN" George Newsome and Paul Bonenfant, Lucent, Jan. 1999.

[3] ANSI T1X1.5/99-003, "A Proposed Implementation for a Digital 'Wrapper' for OCh Overhead," James Ballintine, Lucent, Jan. 1999.

[4] ANSI T1X1.5/99-004, "Optical Channel Overhead Carried on the Optical Supervisory Channel," George Newsome and Paul Bonenfant, Lucent, Jan. 1999.

[5] ANSI T1X1.5/99-146, "Proposed OCh-OH Assignments for the OCh Frame," James Ballintine, Lucent, May 1999.

[6] Bellcore, TR-NWT-233, "Digital Cross Connect System," Nov. 1992.

[7] Bellcore, TR-NWT-917, "Regenerator," Oct. 1990.

[8] Bellcore GR-1377, "SONET OC-192 Transport Systems Generic Criteria," Issue 3, Aug. 1996.

[9] IEC Publication 825-1, "Safety of laser products—Part 1: Equipment classification, requirements and user's guide."

[10] IEC Publication 825-2, "Safety of laser products—Part 2: Safety of optical fibre communication systems."

[11] IEC Publication 1280-2-1, "Fibre optic communication subsystem basic test procedures; Part 2: Test procedures for digital systems; Section 1—Receiver sensitivity and overload measurement."

[12] IEC Publication 1280-2-2, "Fibre optic communication subsystem basic test procedures; Part 2: Test procedures for digital systems; Section 2—Optical eye pattern, waveform and extinction ratio measurement."

[13] ITU-T Recommendation G.650, "Definition and test methods for the relevant parameters of single-mode fibres," 1996.

[14] ITU-T Recommendation G.652, "Characteristics of a single-mode optical fiber cable," April 1997.

[15] ITU-T Recommendation G.653, "Characteristics of a dispersion-shifted single-mode optical fiber cable," April 1997.

[16] ITU-T Recommendation G.655, "Characteristics of a non-zero dispersion-shifted single-mode optical fiber cable," Oct. 1996.

[17] ITU-T Recommendation G.661, "Definition and test methods for the relevant generic parameters of optical fiber amplifiers," Nov. 1996.

[18] ITU-T Recommendation G.662, "Generic characteristics of optical fiber amplifier devices and sub-systems," July 1995.

[19] ITU-T Recommendation G.663, "Application related aspects of optical fiber amplifier devices and sub-systems," July 1995.

[20] ITU-T Draft Recommendation G.664, "General Automatic Power Shut-down Procedure for Optical Transport Systems," Oct. 1998.

[21] ITU-T Recommendation G.671, "Transmission characteristics of passive optical components," Nov. 1996.

[22] ITU-T Recommendation G.681, "Functional Characteristics of Interoffice and Long-Haul Line Systems Using Optical Amplifiers, Including Optical Multiplexers," June 1986.

[23] ITU-T Draft Rec. G.691, "Optical Interfaces for Single Channel SDH Systems with Optical Amplifiers, and STM-64 Systems," Oct. 1998.

[24] ITU-T Draft Rec. G.692, "Optical Interfaces for Multi-channel Systems with Optical Amplifiers," Oct. 1998.

[25] ITU-T Recommendation G.707, "Network node interface for the synchronous digital hierarchy," 1996.

[26] ITU-T Draft Recommendation G.709, "Network Node Interface for the Optical Transport Network (OTN)," Oct. 1998.

[27] ITU-T Draft Recommendation G.795, "Forward error correction for submarine applications," 1996.

[28] ITU-T Draft Recommendation G.798, "Characteristics of Optical Transport Networks (OTN) Equipment Functional Blocks," Oct. 1998.

[29] ITU-T Recommendation G.805, "Generic Functional Architecture of Transport Networks," Oct. 1998.

[30] ITU-T Draft Recommendation G.871, Framework for Optical Networking Recommendations," Oct. 1998.

[31] ITU-T Draft Recommendation G.872, "Architecture of Optical Transport Networks," Oct. 1998.

[32] ITU-T Draft Recommendation G.873, "Optical Transport Network Requirements," Oct. 1998.

[33] ITU-T Draft Recommendation G.874, "Management Aspects of the Optical Transport Network Element," Oct. 1998.

[34] ITU-T Draft Recommendation G.875, "Optical Transport Network Management Information Model for the Network Element View," Oct. 1998.

[35] ITU-T Recommendation G.911, "Parameters and calculation methodologies for reliability and availability of fibre optic systems," 1993.

[36] ITU-T Recommendation G.955, "Digital line systems based on the 1544 kbit/s and the 2048 kbit/s hierarchy on optical fibre cables," 1993.

[37] ITU-T Recommendation G.957, "Optical interfaces for equipments and systems relating to the synchronous digital hierarchy," 1995.

[38] ITU-T Recommendation G.958, "Digital line systems based on the synchronous digital hierarchy for use on optical fibre cables," 1994.

[39] ITU-T Draft Recommendation G.959, "Optical Networking Physical Layer Interfaces," Feb. 1999.

[40] Bellcore GR-253, "Synchronous Optical Network [SONET) Transport Systems: Common Generic Criteria," Issue 2, Dec. 1995.

PART V
DWDM CURRENT ISSUES AND RESEARCH

Dense wavelength division multiplexing (DWDM) is a technology that promises to increase the bandwidth per fiber as the bit rate and as the number of wavelength increase. DWDM systems and networks are applicable in long-haul applications, metropolitan, local area networks as well as in access networks. Systems with 6, 40, 80, and 120 wavelengths are reality and at 10 Gbps (or 40 Gbps) per channel, their total bandwidth is at an amazing 400 Gbps, 800 Gbps, and 1.2 Tbps, respectively. A bandwidth at 1 Tbps could transmit the contents of most volumes of the largest library in only 1 second. In addition, DWDM promises long fiber spans (100 km or more) without amplification. The significance of this is obvious if one considers that a synchronous optical network (SONET) repeater, for example, may cost thousands of dollars per fiber, per 40 km, in addition to maintenance cost. Figure V.1 illustrates some of the recent DWDM experiments, the number of channels used, the total bandwidth, and the fiber span with the type of amplifier used. In addition, experiments have been conducted by various groups and consortia such

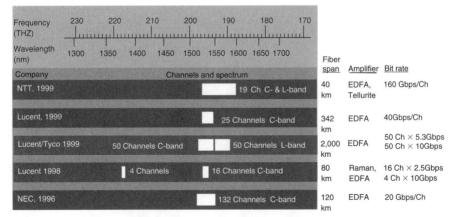

Figure V.1 Some recent DWDM experiments.

as for example the "All-Optical Networking Consortium" (www.ll.mit.edu/con), MONET (www.bell-labs.com/project/MONET), MTONC (www.ntonc.org), ACTS (www.intec.rug.ac.be.horizon/photonic/html), Columbia University Lightwave Group (www.ctr.columbia.edu/~georgios/lightwave.html), and others. Transmitting over longer distances, more bandwidth and more wavelengths in a fiber is a news item that does not go unnoticed.

CHAPTER 17

STATE OF THE ART

17.1 INTRODUCTION

Dense wavelength division multiplexing (DWDM) is a technology that depends heavily on optical components, many of which are state of the art, produced in low-volumes, and thus costly. Consequently, it is reasonable that research continues to develop new and better performing optical components as well as to develop integrated optical compact components at low cost. Amplifiers, multiplexers, filters, signal conditioners, transmitter arrays, and receiver arrays are among the items in development. These components should perform such that center frequencies and power level are compatible, conforming to standard physical interfaces. In addition, standard transport protocols and network management standards are necessary for interoperability and uniform quality of service. This chapter addresses some areas where intense research is conducted. Areas not mentioned are not less important; we simply cannot mention them all.

17.2 CURRENT ISSUES

17.2.1 Lasers and Receivers

Low-cost lasers are important in many applications. Some researchers are even experimenting with organic compounds to create inexpensive high-density plastic lasers and other components. High-power tunable lasers that are inexpensive and laser arrays with narrow line width and sufficient optical power for DWDM applications is another activity. Tunable receivers and receiver arrays at low cost are in development. In the same venue, some techniques generate hundreds of wavelength channels with a single laser.

17.2.2 Optical Cross-Connect

As the number of wavelengths increases to numbers exceeding 200 and approaching 1000, 1000 × 1000 low-loss, non-blocking, and fast-switching optical cross-connect devices are a challenge. Today, there are interesting proposals to produce such a device, however, which becomes a commercial product remains to be seen.

17.2.3 Optical Add-Drop Multiplexers

Low-cost optical add-drop multiplexers (OADMs) are key components in optical networks. OADM devices allow to drop-off and add wavelengths selectively, and pass through all other wavelengths. Low-loss and low-cost OADM devices that add/drop groups of wavelengths on a selective basis are another challenge.

Fibers will soon be connected to the desktop computer and multimedia devices. The bit rate to the home at 64 Kbps in the 1960s will be higher than 1.5 to 2 Mbps in the 2000s (in some cases it may be up to 50 Mbps). These applications will demand extremely low-cost and reliable optical devices (transmitters, receivers, and filters).

17.2.4 Optical Memories and Variable Delay Lines

Optical delay lines consist of fiber cut at lengths that, based on travel time of light in the fiber medium, can delay light by a fixed amount of time. This principle is already used in monolithic interferometers. However, compact optical devices that can store a light pulse of as long as needed would construct a true optical memory and a variable delay. Such devices would be used to treat light pulses in a similar manner as electronic pulses and construct optical integrated sub-systems with time division concepts as well as computation properties.

17.2.5 Non-Intrusive Optical Monitoring

Non-intrusive optical signal monitoring is difficult to perform but important. The optical signal needs to be monitored for power, noise, "eye" closure (enough power to be detected by the receiver), wavelength accuracy, and line width. In addition, if a wavelength channel carries supervisory information, including telemetry, some information needs to be terminated whereas some other needs to be passed transparently. In general, non-intrusive optical monitoring reduces the amount of opto-electronics, reduces latency, and increases reliability.

17.2.6 DWDM System Dynamic Reconfigurability

System dynamic reconfigurability implies wavelength and bandwidth management and thus, tunable optical devices (lasers, receivers, and filters).

17.2.7 Optical Backplanes

The incoming optical signal at a port will be monitored and the optical signal will be directly coupled to an optical backplane that routes the signals to another unit (such as an optical cross-connect fabric) of the system. Optical backplanes provide a cost-effective and compact solution to an all-optical system.

17.2.8   Standards

Currently, standards have been issued (see References), others are being drafted, and others are in the proposal phase. As DWDM evolves, more proposals are expected to be submitted to address emerging issues on all aspects of DWDM systems and networking. The standards bodies are evaluating the proposed standards.

17.2.9   Network Issues

DWDM in optical networks is new territory and thus many issues emerge that have not been addressed before. These issues boil down to performance, efficiency, flexibility, reliability, scalability, and cost. Currently, there is a vast amount of work in progress to resolve these issues, and thus, we feel that we should identify some of them. For example:

- Are all nodes in the DWDM network optically transparent or are they opaque?
- If they are transparent, how do we establish end-to-end (from optical source to destination) wavelength connectivity?
- How do we determine the optimum number of optical components on the end-to-end optical connection (the number of optical components may not be the same from one end to the other) throughout the network?
- How do we execute performance monitoring (PM) in the optical regime?
- What are the rules and mechanisms for fault detection, fault avoidance, and fault restoration on the optical node level, on the optical network level, on the fiber level, and on the wavelength level?
- What are the rules and the mechanisms for DWDM network survivability?
- How do we assure service reliability, service integrity, and quality of service (QoS) in DWDM?
- What are the mechanisms for optical network management?
- How do we transport over the same DWDM network a variety of services (Internet protocol [IP], synchronous optical network/synchronous digital hierarchy [SONET/SDH], asynchronous transfer mode [ATM], Ethernet-type, and others)?
- How do we assign or reassign wavelengths across a DWDM optical network?
- How do we assure security of network and of data?
- As DWDM systems are further deployed and evolve, how do we cope with new emerging issues?

17.2.10   Ultra-High-Speeds at Longer Spans

DWDM systems enable a tremendous bandwidth per fiber. However, lower cost-pressure and competition provide fuel to research and to thinking. Once a speed is achieved, a higher speed is contemplated. Once transmission over a longer fiber span without amplification is achieved, a longer span yet is planned for. Currently, 40 Gbps at 8×80 km spans (with amplification) is reality. If the signal integrity, device noise and loss improve, then optical signal loss, signal noise and bit-error-rate reduce allowing longer yet fiber spans (for the same receiver sensitivity as before). In addition, improvements in forward error correction techniques further reduce BER, and further extend the fiber span (digital wrapper is one example).

17.2.11   Opaque Systems

DWDM technology increases the aggregate bandwidth in a fiber, and large systems terminate many fibers. Thus, the aggregate system bandwidth is the sum of aggregate bandwidth of each fiber. For example, a system with 10 fibers, 40 wavelengths/fiber, and 2.5 Gbps/wavelength has an aggregate bandwidth of 1 Tbps. Presently, an all-optical switching system with a capacity of Tbps is not economical. System cost is dominated by optical device cost and by ultra-fast electronic devices for clock recovery, signal equalization, framing, synchronization, and switching. Thus, systems at these capacity levels are by and large electro-optical (opaque) systems; that is, the system itself is electronic and the interfaces and transmission medium is optical. A possible Tbps opaque system is shown in Figure 17.1.

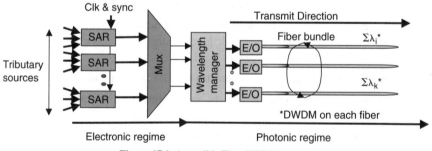

Figure 17.1 A possible Tbps DWDM system.

17.3   ULTRAFAST PATTERN RECOGNITION

One of the key functions in ultra-fast ultra-high bandwidth systems is real-time pattern recognition. By pattern recognition it is meant framing decoding, IP/ATM header fields decoding, error codes decoding, address (source/destination) decoding, and so on. At bit-rates of 10 Gbps (or 40 Gbps), ultra-fast digital electronic circuitry with psec switching capability is required at the high-speed physical layer (pattern recognition in the optical regime—all photonic and without electronics—has not been cost-effectively implemented, yet). Thus, depending on data traffic type, it may be required to recognize millions of patterns per second and perhaps translate each one to another pattern.

This ultra-fast electronic "recognizer" circuitry should not be complex; it may be limited to a clock circuitry and a simple shift register to capture a byte or a word in real time. Reading bytes or words reduces the recognition speed by 8 or 16 times the bit rate. Thus, the "recognizer" can operate a little slower in the nsec regime (and not in the psec).

Devices that can perform fast pattern recognition and translation are known, such as content addressable memories (CAM). When a pattern is applied at the parallel data input of the CAM, the device recognizes it and translates it to another pattern, if needed. The complete operation takes place in one clock cycle. However, commercially available CAMs operate in the order of 100 ns, the pattern set is limited, and the power consumption is relatively high, increasing complexity and thus cost of the system.

A different approach uses fast random access memory (RAM) devices with an access cycle of less than 4 ns, and capable to recognize and translate millions of patterns. This simple approach, known as *associative RAM-based CAM* (AR-CAM), accomplishes pattern recognition and translation at giga-pattern/sec cost effectively (Figure 17.2).

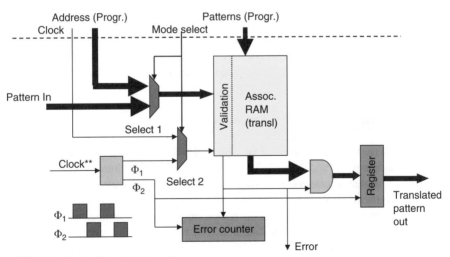

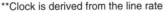
**Clock is derived from the line rate

Figure 17.2 Implementation of an associative RAM-based CAM (AR-CAM).

17.3.1 Example: SONET/SDH

SONET and SDH systems are based on synchronous frame communication principles. Each frame is repeated every 125 µs. The first bytes of a frame (two bytes in
an OC-3, 8 bytes in an OC-12) contain a fixed pattern that is used for synchronization purposes. Other bytes are used for error control, pointers in the payload area,
protection switching, and so on. See Table 14.2 for SONET and SDH rates.

A signal at ~10 Gbps that consists of 196 OC-3 multiplexed signals presents a
challenge in recognizing synchronization patterns and other patterns in the overhead
section of OC-3 frames. AR-CAMs with an 8-bit–wide address bus can cope comfortably with such high pattern recognition rate.

17.3.2 Example: ATM

ATM consists of 53-byte frames. Unlike STM, they do not all arrive synchronously.
However, ATM cells may have been mapped onto the STM payload. ATM cells consist of a 5-byte header and a 48-byte payload. The five bytes of the ATM-cell header
are partitioned (in the case of network-to-network interface or NNI) as follows:

- Virtual path identifier: 12 bits
- Virtual channel identifier: 16 bits
- Payload type identifier and cell loss priority: 4 bits
- Head error control: 8 bits

In a high cell-rate STM case, there may be 350,000 ATM cells per second. That is,
pattern recognition in 1.4 µs is required. However, assuming that there are 16 incoming sources, each with 350,000 cells/s, then recognition time is 8.5 ns. A single
AR-CAM could accomplish this task very comfortably, whereas a CAM could not.
Thus, ATM cells may be quickly recognized and rerouted with the minimum amount
of latency.

17.3.3 Example: Internet Protocol

IP packets based on the IP protocol version 4 (IPv4) consist of an IP header (6×32
bits) and a datagram (up to 65,535 octets) and similarly for future IP versions such
as IPv6. A router fragments the datagram and attaches to each one an IP packet
header. Fragments may not be of equal length. Based on the network used (SONET/
ATM/other) to transport IP packets, the packet may be further segmented by the segmentation and reassembly (SAR) function. The receiving terminal reassembles all
fragments, based on flags and offset (flags and offset are contained in the IP header).
The IP header contains information such as the following:

- Version field (IP format, version of protocol): 4 bits

- Internet header length (measured in 32-bit words): 4 bits
- Type of service (QoS): 8 bits
- Total length (of datagram, up to 65,535 octets): 16 bits
- ID (unique for each datagram used to reassemble): 16 bits
- Flags (O, DF, DM): 3 bits
- Fragment offset (up to 8,192 fragments): 12 bits
- Time to live (time to remain on Internet): 8 bits
- Protocol (upper layer protocol): 8 bits
- Header checksum: 16 bits
- Source addr.: 32 bits (IPv4), 128 bits in *colon hexadecimal* (IPv6)
- Destination addr.: 32 bits (IPv4), 128 bits in *colon hex* (IPv6)
- Options & padding: 32 bits

Thus, AR-CAMs may be used to recognize multiple IP packets fast (within a clock cycle) with a negligible amount of latency, thus addressing one of the optical networks issue, that is fast routability (via fast recognition).

17.4   CURRENT RESEARCH: WAVELENGTH BUS

Current DWDM systems have a number of wavelengths (channels) in a fiber but each wavelength is allocated for one channel. Therefore, the total bandwidth capacity of the DWDM fiber is the sum of bandwidth of each channel. To maximize the efficiency of the bandwidth per fiber, wavelengths may be organized in parallel buses (e.g., five buses each consisting of 8 wavelengths), or fewer buses and individual wavelengths to meet different requirements and provide compatibility with existing systems.

Now, consider a multiplicity of data tributaries. In addition, consider that bytes from each tributary are in parallel (not serial) and the tributaries are byte-multiplexed, forming a multiplexed 8-wavelength bus. The parallel multiplexed data is now transmitted over 8 wavelengths of an 8-wavelength bus.

All wavelengths of a bus carry modulated information at the same bit rate (e.g., 10 Gbps). In this case, the total bandwidth of the bus is $8 \times 10 = 80$ Gbps. Because tributaries are multiplexed, many tributaries and each at a different rate may be multiplexed, up to a total aggregate of 80 Gbps. This method establishes flexibility, scalability, and efficient bandwidth utilization that typically is not readily achieved with traditional DWDM systems where, for example, 8 wavelength channels would each carry data at a different rate. In addition, an 8-wavelength bus allows for more than eight users to share the total aggregate bandwidth, as opposed to traditional DWDM that allows for as many users as the number of wavelengths in the fiber (e.g., eight wavelengths or channels for eight users).

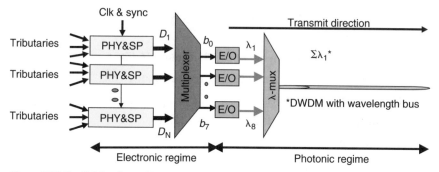

Figure 17.3 Parallel data buses (D_1-D_N) are multiplexed to form a high-speed high-aggregate band-width parallel bus (b_0-b_7) each rail of which is launched into the fiber to construct a par-allel wavelength bus $(\lambda_1-\lambda_8)$.

Figure 17.3 illustrates a multiplicity of tributaries that are terminated at a phys-ical interface (PHY) and if serial data are converted into parallel (SP), D_i. Then, all parallel data are multiplexed by the multiplexer unit to form a high-speed high-aggregate bandwidth parallel bus (b_0-b_7), each rail of which modulates a laser transmitter to form a parallel wavelength bus $(\lambda_1-\lambda_8)$, each rail transmitting at the same rate.

In the receive direction (Figure 17.4), the reverse takes place. A parallel wave-length bus $(\lambda_1-\lambda_8)$ is received and converted to an electrical parallel bus (b_0-b_7), and since each rail is at the same rate, only one clock circuitry is necessary. The par-allel bus feeds a fast recognizer (AR-CAM) that recognizes the target destination of each multiplexed channel (packet, cell or time-slot), and in conjunction with a de-multiplexer, each payload is delivered to its target destination.

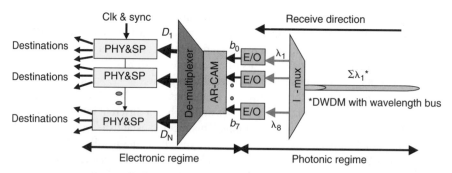
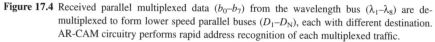

Figure 17.4 Received parallel multiplexed data (b_0-b_7) from the wavelength bus $(\lambda_1-\lambda_8)$ are de-multiplexed to form lower speed parallel buses (D_1-D_N), each with different destination. AR-CAM circuitry performs rapid address recognition of each multiplexed traffic.

REFERENCES

[1] S.V. Kartalopoulos, *Understanding SONET/SDH and ATM: Communications Networks for the next millennium*, IEEE Press, New York, N.Y., 1999.

[2] R. Ramaswami, and K.N. Sivarajan, *Optical Networks*, Morgan Kaufmann Publ., San Francisco, CA, 1998.

[3] B. Mukherjee, *Optical Communication Networks*, McGraw-Hill, 1997.

[4] I.P. Kaminow, ed., and T.L. Koch, ed., *Optical Fiber Communications IIIA and Optical Fiber Communications IIIB*, Academic Press, 1997.

[5] E. Traupman, P. O'Connell, G. Minnis, M. Jadoul, and H. Mario, "The Evolution of the Existing Infrastructure," *IEEE Communications Mag.*, vol. 37, no. 6, 1999, pp. 134-139.

[6] A.G. Malis, "Reconstructing Transmision Networks Using ATM and DWDM," *IEEE Communications Mag.*, vol. 37, no. 6, 1999, pp. 140–145.

[7] T-H Wu, *Fiber Network Service Survivability.* Artec House, Boston, 1992

[8] L. Boivin, M.C. Nuss, W.H. Knox, and J.B. Stark, "206-Channel chirped-pulse wavelength-division multiplexed transmitter," *Electronics Letters*, vol. 33, no. 10, pp. 827–828, 1997.

[9] J.M. Simmons, et al., "Optical Crossconnects of Reduced Complexity for WDM Networks with Bidirectional Symmetry," *IEEE Photonics Technology Letters*, vol. 10, no. 6, June 1998, pp. 819–821.

[10] E.A. De Souza, et al., "Wavelength-division multiplexing with femtosecond pulses," *Optics Letters*, vol. 20, no. 10, 1995, pp. 1166–1168.

[11] S.V. Kartalopoulos, "An Associative RAM-based CAM and its Application to Broad-Band Communications Systems," *IEEE Trans. Neural Networks,* vol. 9, no. 5, 1998, pp. 1036-1041.

[12] S.V. Kartalopoulos, "Ultra-fast Pattern Recognition in Broadband Communications Systems," *ISPACS'98 Conference Proceedings,* Melbourne, Australia, November 1998.

[13] A. Asthana et al., "Towards a Gigabit IP Router," *J. High-Speed Networks,* vol. 1, no. 4, 1992.

[14] S.V. Kartalopoulos, "The λ-bus in Ultra-fast DWDM Systems," TBP.

[15] S.V. Kartalopoulos, "Synchronization Techniques Ultra-fast DWDM Systems: The λ-bus TBP."

[16] S.V. Kartalopoulos, "Add-Drop with Ultra-fast DWDM/λ-bus," TBP.

[17] S.V. Kartalopoulos, "Increasing Bandwidth Capacity in DWDM/λ-bus Systems," TBP.

[18] S.V. Kartalopoulos, "Cryptographic Techniques with Ultra-fast DWDM/λ-bus Systems," TBP.

[19] C.A. Brackett, "Dense Wavelength Division Multiplexing Networks: Principles and Applications," *IEEE JSAC,* vol. 8, no. 6, Aug. 1990.

[20] Internet study group: http://www.internet2.edu.

[21] H. Yoshimura, K-I. Sato, and N. Takachio, "Future Photonic Transport Networks Based on WDM Technologies," *IEEE Communications Magazine,* vol. 37, no. 2, Feb. 1999, pp. 74–81.

[22] L.H. Sahasrabuddhe, and B. Mukherjee, "Light-Trees: Optical Multicasting for Improved Performance in Wavelength-Routed Networks," *IEEE Communications Magazine,* vol. 37, no. 2, Feb. 1999, pp. 67-73.

[23] M.A. Marsan, A. Bianco, E. Leonardi, A. Morabito, and F. Neri, "All-Optical WDM Multi-Rings with Differentiated QoS," *IEEE Communications Magazine,* vol. 37, no. 2, Feb. 1999, pp. 58–66.

[24] Y. Pan, C. Qiao, and Y. Yang, "Optical Multistage Interconnection Networks: New Challenges and Approaches," *IEEE Communications Magazine,* vol. 37, no. 2, Feb. 1999, pp. 50–56.

[25] K. Sato, *Advances in Transport Network Technologies—Photonic Networks, ATM and SDH,* Artec, 1996.

[26] N. Takachio, and S. Ohteru, "Scale of WDM transport network using different types of fibers," *IEEE JSAC,* vol. 16, no. 7, 1998, pp. 1320–1326.

[27] B. Mukhergie, *Optical Communications Networks,* McGraw-Hill, New York, 1997.

[28] P.E. Green, Jr., *Fiber Optic Networks,* Prentice Hall, Englewood Cliffs, N.J., 1993.

[29] M. A. Marsan et al., "Daisy: a Scalable All-Optical Packet Network with Multi-Fiber Ring Topology," *Computer Networks and ISDN Systems,* vol. 30, 1998, pp. 1065–82.

[30] I. Gidon, and Y. Ofek, "MetaRing—a Full-Duplex Ring with Fairness and Spatial Reuse," *IEEE Trans. Communications,* vol. 41, no. 1, Jan. 1993, pp. 110-20.

[31] S. Ohteru, and K. Inoue, "Optical Time Division Multiplexer Utilizing Modulation Signal Supplied to Optical Modulation as a Reference," *IEEE Photon,* vol. 8, no. 9, 1996, pp. 1181-1183.

[32] J.R. Freer, *Computer Communications and Networks,* IEEE Press, 1996.

[33] R. Handel and M.N. Huber, *Integrated Broadband Network,* Addison Wesley, 1991.

[34] R.D. Gitlin, J.F. Hayes, and S.B. Weinstein, *Data Communications Principles,* Plenum, New York, 1992.

[35] S.V. Kartalopoulos, "A Manhattan Fiber Distributed Data Interface Architecture," *Globecom'90,* San Diego, December 2-5, 1990.

[36] S.V. Kartalopoulos, "Disaster Avoidance in the Manhattan Fiber Distributed Data Interface Network," *Globecom'93,* Houston, TX, December 2, 1993.

[37] S.V. Kartalopoulos, "A Plateau of Performance?" *IEEE Communications Magazine,* Sept. 1992, pp. 13-14.

[38] A.E. Willner, "Mining the optical bandwidth for a terabit per second," *IEEE Spectrum,* April 1997, pp. 32-41.

[39] S.V. Kartalopoulos, *Understanding Neural Networks and Fuzzy Logic,* IEEE Press, New York, NY, 1995.

[40] Members of the Technical Staff, *Transmission Systems for Communications,* Bell Telephone Laboratories, 1982.

[41] J. Nellist, *Understanding Telecommunications and Lightwave Systems,* IEEE Press, 1996.

[42] W.Y. Zhou and Y. Wu, "COFDM: An Overview," *IEEE Trans. Broadcasting,* vol. 41, no. 1, Mar. 1995, pp. 1-843.

[43] K-I. Kitayama, "Code Division Multiplexing Lightwave Networks Based upon Optical Code Conversion," *IEEE J. on Selected Areas in Communications,* vol. 16, no. 7, Sept. 1998, pp. 1309–1310.

[44] T. Shiragaki, et al., "Optical Cross-Connect System Incorporated with Newly Developed Operation and Management System," *IEEE J. on Selected Areas in Communications,* vol. 16, no. 7, Sept. 1998, pp. 1179–1189.

[45] S. Johansson, et al., "A Cost-Effective Approach to Introduce an Optical WDM Network in the Metropolitan Environment," *IEEE J. on Selected Areas in Communications,* vol. 16, no. 7, Sept. 1998, pp. 1109–1122.

[46] Y. Miyao, and H. Saito, "Optimal Design and Evaluation of Survivable WDM Transport Networks," *IEEE J. on Selected Areas in Communications,* vol. 16, no. 7, Sept. 1998, pp. 1190–1198.

[47] B. Van Caenegem, W. Van Parys, and P.M. Demeester, "Dimensioning of Survivable WDM Networks," *IEEE J. on Selected Areas in Communications,* vol. 16, no. 7, Sept. 1998, pp. 1146–1157.

[48] O. Crochat, and J-Y. Le Boudec, "Design Protection for WDM Optical Networks," *IEEE J. on Selected Areas in Communications,* vol. 16, no. 7, Sept. 1998, pp. 1158–1165.

[49] M.W. Maeda, "Management and Control of Transparent Optical Networks," *IEEE J. on Selected Areas in Communications,* vol. 16, no. 7, Sept. 1998, pp. 1008–1023.

[50] E. Karasan, and E. Ayanoglu, "Performance of WDM Transport Networks," *IEEE J. on Selected Areas in Communications,* vol. 16, no. 7, Sept. 1998, pp. 1081–1096.

STANDARDS

[1] ANSI T1X1.5/99-002, "A Proposal for Providing Channel-Associated Optical Channel Overhead in the OTN," George Newsome and Paul Bonenfant, Lucent, Jan. 1999.

[2] ANSI T1X1.5/99-003, "A Proposed Implementation for a Digital 'Wrapper' for OCh Overhead," James Ballintine, Lucent, Jan. 1999.

[3] ANSI T1X1.5/99-004, "Optical Channel Overhead Carried on the Optical Supervisory Channel," George Newsome and Paul Bonenfant, Lucent, Jan. 1999.

[4] ANSI T1X1.5/99-146, "Proposed OCh-OH Assignments for the OCh Frame," James Ballintine, Lucent, May 1999.

ACRONYMS

10BaseT = 10 Mbps over Twisted Pair; an Ethernet standard (IEEE 802.3)
100BaseT = 100 Mbps over Twisted Pair; an Ethernet standard (IEEE 802.3)
1000BaseT = 1000 Mbps over Twisted Pair; an Ethernet standard (IEEE 802.3ab)
2B1Q = Two Bits to One Quarternary
2FSK = Two-level Frequency Shift Keying
3R = Reshaping, Retiming, and Reamplifying
4B/5B = Four Bit to Five Bit coding
4FSK = Four-level Frequency Shift Keying
7B/8B = Seven bit to eight bit
8B/10B = Eight Bit to Ten Bit coding

AAL = ATM Adaptation Layer
ACK = Acknowledgment
ACTS = Advanced Communications Technology and Services
ADM = Add-Drop Multiplexer
ADSL = Asymmetric Digital Subscriber Line
AH = Applications Header
AIS = Alarm Indication Signal; aka blue alarm
AIU = Access Interface Unit
Al = Aluminum
AMI = Alternate Mark Inversion
AN = Access Node
ANSI = American National Standards Institute
AON = All Optical Network
AOTF = Acousto-Optic Tunable Filter
AP = Access Point; Adjunct Processor

APD = Avalanche Photo-Detector; Avalanche Photodiode
APON = ATM-based broadband PON
APS = Automatic Protection Switching
AR = Antireflective
As = Arsenic
ASE = Amplified Spontaneous Emission; Amplifier Spontaneous Emission
ASK = Amplitude Shift Keying
ASP = Adjunct Service Point
ATM = Asynchronous Transfer Mode
ATU = ADSL Transceiver Unit
AU = Administrative Unit
AWG = Array Waveguide Grating

B6ZS = Bipolar six Zero Substitution
B8ZS = Bipolar eight Zero Substitution
BBER = Background Block Error Ratio
BCD = Binary Coded Decimal; Blocked Calls Delayed
BER = Bit Error Rate
BFSK = Binary FSK
BICI = Broadband Inter-Carrier Interface
BIM = Byte Interleaved Multiplexer
BIP = Bit Interleaved Parity
BIP8 = Bit Interleaved Parity 8 field
BPF = Band-Pass Filter
Bps = Bits per second
BPSK = Binary PSK
BV = Bipolar Violation

CAC = Call Admission Control
CAM = Content Addressable Memory
CAP = Carrierless Amplitude Phase; Competitive Access Provider
CATV = Cable Television
CBR = Constant Bit Rate
CDC = Chromatic Dispersion Coefficient
CDMA = Code Division Multiple Access
CDV = Cell Delay Variation
CELP = Code Excited Linear Prediction
CER = Cell Error Rate
CIU = Channel Interface Unit
CLP = Cell Loss Priority
CLR = Cell Loss Rate
CM = Communications Module
CMI = Coded Mark Inversion

CMOS = Complementary Metal Oxide Semiconductor
CPDWM = Chirped Pulse WDM
CPRING = Client Protection Ring
CRBS = Cell Relay Bearer Service
CRC = Cyclic Redundancy Check
CS = Convergence Sublayer; Channel Spacing
CSA = Carrier Serving Area
CTD = Cell Transfer Delay
CTI = Computer Telephony Integration
CU = Channel Unit
CV = Coding Violation
CW = Continuous Wave
CWDM = Coarse Wavelength Division Multiplexer

DA = Dispersion Accommodation
dB = Decibel
dBm = Decibel with 1 mWatt reference level
DBR = Distributed Bragg Reflector
DCF = Dispersion Compensated Fiber; Distributed Coordination Function
DCS = Digital Cross-connect System
DES = Data Encryption Standard
DFB = Distributed Feedback
DFCF = Dispersion-Flattened Compensated Fiber
DFF = Dispersion-Flattened Fiber
DFI = Domain Format Identifier
DGD = Differential Group Delay
DMTF = Desktop Management Task Force
DPA = Dynamic Packet Assignment
DSCF = Dispersion-Slope Compensated Fiber
DSF = Dispersion Shifted Fiber
DSn = Digital Signal level n; $n = 0, 1, 2, 3$
DTF = Dielectric Thin Film
DWDM = Dense Wavelength Division Multiplexing
DWE = Dynamic Wavelength Equalizer

E1 = A wideband digital facility at 2.048 Mbps, aka CEPT-1
E3 = A broadband digital facility at 34.368 Mbps, aka CEPT-3
EBC = Errored Block Count
EC = Echo Canceller; Embedded Channel
EDFA = Erbium-Doped Fiber Amplifier
EML = Element Management Layer
E-n = European signal level n ($n = 1, 2, 3,$ and 4)
E/O = Electrical to Optical

F = Fluoride
FBG = Fiber Bragg Grating
FBS = Fiber Bundle Switch
FDDI = Fiber Distributed Data Interface
FDM = Frequency Division Multiplexing
FITL = Fiber In The Loop
FOA = Fiber Optic Amplifier
FOT = Fiber Optic Terminal
FOTS = Fiber Optic Transmission System
FPI = Fabry-Perot Interferometer
FPM = Four Photon Mixing
FPS = Fast Packet Switching
FR = Frame Relay
FSK = Frequency Shift Keying
FT = Fixed Transmitter
FTTB = Fiber To The Building
FTTC = Fiber To The Curb
FTTCab = Fiber To The Cabinet
FTTD = Fiber To The Desk
FTTH = Fiber-to-the-Home
FTTO = Fiber To The Office
FTTT = Fiber To The Town
FWM = Four-Wave Mixing

Ga = Gallium
Gbps = Gigabits per second = 1,000 Mbps
GEF = Gain Equalization Filter
Ghz = Gigahertz (10^9 Hz)
GRIN = Graded Index fiber
GRIN-rod = Graded Index Rod
GVD = Group Velocity Dispersion

IF = Interference Filter
IC = Integrated Circuit; Interference Canceller
ICI = Inter-Carrier Interface
IEEE = Institute of Electrical and Electronics Engineers
IETF = Internet Engineering Task Force
IM/DD = Intensity Modulation with Direct Detection
In = Indium
IP = Internet Protocol
IPv6 = Internet Protocol version 6
IR = Infrared
ISI = Inter-Symbol Interference
ITU = International Telecommunications Union
ITU-T = ITU Telecommunications standardization Sector

Kbps = Kilobits per second = 1,000 bps
K×N = *K*-input, *N*-output Port

LA = Line Amplifier
LAN = Local Area Network
LD = Laser Diode; Long Distance
LED = Light Emitting Diode
$LiNbO_3$ = Lithium Niobate
LPF = Low Pass Filter

M1 = Level 1 Multiplexer
MAN = Metropolitan Area Network
MBE = Molecular Beam Epitaxy
Mbps = Megabits per second (1000 Kbps)
MBS = Maximum Burst Rate
MCVD = Modified Chemical Vapor Deposition
MEMS = Micro-Electro-Mechanical System
MFL = Multi-frequency cavity Laser
Mhz = Megahertz (10^6 Hertz)
MO = Managed Object
MOCVD = Metal Organic Chemical Vapor Dispersion
MONET = Multiwavelength Optical NETworking
MPOA = Multi-Protocol Over ATM
MQW = Multiple Quantum Well
MQWL = Multiple Quantum Well Lasers
msec = milliseconds
μsec = microseconds
mW = milliWatts

NAP = Network Access Provider
NAU = Network Addressable Unit
NC = Network Connection
Nd = Neodymium
NE = Network Element
NEXT = Near End Cross Talk
NF = Noise Figure
NGI = Next Generation Internet
NIC = Network Interface Card
NIU = Network Interface Unit
nm = nanometer
NRZ = Non Return to Zero
nsec = nanosecond
NT = Network Termination
NZDF = Nonzero Dispersion Fiber

OA = Optical Amplifier
OAM = Operations, Administration and Management
OADM = Optical ADM
OAMP = OAM and Provisioning Services
OAR = Optically Amplified receiver
OAS = Optical Amplifier Section
OAT = Optically Amplified Transmitter
OC = Optical Carrier
OCDM = Optical Code Division Multiplexing
OCh = Optical Channel
OCn = Optical Carrier level n (n=1, 3, 12, 48, 192)
ODL = Optical Data Link
ODU = Optical Demultiplex Unit
O/E = Optical to Electrical conversion
OEIC = Opto-Electronic Integrated Circuit
OFA = Optical Fiber Amplifier
OFD = Optical Frequency Discriminator
OFDM = Optical Frequency-Division Multiplexing; Orthogonal Frequency-
    Division Multiplexing
OFS = Optical Fiber System
OH = Overhead; Hydroxile
OLC = Optical Loop Carrier
OLS = Optical Line System
OMU = Optical Multiplex Unix
ONTC = Optical Networks Technology Consortium
ONU = Optical Network Unit
OOK = On-Off Keying
OPLL = Optical Phase-Locked Loop
OPS = Optical Protection Switch
ORL = Optical Return Loss
OS = Operating System
OSC = Optical Supervisory Channel
OSNR = Optical Signal-to-Noise Ratio
OTDM = Optical Time Division Multiplexing
OTE = Optical Terminating Equipment
OTS = Optical Transmission Section
OTU = Optical Translator Unit
OVD = Outer Vapor Deposition
OXC = Optical Cross-Connect

P = Phosphorus
PD = Photodiode; Propagation Delay
PDFA = Praseodymium-Doped Fiber Amplifier
PDL = Polarization Dependent Loss

PDN = Packet Data Network
PFCB = Per-Fluoro-Cyclo-Butane
PHASARS = phased-array gratings
PHY = Physical Layer
PIC = Photonic Integrated Circuit
PIN = Positive Intrinsic Negative photodiode
PLC = Planar Lightwave Circuit
PLL = Phase-Locked Loop
PM = Performance Monitoring
PMD = Polarization Mode Dispersion
PMF = Polarization-Maintaining Fiber
POP = Point Of Presence
PPP = Point-to-Point Protocol
PPS = Path Protection Switching
PRK = Phase Reversal Keying
PSK = Phase-Shift Keying
PVC = Permanent Virtual Circuit
PVP = Permanent Virtual Path

QAM = Quadrature Amplitude Modulation
QoS = Quality of Service
QPSK = Quadrature PSK; Quartenary PSK; Quadriphase PSK

RF = Radio Frequency
RS = Reduced Slope
RSVP = Resource reSerVation setup Protocol
RZ = Return to Zero

SAP = Service Access Point
SAR = Segmentation And Re-assembly
SBS = Stimulated Brillouin Scattering amplifiers
SCR = Sustainable Cell Rate
SDH = Synchronous Digital Hierarchy
SDM = Space Division Multiplexing
SDSL = Symmetric DSL
SEED = Self Electro-optic Effect Device
SFL = Single-frequency laser
SI = Step Index
SLA = Service Level Agreement
SLM = Synchronous Line Multiplexer
SM = Switching Module
SMDS = Switched Multi-megabit Digital Services
SMF = Single Mode Fiber
SMN = SONET Management Network; SDH Management Network

SN = Sequence Number; Service Node
SNA = Systems Network Architecture
SNAP = Sub-Net Access Protocol
SNCP = Sub-Network Connection Protection
SNMP = Simple Network Management Protocol
SNR = Signal to Noise Ratio
SOA = Semiconductor Optical Amplifier
SOHO = Small Office/Home Office
SONET = Synchronous Optical Network
SPM = Self Phase Modulation
SPRING = Shared Protection Ring
S-PVC = Soft PVC
SRS = Stimulated Raman Scattering
SRTS = Synchronous Residual Time Stamp
SS7 = Signaling System #7
SSAP = Source Service Access Point; Session Service Access Point (ISO)
SSMF = Standard Single Mode Fiber
SSR = Side mode Suppression Ratio
STB = Set Top Box
SVC = Switched Virtual Circuit

T1 = A digital carrier facility used to transmit a DS1 signal at 1.544 Mbps
Tbps = Terabits per second = 1,000 Gbps
TCM = Tandem Connection Maintenance; Trellis Code Modulation
TCP = Transmission Control Protocol
TCP/IP = Transmission Control Protocol/Internet Protocol
TDM = Time Division Multiplexing
TE = Terminal Equipment; Transverse Electric
TEC = Thermo-Electric Cooler
tFWM = Temporal FWM
Thz = Tera-hertz (1000 GHz)
TM = Terminal Multiplexer; Transverse Magnetic
TOF = Tunable Optical Filters
TST = Time-Space-Time switch
TU = Tributary Unit

UBR = Unspecified Bit Rate
UDP = User Datagram Protocol
UI = Unit Interval
UHF = Ultra-High Frequency
UNI = User to Network Interface
URL = Uniform Resource Locator
UV = Ultraviolet

VAD = Vapor-phase Axial Deposition
VBR = Variable Bit Rate
VC = Virtual Channel
VCC = VC Connection
VDSL = Very-high-bit rate DSL
VLAN = Virtual LAN
VOA = Variable Optical Attenuator
VoIP = Voice over IP
VP = Virtual Path
VPC = VP Connection

WADM = Wavelength Add-Drop Multiplexer
WAN = Wide Area Network
WDM = Wavelength Division Multiplexing
WGR = Waveguide Grating Router
WIS = Wavelength Independent Switch
WIXC = Wavelength Interchanging Cross-connect
WPON = WDM PON
WSC = Wavelength Selective Coupler
WSS = Wavelength Selective Switch
WSXC = Wavelength Selective Cross-Connect
WORM = Write Once, Read Many

xDSL = any-DSL

YIG = Yttrium Iron Garnet

ANSWERS

CHAPTER 1

1. Depending on growth expectation, and economics:
   A. Increase the bit rate to 4 × 2.5 Gbps and use four fibers each at 2.5 Gbps, or, increase the bit-rate to 10 Gbps and use one fiber, or use 10 wavelengths in a single-fiber, each at 1 Gbps, or use 4 wavelengths in a single fiber each at 2.5 Gbps.
   B. Increase the bit rate to 10 Gbps and use one fiber, or use 10 wavelengths in a single fiber, or install additional fiber through the pipe and use each at 1 Gbps.
   C. Increase the bit rate to 10 Gbps and use one fiber, or use 10 wavelengths in a single fiber.

2. The glassplate is transparent for wavelengths in the blue range. It is opaque for all other wavelengths.

3. Because the blue plate is transparent to blue light only and it is opaque to red and thus it lets no red light through it. Similarly, the red plate is transparent to red light only and it is opaque to blue. Thus, one would expect no light (dark) through the two plates.

4. The covered surface reflects photons while the painted black surface absorbs them. Thus, one expects to find the black surface much warmer than the aluminum covered.

CHAPTER 2

1. Light never stops by itself unless it encounters a strong field (one of the reasons we can view distant galaxies). Based on the interaction with the field, it may transfer some of its energy or all of it.

2. What really changes is the wavelength.

3. No. Vacuum has $n = 1$, everything else has n greater than 1.

4. Yes, there would be a reflected ray.

5. $\Theta_t > \Theta_i$,

6. $\lambda_K < \lambda_J$

7. A mirage.

8. Due to refraction, the bottom appears to be closer to the surface although it is deeper.

9. This is a graphical exercise—no answer.

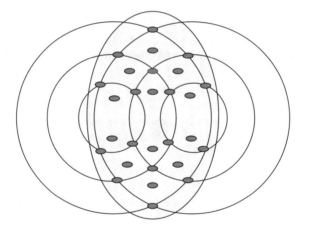

(Diagram simplified for clarity)

10. As the mirror moves alternating bright and dark spots are expected to form, based on the path difference between the two rays B and C.

11. No. It will propagate forever in a straight (per general relativity) line.

12. Although a photon has mass, it also behaves like a wave. Thus, capturing a photon is not like grabbing in space a moving ball and close it in a box. It is merely captured by means of an atom that is raised to a higher energy level and the added energy is later released in the form of a photon. When a photon interacts with an atom, it may either be absorbed by it, it may cause it to release more photons, or it may be deflected by it.

13. $\lambda = 155.459$ nm.

CHAPTER 3

1. The speed of pulses in the fiber is $v = c/n = 3 \times 10^{10}$ cm/sec/1.5 = 2×10^{10} cm/sec.

   The travel time throughout the fiber is: $t = L/v = 10^5$ cm/2 $\times 10^{10}$ cm/sec = 5×10^6 psec.

   The period of each bit is 1/10 GHz = 100 psec. Thus, the fiber bit capacity is 5×10^6 psec/100 psec = 50,000 bits.

2. A larger critical cone implies that part of the photonic energy is not coupled into the fiber, and thus, energy is lost.

3. NA = $\sqrt{(1.48^2 - 1.46^2)} = 0.242487$, and $\Theta_{NA} = \sin^{-1}$ (NA) = 14.03^0

4. Clearly, the single-mode fiber core is more than 5 times smaller than the multiple-mode fiber core. Therefore, the cone of the single mode fiber is much smaller.

5. From $\Delta\tau = \tau_2 - \tau_1$, the spread is calculated to $60 - 30 = 30$ psec. For $k = 3$, the bit rate calculated limit is by $R_b < 1/(k\Delta\tau)$ to 1/3 $\times$ 30 psec $\sim 1/100 \times 10^{-12} = 10^{10} = 10$ Gbps.

6. The OH radical is a dipole with resonant frequency that matches the frequency that corresponds to the wavelength of 1385 nm.

7. The total fiber length is 60 km. Thus the total attenuation is 60 $\times$ 0.1 = 6 dB. The total loss due to connectors, two at the ends and three interconnecting is 5 $\times$ 0.1 = 0.5 dB. Thus the total power loss over the link is 6 + 0.5 dB = 6.5 dB.

8. False. As channel-spacing increases, four-wave mixing contribution decreases.

CHAPTER 4

1. For the relationship that satisfies the values for $\lambda = (2dn)/m$ for the *resonant wavelengths* of a Fabry-Perot resonator the distance d is calculated.

   $d = \lambda m/2n = 1400/2$ nm = 700 nm.

   $R = 0.7$.

   $R = 0.3$.

2. The finesse is estimated by the relationship $F = (\pi R)/[2(1-R)]$.

   (a) $F = (3.14 \times 0.9)/[2(1 - 0.9)] = 14.13$.

   (b) $F = (3.14 \times 0.3)/[2(1 - 0.2)] = 2.35$.

3. 750 nm is half the wavelength of 1300 nm. Thus, the Bragg grating is 5th order for this wavelength.

4. For $n = 1$ (first order) and for $d = 700$ nm, then $\lambda_B = 2 d/n = 2(700/1) = 1400$ nm.

CHAPTER 5

1. There are two, *passive* and *active*.
2. Yes, passive.
3. False. It is an optical demultiplexer.
4. True.
5. Yes.
6. True.
7. They rotate the polarization mode of a specific wavelength from TE to TM.
8. A wavelength demultiplexer.

CHAPTER 6

1. Two, the continuous wave with external modulator and the directly modulating light source.
2. To either; a laser source may be directly or externally modulated.
3. Yes. An LED is a special diode device that emits light.
4. As temperature rises, the LED spectrum shifts and its intensity decreases.
5. They are most suitable in multimode fiber applications.
6. The speed of light within the dielectric material is slower as compared with that in the free space. Thus, the traveled distance in the unit of time is shorter in the dielectric than that in the free space. Comparatively, few Angstroms traveled in the dielectric correspond to many Angstroms in the free space.
7. At minimum they are an active region (where stimulated emission takes place), an optical waveguide (to limit light in a single direction), and optical feedback (a cavity in which light bounces back and forth for gain and filtering purposes).
8. Chirping is minimized if external modulation is used.
9. Resonant cavities may be of the Mach-Zehnder or Fabry-Perot type.
10. The very small thickness of its active region, 50 to 100 Angstroms.
11. Fast tuned (<3 nsec), accurate optical channel spacing, low insertion loss, simultaneous operation of all wavelengths.
12. False. They perform best in the 1550 nm region.

CHAPTER 7

1. Natural: *rods* and *cones* of the eye retina, and chlorophyll. Artificial: Photoresistor and semiconductor PIN.

2. The capacitance of the reversed biased PIN photodiode is a limiting factor to its response (and switching speed).

3. False. It has a high gain.

CHAPTER 8

1. A regenerator converts the optical signal into an electrical signal, conditions and amplifies the electrical, and then converts the electrical into an optical signal. An optical amplifier amplifies an attenuated optical signal directly.

2. An SOA is a semiconductor laser-type device that requires electrical current to excite its electron-hole pairs. An EDFA is an erbium-doped fiber that requires another exciting source of light, known as the pump.

3. In EDFAs, even if no incoming signal is present, there is always some output signal as a result of some excited ions in the fiber; this output is known as amplified spontaneous emission and is spontaneous noise.

4. The light source is either 980 nm or 1480 nm. It is known as *the pump.*

5. They are classified in power *amplifiers,* placed at the output of a laser source, *preamplifiers* placed before the receiver, and *line amplifiers* placed somewhere between the source and the receiver.

6. A wavelength converter is an optical or semiconductor device that receives a signal at one wavelength and it converts it into another.

7. See Section 8.3.2 for description.

8. A wavelength shifter is a dispersion-shifted fiber device in which a pump and a data signal, at different wavelengths, interact to produce a third modulated signal at a wavelength approximately equal to the lower wavelength shifted by the difference of the pump and signal wavelengths.

9. The probe signal is modulated and the pump source is continuous.

10. It requires an interference filter (IF) that acts as a band-pass filter.

CHAPTER 9

1. An OPLL device consists of a tunable laser source, a filter, and a photodiode bridge.

2. Five of the most desirable characteristics of optical couplers are: high isolation, low coupling power loss, no signal reflectivity, no signal absorption, and no through phase shift.

3. Interferometry. Two waves, one from the ring and one from the fiber, encounter each other and depending on their phase interfere constructively or destructively at the coupler.

4. An optical isolator is a device that transmits optical power (of a band of wavelengths) in one direction more than the other direction.

5. It is a device that is based on the property of certain materials to rotate the polarization of a wave by an angle.

6. Yes. A rotator with polarizers may be used to construct an optical isolator.

CHAPTER 10

1. Each row should have only one 1.

2. If more than one 1, then two inputs are directed to the same output—hence collision.

3. Each column should have only one 1.

4. More than one 1s in the same column indicated that an input is broadcasted to more than one outputs. However, the signal amplitude is divided by the number of outputs. Hence, the value "1" in the matrix does not represent the output amplitude of the signal.

5. Only when the inputs are at different wavelength, such as WDM.

6. Each row can have more than one 1, if each input is at different wavelength. Then, two or more inputs are directed to the same output where wavelength division multiplexing takes place.

7. More than one 1 in the same column indicates that an input is directed to more than one outputs. However, the signal intensity is divided by the number of outputs. Hence, the value "1" in the matrix does not represent the output amplitude of the signal.

8. The fastest, in the order of nanoseconds, are semiconductor-based switching devices, such as the $LiNbO_3$. Acousto-optic and MEM devices are in the order of microseconds, and thermo-optic devices in the order of milliseconds.

CHAPTER 11

1. The main function of an optical multiplexer is to couple two or more wavelengths into the same fiber.

2. In general, yes. This is based on the theory that light travels in either direction the same.

3. The prism-based and the diffraction grating demultiplexer.

4. Yes, it is possible with an optical add-drop multiplexer.

5. Yes. Its application is illustrated in Figure 10.6.

6. Yes. With reference to Figure 10.6, conceptually as many wavelengths may be dropped-off and added by using an equal number of 2 × 2 switches.

7. Adding a second circulator would accomplish Add/Drop multiplexing, as shown in Figure.

CHAPTER 12

1. The term "coherent" in optical transmission indicates that another light source is used as the local oscillator.

2. The phase, the frequency, or the amplitude of a carrier signal.

3. It is known as intensity modulation with direct detection (IM/DD).

4. FSK and PSK.

5. The coherent techniques improve receiver sensitivity by $\sim$20 dB and thus they allow for longer fiber spans.

6. An electrical RZ signal oscillates between a negative and a positive voltage. An optical signal changes from high intensity to zero intensity. In optical signal, each logic ONE is about 1/3 of the bit period ON and 2/3 OFF. A logic zero is 3/3 of the bit period OFF.

7. No, in the sense of bipolar electrical signals.

8. 2.5 Gbps.

CHAPTER 13

1. The design and the principle of detection between a PSK and FSK are different. Therefore, it seems unlikely that a PSK receiver would reliably detect a FSK signal.

2. Twelve states.

3. Due to attenuation, the received light is counted in single digit photons. Consequently, the incoming signal should be coupled with the receiver with no losses, the signal should be dispersion compensated, the sensitivity of the receiver should be very high as well as its stability.

4. Both frequencies are the same and they interact interferometrically to decode the signal.

5. An optical (tunable) filter.

INDEX

237

ABOUT THE AUTHOR

Stamatios V. Kartalopoulos is currently with the Advanced Optical Networking Group of Lucent Technologies, Bell Labs Innovations, formerly known as AT&T. He holds a B.Sc. in Physics, a graduate Diploma in Electronics, and an M.Sc and Ph.D. in Engineering Science.

His most recent contributions in the area of communications are in DWDM Systems, IP Optical Networks, SONET/SDH and ATM systems, and ultrafast pattern recognition. Since 1979 he has made technical contributions to digital loop carrier systems, local area networks, fiber networks, satellite systems, and intelligent signal processing, including neural networks and fuzzy logic. His other contributions have been toward the definition, development, and management of advanced real-time, high-speed communications architectures and their implementation using VLSI and/or microprocessors, and the definition and development of high-speed and robust communications protocols.

Dr. Kartalopoulos has recently lectured on DWDM technology, on SONET/ SDH and ATM systems as well as neural networks and fuzzy logic at several seminars. Prior to employment with AT&T, he taught undergraduate and graduate courses and conducted research on the dynamic phenomena of optical materials, electro-optic devices, digital and analog computers, and searching algorithms.

Dr. Kartalopoulos is the author of *Understanding SONET/SDH and ATM* (IEEE Press, 1999) and *Understanding Neural Networks and Fuzzy Logic* (IEEE Press, 1996). In addition, he has published numerous articles and has been awarded many patents, several in optical communications systems. He has also been a guest editor of the IEEE *Communications Magazine* and an associate editor of the *Transactions on Neural Networks*. In addition, he has served as vice president of the IEEE Neural Network Council and was a member of the IEEE USA Board.

A member of the IEEE, Dr. Kartalopoulos chairs the IEEE Communications Society to the Technical Emerging Technologies Committee, he represents ComSoc to the Technical Activities Board (TAB) New Technology Directions Organization, and is a member of the IEEE Press Board. Prior to this, he chaired the Signal Processing and Electronics Committee. He is also a member of the IEEE Communications Society Transmission, Access, and Optical Systems Committee.